The Classic Television Reference

Stories Behind Those Exciting Shows.
A Mirror of Societal Changes, via the Tube.
From Nostalgia to Business Applicability.

By **Hank Moore**
Futurist, Corporate Strategist™

Skyward Publishing
NEW YORK • LONDON • DALLAS

For quantity purchases, contact:
Skyward Publishing, Inc.
813 Michael Street
Kennett, MO 63857
E-mail: info@skywardpublishing.com
Web site: http://www.skywardpublishing.com

Library of Congress Cataloging-in-Publication Data

Moore, Hank.
The classic television reference : stories behind those exciting shows : a
mirror of societal changes, via the tube, from nostalgia to business applicability / by Hank Moore.
p. cm.
ISBN-13: 978-1-881554-46-2 (pbk.)
1. Television broadcasting—United States—Miscellanea. I. Title.

PN1992.3.U5M624 2005
384.55'0973—dc22   2005013020

First Printing
Printed in the United States of America

Entire book design and original cover illustration by lyledidthis.com
http://www.lyledidthis.com

Artwork reproduced from public domain sources
and the author's photo archives.

Foreword

By Hank Moore

Futurist, Corporate Strategist™

This is primarily an entertainment book. It is secondarily a business book because it looks at the "hows and whys" of the television industry. It also makes analogies from 50 years of TV show content to the core values held by executives and the ways in which organizations may be better operated today.

Nowadays, as a futurist and Corporate Strategist™ , I am a senior organizational advisor and the author of business books, monographs, strategic plans and research documents. I speak at business conferences around the world and conduct Executive Think Tanks, the result being that client businesses pursue more creative, effective and profitable endeavors.

The early years of my career were spent in and around the entertainment industry. I started as a disc jockey in 1958 and pioneered radio's "oldies show" concept a year later. It was my great pleasure to create and host rock n' roll, jazz, country, big band, soul and easy listening oldies shows. Through the next 24 years in radio, I met giants of the music industry, emceed concerts with great stars and produced 200+ documentaries on rock n' roll, pop, country, soul and jazz music art forms and their performers.

In the mid-1960s, I began writing for newspapers and magazines, with "beats" being business, education, healthcare and entertainment. I went to Hollywood, New York and other entertainment centers to interview stars, directors, producers, writers and other creators for television. From 1969-1972, I edited TV Digest, a weekly magazine and wrote about the genre for other publications, from the London Times to TV Guide, from the Austin American-Statesman to Rolling Stone.

These chapters reflect 35 years of research on the shows and stars of television. These chapters reflect the contexts in which the medium of television has grown. Each reflects from the Big Picture perspective upon specific aspects of classic television. The appendix of this book draws from actual interviews that I conducted and wrote during the period of 1969-1972.

I grew up in a one-TV-station town. It carried material from all three networks, plus syndicated filmed shows and local programming. Thus, I was exposed to a plethora of everything in the 1950s, and most everything was broadcast on a delayed basis.

With the advent of home VCRs, I began acquiring most of the shows that I had missed as a youth. Today, I have a library of 30,000 titles, mostly classic television. I think that black and white TV is a distinct art form. I watch those shows today with new insights and revisit the values that the classic shows taught.

Cable television has done a good job of exposing new and old audiences alike to the classic shows. I wish to thank Ted Turner, Nick at Night, the Family Channel, the Game Show Network, TV Land, Encore, the Nostalgia Channel, the Sci-Fi Channel and others for popularizing this genre in modern times.

There are many other classic TV shows (especially black and white series) that are not shown today, and they really should be exhibited. Today's cable viewers are seeing only a fraction of the quality programming that was produced. It's a good sampler, which whets appetites for video sales through catalogs like Shokus, Radio Spirits, Grapevine Video, Discount Video Tapes, VCI, Captain Bijou and others.

Special dedications go to my wife (April), my sisters (Janie Taylor and Julie Moore) and my grandchildren (Courtney Hamlyn, Alexandra Zepeda, Henry Wilson, Austin Zepeda, Tad Hamlyn, Thomas Zepeda, Erin Hamlyn and AnnaMarie Zepeda).

Dedications go to other family members, including Sally Choate, Bill Garrett, Byron Garrett, Lucile Garrett, Tina Mabe Hamlyn, Jesse Mueller, Larry Mueller, Lizzie Mueller, Bill Taylor, Deborah Taylor, Jon Taylor, Tamra Wilson, Danielle Zepeda, Johnny Zepeda, John Zepeda and Rebecka Zepeda.

Professional dedications and acknowledgments go to my media mentors (Cactus Pryor, Bob Gooding, Bill Moyers) and my media heroes (Desi Arnaz, Lucille Ball, Dick Clark, Leonard Goldenson,

William S. Paley, Dick Powell, Aaron Spelling, Ed Sullivan, Lew Wasserman).

Friends and colleagues whom I wish to salute in this book include Kathleen Ballanfant, Robert Battle, Deborah Beaman, Bob Benedik, John Benske, Torre Blomgren, Dennis Bonsignore, Tom Britton, Randy Brower, John Bustin, Ken Campanile, Chris Campbell, Tony Castiglie, Richard Dacre, Daniel Dedmon, Jeff DeHart, John Dorsa, Colin Duff, Michael Eisner, Dr. Ron Evans, Elroy Forbes, Felix Fraga, Dr. George Glass, Royce Guinn, Jackie Hall, Alan Heinecke, Michael Hick, John Hill, Bob Hinsley, Gary Hoffman, John Jett, Lady Bird Johnson, Jon King, Tom Kleinschmidt, Rich Latimer, Keith LeBlanc, Rick Lee, Jonathan Lel, Dr. Bruce Leslie, Daniel Lim, Mike Linares, Alex Lopez-Negrete, Bertil Lundgren, Boyd Magers, Henry Marks, Sue Marlow, Dan Matheson, Sal Mauriello, Stark Maynard, Jeff McClain, Jim McKinley, Tony Mechele, Aaron Mintz, David Moore, Paul Munoz, Dolly Nana'ah, Denise Patrick, Steve Peel, Tom Perrone, Greg Prevost, Derek Redmond, Robert Rivera, Carter Rochelle, Steve Russo, Lyle Ruybalid, Richard Schurch, Mike Scott, Jack Shabot, Ed Shane, Stuart Shostak, Bruce Simon, Howard Sine, David L. Smith, Joan Spitz, Mike Stoll, Carole Keeton Strayhorn, Ed Stuart, Rich Tiller, James Todd, Gene Tognacci, Tise Vahimagi, Judi Wegley, Joanne Weiland, Chuck Wheeler and Barney Zick.

This book serves to contextualize all those shows and the pop culture in which they exist. Memories reside in our souls and are not ranked according to Arbitron ratings or box office grosses. We fondly recall images dear to our lives. And we even recall the continuing images (shows and advertising) that we just cannot delete from our sub-consciousness. And we keep singing, whistling and quoting those old theme songs.

Among the stars and television industry leaders interviewed by Hank Moore in combining this body of work were Roy Acuff, Claude Akins, Eddie Albert, Alan Alda, Steve Allen, Herb Alpert,

Nancy Ames, Cleveland Amory, Dana Andrews, Tige Andrews, Roone Arledge, Desi Arnaz Jr., James Arness, Eddy Arnold, Ed Asner, Max Baer, Lucille Ball, John Banner, Adrienne Barbeau, Richard Basehart, Meredith Baxter, Milton Berle, Shelley Berman, Chuck Berry, Ted Bessell, David Birney, Joey Bishop, Bill Bixby, Frank Blair, Janet Blair, Dan Blocker, Pat Boone, Shirley Booth, Walter Brennan, Lloyd Bridges, David Brinkley, James Brolin, Yul Brynner, Carol Burnett, Raymond Burr, Sebastian Cabot, Glen Campbell, Truman Capote, Macdonald Carey, Diahann Carroll, Angela Cartwright, Johnny Cash, David Cassidy, Jack Cassidy, Dick Cavett, John Chancellor, Dick Clark, Lee J. Cobb, Michael Cole, Gary Collins, Mike Connors, Robert Conrad, William Conrad, Michael Constantine, Tim Conway, Bill Cosby, Joseph Cotten, Howard Cosell, Broderick Crawford, Bob Cousse, Bob Crane, Richard Crenna, Walter Cronkite, Bill Cullen, Bob Cummings, Ken Curtis, Dan Dailey, John Davidson, Ann B. Davis, Roger Davis, Richard Dawson.

Also, Don DeFore, Pete Deuel, Roy Disney, Placido Domingo, Fats Domino, Donna Douglas, Michael Douglas, Hugh Downs, James Drury, James Duffy, Buddy Ebsen, Barbara Eden, Ralph Edwards, Michael Eisner, Duke Ellington, Chad Everett, Shelley Fabares, Peter Falk, Farrah Fawcett, Ella Fitzgerald, Art Fleming, Joe Flynn, Henry Fonda, Glenn Ford, Steve Forrest, John Forsythe, Chet Forte, Redd Foxx, James Franciscus, Jonathan Frid, Robert Fuller, Eileen Fulton, Eva Gabor, Joe Garigiola, Dave Garroway, Christopher George, Frank Gifford, Benny Goodman, Julian Goodman, Gale Gordon, Curt Gowdy, Kirby Grant, Lee Grant, Peter Graves, Lorne Greene, Rosey Grier, Merv Griffin, Andy Griffith, Clu Gulager, George Hamilton, Valerie Harper.

Also, David Hartman, Don Hastings, Lloyd Haynes, Florence Henderson, Audrey Hepburn, Don Herbert, Don Hewitt, Pat Hingle, Hal Holbrook, Bob Hope, Chuck Howard, Ron Howard, Rock Hudson, Tab Hunter, Keith Jackson, David Janssen, Peter Jennings, Chuck Jones, Dean Jones, Shirley Jones, Casey Kasem, Bob Keeshan, Brian Keith, Zalman King, Werner Klemperer, Jack Klugman, Don Knotts, Sid & Marty Krofft, Michael Landon, Tom

Landry, Glen Larson, Norman Lear, Brenda Lee, Pinky Lee, Michael Lembeck, Sheldon Leonard, Art Linkletter, Jack Linkletter, Peggy Lipton, Little Richard, Stanley Livingston, Julie London, Richard Long, Jack Lord, Marjorie Lord, Lawrence Luckinbill, Allen Ludden, Keye Luke, Peter Lupus, Paul Lynde, Gavin MacLeod, Fred MacMurray, Patrick Macnee, George Maharis, Lee Majors, Karl Malden, John Mantley, Andrea Marcovicci, E.G. Marshall, Dean Martin, Strother Martin, Jerry Mathers, Tim Matheson.

Also, Johnny Mathis, Bill Mauldin, Paul McCartney, Doug McClure, Marilyn McCoo, Frank McGee, Jim McKay, Rod McKuen, Ed McMahon, Don Meredith, Lee Meriwether, Donna Mills, Juliet Mills, Martin Milner, Yvette Mimieux, Elizabeth Montgomery, Mary Tyler Moore, Greg Morris, Bill Moyers, Ben Murphy, Jim Nabors, Joe Namath, Ed Nelson, Ozzie Nelson, Ricky Nelson, Leonard Nimoy, Robert Northshield, Hugh O'Brien, Carroll O'Connor, Roy Orbison, Buck Owens, Patti Page, Fess Parker, Bert Parks, Pat Paulsen, Stefanie Powers, Elvis Presley, Andre Previn, Ray Price, Vincent Price, Tony Randall, Dan Rather, Martha Raye, Maureen Reagan, Donna Reed, Robert Reed, Rob Reiner, Burt Reynolds, Nelson Riddle, Tex Ritter, Pernell Roberts, Cliff Robertson, Kenny Rogers, Roy Rogers, Cesar Romero, Linda Ronstadt, Diana Ross, Bill Russell, Irene Ryan, Dick Sargent, Vidal Sassoon, Chris Schenkel.

Also, Peter Sellers, Doc Severinsen, William Shatner, Bobby Sherman, Phil Silvers, O.J. Simpson, Frank Sinatra, Sonny and Cher, Aaron Spelling, Kay Starr, Ringo Starr, Milburn Stone, Gale Storm, Sally Struthers, Ed Sullivan, Burt Sugarman, Frank Sutton, Loretta Swit, Fran Tarkenton, Danny Thomas, Marlo Thomas, Richard Thomas, Lily Tomlin, Mel Torme, Conway Twitty, Jack Valenti, Karen Valentine, Dick Van Patten, Mitch Vogel, Robert Wagner, Lyle Waggoner, Robert Walden, Cornelia Wallace, Barbara Walters, Lesley Ann Warren, Dionne Warwick, Lawrence Welk, Av Westin, James Whitmore, Andy Williams, Barry Williams, Clarence Williams III, Chill Wills, Natalie Wood, Jane Wyatt, Robert Young, Efrem Zimbalist Jr.

Table of Contents

Quotes, lessons learned and knowledge gleaned from the experience of growing up with tube talk.

Music from the Back of the Mind. Recalling advertising jingles, song hits, TV theme songs and associated musical memories paints a panorama of life.

Texture for Perspectives on Life. The Witty, the Glib and the Pertinent.

They rounded out popular TV schedules.

Essays, interviews and profiles written by Hank Moore in television's Golden Age. Period-piece reprinted articles from 1969-1972 that investigate TV's impact on the Baby Boom culture. Recollections of major TV stars, including Lucille Ball, Frank Sinatra, Jack Lord, Lawrence Welk, Dick Clark, Ed Sullivan, Dean Martin, Hugh Downs, Burt Reynolds, Howard Cosell, Merv Griffin, Peter Graves, Lee J. Cobb, Carol Burnett, Frank McGee, Glen Campbell, Norman Lear, Mary Tyler Moore, Eddie Albert, Eva Gabor, Walter Cronkite, Fess Parker, Buddy Ebsen, Diahann Carroll and others. Overall themes and social significance of selected shows. Shows the applicability of classic shows and their teachings to modern life

1

The Hybrid Medium

How Television Got Equality and Dominance Over Movies, Theatre and Radio.

Television represents many things to many people. It is a hybrid of cultural tastes and mores...the best and the worst. The fact that it is a successful amalgamation of various other art forms and information sources makes it well worth examining in a new light.

Television was actually conceived before radio was developed. However, technological experimentations took years longer. When TV became commercially operable, radio was the dominant medium and had set format standards. Variety shows, though extensions of vaudeville, were customized for broadcasting, with sketches, guest stars, duets and other ingredients added. Situation comedies, westerns, anthologies and dramatic series bloomed during the 1930s and 1940s.

The early days of television represented radio with pictures added. People watched anything, due to curiosity and the newness of the medium. The art came when touches of other media were added.

The first decade of TV was dominated by New York influences, culture and presence. Management of the major networks was centered in New York and had vested interests in keeping New York as the production hub.

That was fine with Hollywood for awhile, as the major studios saw TV as zapping movie attendance and nothing more than a vehicle to promote films. Hollywood was somewhat the same mindset with radio, though reduced time demands enabled the top stars, directors and talents to contribute to the crystal-set medium. Hollywood put out the hype that TV was of lesser quality and importance than movies...a fallacy that many people still believe.

In the late 1940s and early 1950s, Broadway theatre was the highest hierarchy of the entertainment world, though it embraced radio and TV as being fertile sources of work for actors, proving grounds for emerging playwrights and experimentation zone for storytelling concepts. The Broadway community embraced TV dramas, bringing technique, quality and creativity to live anthologies.

Live dramatic programs featuring New York theatre actors served to catapult their careers (Julie Harris, Richard Kiley, James Whitmore, Eli Wallach, Jack Warden, Jessica Tandy, Hume Cronyn, Kim Hunter, Cyril Ritchard, Yul Brynner) on both coasts. Some made their ultimate marks on the silver screen (Charlton Heston, James Dean, Paul Newman). Others became the royalty of home viewers (John Forsythe, Leslie Nielsen, Elizabeth Montgomery, Carroll O'Connor, Jack Klugman, Tony Randall, Robert Culp, E.G. Marshall, William Shatner).

Variety shows had a distinctive New York feel, from Ed Sullivan introducing notables from the audience to Perry Como's sophisticated class. Soap operas and game shows had east coast orientations to them. Repertory companies produced and appeared in live sitcoms and children's shows. New York was and still is the information-media center, and newscasts, documentaries, timely events, sports coverage and discussion-panel shows hit "art form" status...formats that are still followed to this day.

As viewers watched a primary diet of live New York-originated programming, the influences of film began whetting future appetites. Early TV had large time chunks to fill, and film inventories of all types (A features, B features, short subjects and cartoons) found new generations of fans.

The hybridization of television began from its onset as a commercial medium. The networks built west coast operations, and Hollywood stars began appearing on live dramas. The first "spectacular" aired in 1953, starring Mary Martin and Ethel Merman, themselves Broadway stars with broadcasting and film appeal. TV-invented spectaculars became known as "specials," and talents from both coasts produced them with finesse, charm and mass-audience appeal.

With the Hollywood establishment resisting in producing series for television, a host of independent filmmakers, production companies and talent assemblages broke new ground, thereby setting precedents for filmed TV that the major studios later adopted and embraced.

Some independents (Dick Powell, Lucille Ball, Ozzie Nelson, Danny Thomas) were graduates of the studio system...seeking to make their marks with quality shows. Others (Desi Arnaz, Frederick Ziv, Bernard Schubert) had been Hollywood mavericks, and pioneering TV film fulfilled their creative thrust. Still others (Walt Disney, Hal Roach, Jerry Fairbanks) were champions of the entrepreneurial mindset and adapted well to the new TV medium. Additional producers of the New York theatre (Alexander Cohen, David Susskind, Worthington Miner, Fred Coe) found new frontiers in the small screen that they could not achieve through the Hollywood hierarchy.

With such diverse talents, track records, driving forces, financial backing, rosters of stars and sheer ambition, the hybridization of TV through filmed product continued to advance throughout the next 20 years.

1950s filmed shows took techniques from 1940s moviemaking. Because tight shooting and post-production schedules were incumbent upon TV production, economies of scale were adopted. The primary influence upon the decade was Film Noir.

TV directors embraced theatrical staging, documentary techniques and the movies' first-take emphasis in getting the best performances in available time. Episodes inter-cut stock footage, movie scenery, studio archives to mount productions that had at least a "B movie" feel. By the end of the decade, TV filmed product usually exceeded that of the movies...in quantity, quality, continuity, audience appeal and marketability.

The second generation of producers (Aaron Spelling, Dick Clark, Herbert B. Leonard, Bruce Geller) took the hybrid nature of TV to the next level. They devised more sophisticated filming techniques, drew larger budgets through their skills at attracting larger audience size, pushed the creative envelope and established track records in crowd pleasing hits.

The second generation of television producers learned from the trailblazers and in turn spawned subsequent generations of film-savvy, marketing-friendly and project-unique mindsets that canonized Hollywood film industry into the TV-movie hybrid that now exists.

Remakes of classic plays and film scripts got the highest tier of Broadway and movie stars (Helen Hayes, Humphrey Bogart, James Stewart, Joan Crawford, Alan Ladd) onto TV. Some radio stars and shows (Arthur Godfrey, Perry Como, Roy Rogers & Dale Evans, Jack Benny, George Burns & Gracie Allen, Bob Hope, Groucho Marx) adapted well to television. Others (Don McNeill, Edgar Bergen, Fibber McGee & Molly) did not.

Some movie stars (Loretta Young, Ronald Reagan, Bette Davis, Jane Wyman, Ann Sothern, Ray Milland, Joan Davis) revitalized careers and often flourished better in TV than they had in formula movies. Some movie stars did occasional TV for the fun of the projects (John Wayne, Elizabeth Taylor, Natalie Wood).

Most film greats of the last four decades started in television. This includes directors (Stephen Spielberg, Ron Howard, Rob Reiner, Mike Nichols, Barry Shear, Robert Altman, John Frankenheimer), producers, writers and actors (Jack Nicholson, Jodie Foster, Harrison Ford, Burt Reynolds, Steve McQueen, Helen Hunt, Charles Bronson, Mia Farrow, Ryan O'Neal).

Some superstars (James Garner, Peter Falk, Lee Marvin, Kathleen Quinlan, Richard Dreyfuss, Lea Thompson, Barbara

Hershey) who began in TV continued to keep active in the medium in parallel to their thriving movie careers.

Some stars who began on the stage, in the movies and on radio took their careers to higher plateaus on TV included Raymond Burr, Jack Lord, Annie Potts, Milton Berle, Donna Reed, Jack Webb, Gene Barry, Lorne Greene, Ida Lupino (actress and TV's first female director), Bill Cosby, Robert Stack, Jackie Cooper, Phil Silvers, Bob Cummings, Richard Boone, Angie Dickinson, Telly Savalas, Faye Emerson, Robert Blake, Broderick Crawford, Richard Carlson, Lloyd Bridges, Eve Arden, Wendell Corey, Rory Calhoun, Dale Robertson, Buddy Ebsen, Rod Cameron, Red Skelton, Robert Young and Bill Williams.

Television created its own superstars...talents who studied, captured and mastered the presence, techniques, methodologies and opportunities of tube stature. These included Rod Serling, David Janssen, Jackie Gleason, James Franciscus, Lee Majors, Carol Burnett, Mike Connors, Mary Tyler Moore, Chuck Connors, Efrem Zimbalist Jr., Larry Hagman, Richard Chamberlain, James Arness, Peter Graves, Barbara Eden, Hugh O'Brian, Robert Conrad, Leonard Nimoy, Stefanie Powers, Vincent Edwards, Bill Bixby, Farrah Fawcett and Chad Everett.

Television bred, fostered and supported the greatest stable of guest stars. Many had started in theatre or films but achieved superstar status by reliably headlining episodic TV. After all, the core of success for Gunsmoke, The Fugitive, Route 66, Wagon Train, Star Trek and others lies in the central characters' interactions with guest stars and featured players.

Among the top guest stars were Darren McGavin, Beverly Garland, Barry Sullivan, Robert Loggia, Lee Grant, Joseph Campanella, Paul Burke, Cloris Leachman, Pernell Roberts, Susan Strasberg, Lloyd Bochner, Suzanne Pleshette, Robert Lansing, Brian Keith, Victor Buono, Patty Duke, William Windom, Vincent Price, Bruce Dern, Vera Miles, Mark Richman, Diane Baker, Boris Karloff, Bradford Dillman and Burgess Meredith. Many of the guest stars previously headlined series. Others came from hybrid theatre, movie and TV backgrounds.

Television brought us the largest stable of character actors, who worked in films as well but are primarily known for faces, expressions, characterizations, attitude, presence and skill. Some busily working characters (Ward Bond, Edmond O'Brien, Edward Asner, Gavin MacLeod, Ted Knight, Thomas Mitchell, Sebastian Cabot, Will Geer, Ellen Corby) became known as stars. Others have memorable faces (Richard Anderson, Nehemiah Persoff, Claude Akins, Whitney Blake, Ben Johnson, Jeanne Cooper, Whit Bissell, Brooke Bundy, Tris Coffin, Jeanette Nolan, Don Stroud, Richard Jaeckel, Michael Ansara, Peter Leeds).

And could we ever forget those talented actors who played "heavies" and "baddies" in the cop shows, westerns and mysteries (Henry Silva, Jack Elam, John Doucette, Myron Healey, Strother Martin, John Marley, Bert Freed).

Music has had a wider berth on television than in the movies and radio combined. Rock stars and shows were part of TV's search for young viewers, who have continued to show their loyalty. From specials to variety shows to music videos, the visualization of music has further stimulated record and concert sales.

Music is the soundtrack to our lives...and not hit songs on the radio and jukeboxes. TV brought us theme songs, music scores, musical cues and commercial jingles. Most of the top musical composers, conductors and arrangers supplied memorable themes and cues for television shows, including Nelson Riddle, David Rose, Billy May, Frank Devol, Bernard Herrmann, Alfred Newman, Franz Waxman, Bill Conti, William Lava, Herschel Burke Gilbert, Joseph Mullendore, John Scott Trotter, Juan Esquival, Fred Steiner, Jerome Moross and Jack Marshall. Top film composers started in TV (John Williams, Jerry Goldsmith) or continued to produce music for TV shows along with film scores (Elmer Bernstein, Henry Mancini).

Television has had a profound and lasting influence on the film industry. By the 1970s, blurs of distinction between the movies, theatre and television had blurred. TV has since been the hybrid entertainment form where talents from other media come together and return often. TV affords scripts and roles not readily available in movies, especially for actors over the age of 40. Appearances on high-rated shows can cross-promote movie roles. The scope and volume of shows enables all talents to find places on the tube.

The studios and independent producers regularly partner with each other, cross-distribute product and accommodate stars' shooting schedules. All of these concepts originated in a bustling television film production industry...one which overtook the movies and rules the Hollywood roost.

SEE TV'S GREATEST ARRAY OF STARS!

THE TV
EMMY
NOMINATIONS
ALL-STAR SHOW

FEATURING SUCH STARS AS...

★ STEVE ALLEN   ★ ARLENE FRANCIS
★ DESI ARNAZ   ★ ERNIE KOVACS
★ GERTRUDE BERG   ★ TONY MARTIN
★ JOHN DALY   ★ JOHNNY MERCER
★ EDDIE FISHER   ★ PHIL SILVERS

...plus many others!

SEE TV'S NOMINEES FOR THE 1956
EMMY AWARDS ON ONE BIG SHOW!

BROUGHT TO YOU BY

OLDSMOBILE
IN BEHALF OF YOUR QUALITY DEALER

SATURDAY EVENING   9:00 P.M.
FEB. 16   CHS. ④ ⑤ ⑦ ⑫

2

Looking for Role Models, Generational Heroes

Why we sought heroes elsewhere.
Why we become our own best role model.

All of us are products of the mass culture in which we grew up. This permeates our business careers and every other aspect of our lives.

We are a confluence of many factors:

• Societal expectations, dreams, failures and also-rans.

• Events beyond our control.

• Home and family.

• Mass media variations on home and family.

• Fads and foibles.

• Legitimate goals versus frivolous fancies.

• Music.

• Perceptions.

- Realities.
- Movies.
- The educational system, not to be confused with lifelong education.
- What we perceive other families have that we do not.
- Social changes and advances in global cultures.
- Television.
- Technology.
- Changing roles that people play in interfacing with each other.
- What constitutes self-improvement.

The same holds true for business and careers. If pop culture was a confusing mish-mash of mixed messages, then so was our business education, or lack of it. Rarely were we taught about such things as:

- Codes of personal conduct.
- Tiers of professionalism.
- The dues paying process.
- Contributing directly and indirectly to the bottom line.
- Expectations of executives.
- Sophisticated nuances of being a successful executive.
- Empowering teams.
- Benchmarking performance, yours and that of others.
- Observing trends and changes in society, the economy and the business marketplace.
- Becoming an active participant, rather than just an observer.
- Championing-mastering change, rather than falling victim to it.
- Standing for something...and being counted-acknowledged.
- Mentoring others.

- Having original ideas.
- Learning how to think for yourself.
- Realizing that thinking for yourself gives you the advantage to make clear decisions.
- Carrying decisions into actions.
- Recognizing the positive by-products of effective decisions.
- Becoming a leader and sustaining leadership potential.
- Effecting a career Body of Work.
- Leaving something meaningful behind.

Continuing to produce, rather than becoming a relic reflection of yourself.

The Ideal Parents

Most of us have fantasized the possibility of our parents being other people. Sometimes, idolized parents were those who already were attached to our friends. Most often, role models were symbols of people we didn't know...but wanted to be like.

Businesses operate the same way as individuals. What looks good on the outside is what we must have and become. Tactics are commonly devised to get what we perceive that someone else has and look like what we assume they appear to be.

Perception becomes reality. The process of chasing the perception becomes an obsession for businesses of all sizes...until reality sets in.

With the advent of television in the 1950s, it was natural that TV families would be held up as ideals. We jokingly wonder how June Cleaver could do the housework in her fancy dress, high heels and pearls. We just knew that Harriet Nelson would make more delicious meals than our own mothers did.

The families on TV situation comedies were all white, middle-class, carried traditional family structures and were mostly based in mythical small towns.

The realities behind the facades now make for fascinating

insights into life, as we saw it portrayed on the television screen. In reality:

- Harriet Nelson could not really cook. She had grown up in hotels and was accustomed to ordering room service.

- Ozzie Nelson had no job on TV, and his wife didn't work outside the home. No explanation was ever made about their means of support. Though his character appeared light on screen, Ozzie Nelson was the true guru of that show. In my mind, he stands with Desi Arnaz as one of the behind-the-scenes geniuses of TV.

- There was dysfunctional behavior, even though we didn't recognize it as such. When Danny Thomas yelled at his kids and spit coffee on the living room floor, it was couched in wisecracks.

- Women were severely stereotyped. Many TV wives appeared to be subservient...yet pursued their own pro-active courses. Laura Petrie always got her way. Lucy Ricardo pursued hijinx. And mother did really "know best," though society would not quite position it that way in the 1950s. Nonetheless, women learned subtle ways to master the system, within the context of good humor.

- While Western sheriffs won at the shootouts, the issues of good versus bad were overly simplistic. Life is mostly shades of gray...which tough strength does not work well against.

- Behind the guns and action, the Westerns really did teach lessons of empowerment and team building. On "Wagon Train" and "Rawhide," people had no choice but to get along and work together. As a team, they fought the elements and usually won.

- Gangsters always got their just deserves in movies and on cop TV shows. We were taught that crime does not pay...and were shown the price for violating property and safety. Jack Webb, Broderick Crawford and other tough cops put the baddies in their place, in no uncertain terms.

Many of us wonder why values like these are not taught now. Where is society headed, we wonder. Whatever happened to Randolph Scott? Where are the new heroes coming from?)

We now realize that many of our childhood idols had demons of their own. Keeping up appearances and being interchangeably confused with their on-screen characters led many a performer toward personal abuse, career burnout and eventual ruin.

Not many taught us about going the distance. Too many actors and singers had short-term careers. That was the design of the system. In business, we must not follow pop culture and train ourselves to last, prosper and get better with age.

As we get older and more cynical, society tends to shoot down its media heroes and watches them stumble and fall, sometimes with interest and joy. We don't expect any of them to measure up to past pedestal status. When one falls from grace, we may either repudiate our past allegiance or justify unrealistic ways to keep them perched up on high.

Having met many major performers and media heroes, I know that raw talent does not directly translate to business savvy and people skills. The Paul McCartneys of the world, who successfully embody it all, are few and far between.

One of my first career idols was Dick Clark, another man who is smart and accomplished in many facets. He had just debuted on "American Bandstand." I was in the fifth grade and started working at a radio station, determined to be Texas' answer to Dick Clark.

A mentor reminded me that none of us should go through life as a carbon copy of someone else. We can admire and embody their qualities but must carve out a uniqueness all our own. Good advice from a 24-year-old Bill Moyers, who stands for me as an ever-contemporary role model.

Corporate executives do not get a rulebook when the job title is awarded. They are usually promoted on the basis technical expertise, team player status, loyalty and perceived long-term value to the company. They are told to assume a role and then draw upon their memory bank of role models.

Top executives have few role models in equivalent positions.

Thus, they get bad advice from the wrong consultants. In the quest to be a top business leader, one quickly reviews how poorly corporate executives were portrayed to the mass culture.

J.R. Ewing ("Dallas") sold every member of his family and work force down the river. He is hardly a CEO role model, though many "good old boys" think how he operated was perfectly acceptable.

Alan Brady ("Dick Van Dyke Show") practiced nepotism with his brother-in-law, Mel Cooley. Brady yelled at everyone and was especially abusive to Mel, in front of others. Creativity was determined by his will. All were expected to parrot his "vision."

Lou Grant ("Mary Tyler Moore Show") drank on the job, was brash, threatened termination, asked pervasive questions and sometimes dated co-workers.

Charlie Townsend ("Charlie's Angels") was never around. He left his staff to their own devices and to supervise themselves. The reasons most employees do not perform as expected is that they are given insufficient direction and time with a mentor, not knowing what is expected of them.

It was never revealed where John Beresford Tipton ("The Millionaire") earned all that money that he gave away to total strangers.

Economic accountability was never a consideration in TV families. They lived well, but we rarely saw the relationship between workplace output to family quality of life. How did Mike Brady ("The Brady Bunch") afford to feed a family of eight, especially with his wife staying at home and not working? He seemed to stay at home much more than the average successful architect.

In reality, most TV lead characters were the employees of someone else. The boss was the brunt of the jokes. Fear of being disciplined was openly communicated to viewers as part of the territory in earning one's way in life.

Ralph Kramden ("The Honeymooners") was not considered to become a supervisor, nor a leader. He exhibited a defeatist attitude that probably kept him from being successful.

Certain characters did their jobs in such a way as that the bosses fell in love with them and eventually married them. Witness Katy Holstrum ("The Farmer's Daughter"), Agent 99 ("Get Smart") and Jeannie ("I Dream of Jeannie"). At one time, some women went into business with such an unrealistic view.

Then, there were those who fostered the notion of "do as I say, not as I do." For example:

We never saw psychologist Bob Hartley ("Bob Newhart Show") conferring with colleagues, attending professional symposia, authoring academic papers or seeking professional help himself. When he wasn't in session, he was joking with the receptionist and the dentist.

Editor Perry White ("Superman") threatened young Jimmy Olsen, "Don't call me chief," when mentoring the eager reporter would have amplified Olsen's service to The Daily Planet. Alas, Olsen was always a tagalong and did not develop as a seasoned reporter, stalling his career.

Marshal Simon Cord (played by Henry Fonda) was always out of town. His "Deputy" (played by Allen Case) was a shopkeeper, who became the town's part-time law and order by default. Part-time jobs and careers are not the same thing.

Money was rarely an issue. We rarely saw families just scraping by, as were most Americans. "The Real McCoys" were farmers...with wealth in spirit and positive will.

There were unexplained quirks, showing insufficient resources necessary to do business. All the detectives on "77 Sunset Strip" drove the same car (a Ford convertible). How did the others get around and earn their livelihood, if a car was essential equipment?

Steve McGarrett ("Hawaii Five-0") drove the same car (a 1967 Mercury Monterey) year after year. With his arrest record, why didn't the department upgrade his equipment?

Jim Anderson was an insurance agent on "Father Knows Best." Yet, he never made evening calls...only working days. Thus, he couldn't sell that many policies and missed his marketplace...not being available at peak times that his customers were.

Ricky Ricardo worked in a nightclub and always went to work during the day, usually being home most evenings.

Becoming Your Own Role Model

Amidst these entertaining analogies is a confluence of ideas in each of our heads. Few of us had modeling for life and career. We learned early glimpses of life from the TV. Along the way, we absorbed others...always influenced by the misperceptions of pop culture.

It is difficult to inventory all the images, sort perceptions versus realities and look new ways at old business tenets. That is what I've done over the last five years, and that is how this book evolved.

This progression of statements, validations and commitments is the premise of this book, which is just the same approach utilized when I work with corporate clients on strategizing and visualizing their future:

- Examine where you came from.
- Retread old knowledge.
- Apply teachings to today.
- Honestly evaluate your path to progress thus far.
- Affix responsibilities, goals and benchmarks to all intended progress.
- Find creative new ways to approach and conduct business.
- Proceed with zeal, commitment, creative instinct and bound-less energy.
- Achieve and reflect upon successes.
- Learn three times more from failure than success.
- Plan to achieve and succeed in the future.

Never stop researching, planning, executing and evaluating. Benchmarks of one phase, project or series of events drive the research and planning for the next phase.

Futurism is not an esoteric concept. After all, It's Almost Tomorrow. But then, it always is.

3

Nostalgic Excursions Through Memories and Culture

Why Good Organizations Click.

Think of any organization or business as being analogous to a successful and highly entertaining television variety show or situation comedy series. To better understand and improve your organization, remember the most successful TV series and the elements which made them work.

1. The Host-Star. Great TV variety show hosts made their presence known, without overshadowing the scope of the show. The best ones showcased talent, were viewer-friendly and did what it took to make the show a continuing and lasting force. The perennial ones were strategically positioned to last, rather than just appearing and staying.

Perry Como prided himself in being able to perform ensemble singing with ease. Certainly a great headline singer, he knew that singing as part of a harmonious group required a different vocal delivery than the opening number he would deliver at the top of the show and in his "spotlight" medley.

A fundamental element of variety shows was the duet. After the guest star delivered a song or two, the host would make lively patter, and the two would croon together. Many guest stars were actors, comics or other performers. However, all got the opportunity to duet with the boss...most performing nobly. Next to Dinah Shore, Patti Page or Andy Williams, any and all performers sounded their best and gave that "extra something."

There were group production numbers. Garry Moore had a segment, "That Wonderful Year." He narrated and occasionally sang, but this segment was designed to showcase his ensemble (Carol Burnett, Durward Kirby, Marion Lorne) and guest stars.

Then, there were the hosts that were good administrators. They did not perform but had a sense of timing, mixing the right ingredients, vision for the show and production values. Media veteran Ed Sullivan knew these elements better than anyone and had the longest running TV variety show (series, 1948-1971; specials, 1971-1974; "best of" compilations still running).

The sitcom star knew that the on-screen family had an obligation to showcase both the whole and each of the parts. Superstars like Mary Tyler Moore, Bill Cosby, Lucille Ball and others had the ability to shine and also become the spotlight which pointed toward the talents of others.

There were ensemble shows like "Cheers," "Family Ties," "The Addams Family," "The Golden Girls," "The Beverly Hillbillies," "Full House" and others. No part of the ensemble could have functioned on his or her own. In these, the team is always the star, with rotating parts featured.

2. Regular Cast, Setting and Other Constants. The ensemble is what makes the show succeed or fail. Remember the "Dick Van Dyke Show," "Make Room for Daddy," "Adventures of Ozzie & Harriet," "Lucy Shows," "Night Court," "Father Knows Best" and others.

Think of favorite long-lasting series and what made them memorable. Each season's batch of episodes represented the following:

- Each cast member interacted with the other.

- The star was pivotal to the ensemble but was also a part of it.

- Each character got their own lead storylines during the course of each season.

- Each character played a supportive role to another's lead storyline.

- Not every character appeared in every storyline, every week. Some were occasionally absent because they did not figure into the story at hand.

- Guest stars appeared but were not the "make or break" ingredient.

- The sets and settings had audience appeal. They were believable within the context of the series premise.

- Some storylines were predictable. Others broke new ground. And a few were dramatic changes of pace, for emphasis, including the trips to new locations.

3. The Guest Stars. All the top stars guest starred on each other's shows. That was a way to assure big names and allow those headliners to do things they necessarily could not do on their own shows. The most successful "guest shots" had diversity in performance, rather than the same old schtick.

Ed Sullivan finally got to perform sketch comedy on Red Skelton's and Flip Wilson's shows. Broadway and opera headliners sported new dimensions when clowning with the likes of Danny Kaye or Spike Jones.

The longest lasting stars were the ones who were equally good at being guest stars, as they were successful headliners. Lucille Ball was the quintessential guest star. Stars like Kathie Lee Gifford ably fulfill that versatility nowadays.

The business analogies here are to effective partnering, collaborations and joint venturing. One is a better member of other people's teams if he or she has captained their own. Doing business on other turfs enables executives to expand and grow.

4. Breadth of Material, Backup Production Techniques and Company. The best remembered shows were strategically planned. Writing was consistently good. Subject topics referred to each show's premise and the integrity of its characters.

What goes on behind the camera is more important that what is in front. A star does not make a show. The team does. Successful series learned the value of loyal crews, technicians who voluntarily went the distance and supervisors who saw the team holistically.

5. The Time Slot—Marketplace Advantage. Scheduling is everything in mass entertainment. A good show in the wrong time slot inevitably is cancelled because it fails to build enough audience. Having the right lead-in and follow-up show help deliver the viewership.

Sitcoms always work best in the first hour, the "family hour." Variety shows and specials always work best in the second hour, the "median mark of the evening." Third hours are always reserved for prestige dramas, containing deep material, adult content and a thought provoking edge to their narratives.

One cannot produce a product or service without regard to their intended marketplace. Studying demographics and continually benchmarking is imperative. Too many companies keep manufacturing products after the demand has ebbed.

6. The Opposition—Competition. In TV, the only way to measure up to a seasoned hit is to break new ground (i.e. build a better mousetrap).

Even the nature of competition is changing. In the old days, three major television networks competed against each other. With the advent of expanded TV channels, cable, video rentals and VCRs, the number of alternatives keep the industry and the consumers from staring at test patterns.

Too many companies think the public will beat a path to their doors. They're blind sighted by the competition and fail to properly consider the alternatives held by prospective customers.

Business must research and comprehend every external influence upon the marketplace. Though most are beyond the company's concern, each constituency, problem and opportunity must be predicted, studied and acted upon. Businesses can no longer perform out of sync with everything else around them.

7. Societal Factors During Their Run. Radio and the phonograph were toys in the 1920s. Within 20 years, they had mainstreamed into the primary artistic media showcases.

Television, though developed for years, signaled the post-World War II era of wonderment and renewed hope. In the early years, the public accepted everything that the box had to offer, without questioning why...and still clamoring for more. The earliest TV series reflected the public's insatiable appetite for anything that sang, danced or joked.

Television grew as an art form and business in the 1950s. Its cultural beacons encompassed the next decades. The seemingly calm years of the 1950s were an undercurrent of social upheaval. Thus, popular entertainment reinforced traditional values while gradually evolving contemporary issues.

The 1960s were transition years, as extreme artistic expressions began to emerge. The emerging youth culture became the largest target of advertisers and, thus, network executives. The 1970s shocked society with stark reality amidst the entertainment genre.

In the 1980s, videotape enabled viewers to watch what they wanted, when they wanted. With tape rentals, pay-per-view and stockpiling private libraries with tapes, consumers became their own programming executives.

Niche marketing hit its zenith in the 1990s. Cable channels (like magazines and radio stations before them) narrowcast each audience and demographic within. New media (CD rom, the Internet) emerged to create alternative information and entertainment resources.

Business has paralleled milestones in the entertainment industry. Additional societal factors include multicultural diversity, workplace literacy, global markets, environmental concerns, political correctness, ethics and values, the changing nature of employee bases, virtual corporations, collaborative joint-venturing and putting the customer first...which comes full-circle to the way business started out to be.

Organizations, which click and sustain a track record, must real-ize the same lessons, which its leaders gleaned as consumers of mass media programs:

- There is nothing more permanent than change.

- Change is 90% beneficial. So, why do people fight what's in their best interests?

- Learn from the past.

- Avoid repeating the same mistakes.

- There exists more knowledge in failure than through repeated successes.

- "Saving face" is not the most important thing.

- Many cancelled TV shows have won prestigious awards. They were just "too good" to be ratings hits.

- Becoming part of an organization involves commitment and responsibility from each of its members.

- Put the customer first, and they will keep you first.

- Get advice from the best consultants, not the wanna-be's.

- Never stop planning.

- Never stop changing.

- Never stop improving.

- Continually research, study, understand and communicate what works well.

- Loyalty and consistency pays off.

- Learn that the guest star should sound better in the song duet than you do.

- Thank the guest stars...on and off the air.

- Even if you're cancelled, thank the network for the run and past support.

- There will always be another show...on another day...for a changing audience...with different creative focus.

4

Bosses and Employees

Reviewing Management Styles
Which Were Modeled For Us Through TV.

Management styles reflect human basic behaviors. Bosses and employees all reflect one of the four basic behavioral styles:

1. The Steady Relater.

- They want to maintain good relationships.

- We're all in this together. So, let's work as a team.

- They like to maintain the status quo and are reluctant to make changes.

- They are drawn to helping professions, focusing upon relationships.

2. The Cautious Thinker.

- The overriding concern is for accuracy.

- Can you provide documentation for the claims?

- They focus first on each task at hand.

- They move slowly and are self-contained.

• They are technicians and are drawn toward exact sciences.

3. The Dominant Director.

• The need is to get the job done.

• I want it done right, and I want it done now!

• They need to make the decisions and be in charge.

• They are managers of organizations and departments.

4. The Interactive Socializer.

• They want to be noticed.

• Let me tell you what happened to me.

• They love variety, hate routine and should be shown the Big Picture.

• They need to be where the action is and choose creative, high profile professions.

Questions Bosses Ask

At some point, most of us experienced either "boss from hell," or the employee who just wouldn't fit into the organization, or the co-worker who persisted in digging his-her own grave.

What was wrong with those people? Why couldn't they get their acts together? Couldn't they realize that going with the flow would have been easier than against it?

Where were they standing when the brains and the people skills were handed out? And, why were our careers cursed by their getting in our paths?

Many people have banes of their professional existence...difficult bosses, employees and co-workers who make life miserable. We do not understand how they got to be that way, usually from being ill-prepared for the job at hand.

Media Role Models

As we grew up, television bosses were our first experience to the catbird seat. Here is an analysis of some of them.

Boss	Title/Company	Characteristics
Arthur Carlson	General Manager, radio station, "WKRP in Cincinnati"	Got job through nepotism. Won't make decisions. Unfocused, ambivalent.
Milburn Drysdale	President, Commerce Bank, "The Beverly Hillbillies"	Too focused on one client. Money, profits only focus.
J.R. Ewing	CEO, oil company, "Dallas"	Unscrupulous. No ethics.
Lou Grant	News Director, WJM-TV "Mary Tyler Moore Show"	Drank on the job. Loud, harassed employees. Uneven temper.
Thurston Howell, III	Chairman, Howell Industries, "Gilligan's Island."	Vain, aristocratic, aloof. Away from business. Stranded on island.
Martin Lane	Newspaper Editor, "The Patty Duke Show"	Crusading, fair journalist. Balanced in home life.
Britt Reid	Newspaper Publisher, "The Green Hornet"	Crusader, on and off the job.
Hannibal Smith	"The A-Team"/soldiers of fortune	Tough. Don't cross him.
Alexander Waverly	Head of secret agent team, "UNCLE"	Fair, visionary. Able to cut through red tape. Empowered employees to take risks, get action.
Perry White	Newspaper editor, The Daily Planet, "Superman"	Criticized employees often. Rare constructive input.

There were some small business role models. We only heard about their work situations but never saw them. Though kind hearted to their families, we never got a sense of the symbiosis of the professional life with the TV screen portrayal.

Employee	Show	Occupation
Jim Anderson	"Father Knows Best"	Manager, General Insurance Co.
Mike Brady	"The Brady Bunch"	Architect
Howard Cunningham	"Happy Days"	Owner, Cunningham Hardware
Sam Drucker	"Petticoat Junction"	Owner, Hooterville General Store

Dale Evans	"Roy Rogers Show"	Cafe proprietor
Herbert T. Gillis	"Dobie Gillis"	Owner, Gillis Grocery Store
James Grumby	"Giligan's Island"	Captain, USS Minnow
Dr. Robert Hartley	"Bob Newhart Show"	Psychologist in private practice
John Herrick	"Waterfront"	Captain, "The Cheryl Ann" (tugboat)
Rebecca Howe	"Cheers"	Manager, Cheers Bar
Clair Huxtable	"The Cosby Show"	Attorney
Fred & Ethel Mertz	"I Love Lucy"	Owners, apartment building
Jim Newton	"Fury"	Owner, Broken Wheel Ranch
Paladin	"Have Gun, Will Travel"	Gunfighter
Josh Randall	"Wanted: Dead or Alive"	Bounty hunter
Kitty Russell	"Gunsmoke"	Owner, Long Branch Saloon
Mel Sharples	"Alice"	Owner, Mel's Diner
Howard Sprague	"Mayberry RFD"	County Clerk
Dr. Alex Stone	"Donna Reed Show"	Pediatrician
Arnold Takahashi	"Happy Days"	Owner, Arnold's Drive-In
Honey West	"Honey West"	Owner, private investigation firm

The real heroes on early TV and, thus, our earliest role models, were hard working, underpaid and diligent employees. With few bosses as role models, we just naturally identified more with competent worker bees.

Employee	Show	Occupation
Agents 86 and 99	"Get Smart"	Secret agents
Pepper Anderson	"Police Woman"	Police sergeant
Ward Cleaver	"Leave It to Beaver"	Businessman, prof. not revealed
Roy Coffee	"Bonanza"	Sheriff
Laverne DeFazio	"Laverne and Shirley"	Bottle capper, Shotz Brewery
Jim Dial	"Murphy Brown"	TV news anchor
Steve Douglas	"My Three Sons"	Engineer
Elsie Ethrington	"The Flying Nun"	Nun, AKA "Sister Bertrille"
Florida Evans	"Good Times"	School bus driver, Roadway Bus Co.
Shirley Feeney	"Laverne and Shirley"	Bottle capper, Shotz Brewery
Fred Flintstone	"The Flintstones"	Dinosaur operator
Arthur Fonzarelli	"Happy Days"	Mechanic, Otto's Auto Orphanage
Chester Good	"Gunsmoke"	Aide to U.S. Marshal
Emily Hartley	"Bob Newhart Show"	School teacher
Tom Hartman	"Mary Hartman"	Factory worker
Amos Jones	"Amos n' Andy"	Cab driver
Dr. Richard Kimble	"The Fugitive"	Obstetrician, on leave of absence

Gerald Kookson	"77 Sunset Strip"	Parking lot attendant
Ralph Kramden	"The Honeymooners"	Bus driver
Susie McNamara	"Ann Sothern Show"	Private secretary
Henry Mitchell	"Dennis the Menace"	Engineer
Rhoda Morgenstern	"Mary Tyler Moore Show"	Retail window decorator
Harry Morton	"Burns & Allen Show"	Real estate salesman
Tony Nelson	"I Dream of Jeannie"	Astronaut
Edward L. Norton	"The Honeymooners"	Sewer worker
Wilbur Post	"Mr. Ed"	Architect
Chester A. Riley	"Life of Riley"	Factory worker
Ann Romano	"One Day at a Time"	Ad agency account executive
Sam	"Richard Diamond"	Small business answering service
Jonathan Smith	"Highway to Heaven"	Angel
Cosmo Topper	"Topper"	Banker
Jack Tripper	"Three's Company"	Chef, Angelino's Italian Restaurant
Dorothy Zbornak	"The Golden Girls"	English teacher

Lonely at the Top

Just as bosses are not properly schooled in supervising other people and juggling multiple roles, they suffer the "lonely at the top" syndrome. Heads of companies receive filtered information from within. They don't know which outside consultants to trust and, as a result, don't use the ones they should.

The process of walking through landmines causes most bosses to learn as they go. Few companies have the luxury of a long executive development curve. Thus, supervisors must compress their growth process, while getting maximum productivity out of their workers.

These truths exist in the workplace:

- Good bosses were good employees. They are consistent and have understanding for both roles.
- Bad bosses likely were not ideal employees. They too are consistent in career history.
- Poor people skills cloud any job performance and overshadow good technical skills.
- The worst bosses do not sustain long careers at the top. Their track record catches up with them.

- Good workers don't automatically become good bosses.
- Just because someone is technically proficient or is an exemplary producer does not mean that he-she will transition to being a good boss. Very few great school teachers like becoming principals, for that reason. Good job performers are better left doing what they do best.
- Administrators, at all levels, need to be properly trained as such, not bumped up from the field to do something for which they have no inclination.
- At some point in our lives, we are better suited to be a boss than to be an employee.
- Leadership and executive development skills are steadily learned and continually sharpened. One course or a quick-read book will not instill them. The best leaders are prepared to go the distance.
- Being your own boss is yet another lesson. People who were downsized from a corporate environment suddenly enter the entrepreneurial world and find the transition to be tough.

Management Traps

The most common fatal flaws of supervisors include:
- Insensitivity and/or abrasiveness to employees.
- Tendency to over-manage.
- Inability to delegate.
- Inflexibility.
- Poor crisis management...are reactive to problems, rather than being pro-active.
- Aloofness.

Bosses traditionally manage things so that workers will do things right. The preferable style is to lead people, so that they will do the right things.

Most workers do not perform up to standards because they are not fully told what is expected. 90% of mistakes are made because of wrong instructions. Failure to communicate and provide training on the front end proves more costly to business in the longrun.

Within the ranks of workers, chain reactions occur. Attitudes create other problems. They may be delegated tasks but are not held accountable. Responsibility rests upon employees, just as it does with their supervisors.

How to Get More

Use the acronym SCORE to motivate staff in the best manner:

• Seek suggestions.

• Comfort employees.

• Offer opportunities.

• Reassure them.

• Encourage risk taking.

The following suggestions are offered to maximize productivity:

• Set and maintain boundaries, while giving employees the latitude to add their own touches and, thus, invest themselves in their jobs.

• Set performance standards, giving reasons, tasks to perform and a vision of what "finished" looks like.

• Assign priorities.

• Have starting and ending times for project assignments, rather than be nebulous.

• Identify your people's strengths and weaknesses.

• Pinpoint staff's strengths in relation to the company's strengths at the soonest possible point.

Employees should aspire to be leaders. Thus, they will become empowered employees and will be ready to assume supervisory duties, when appropriate. Effective leaders:

- Provide vision.
- Inspire commitment.
- Create strategies.
- Encourage, rather than push or force people to do things.
- Realize that, with a team effort, everyone's share of the pie grows.

In summation, as one climbs The Organization Tree (Career Track for Professionals), one must amass skills and knowledge, as well as the:

- Art of being a leader.
- Art of being a boss.
- Art of being a good team member.
- Art of interchanging roles, responsibilities...the mark of a truly valuable professional.

5

Independent Television Producers

Case Studies of Hollywood Adapting to Television.

The biggest problem with business in general is an arrogance that its status quo will be maintained at all costs. By looking the other way, they seemingly avoid the winds of change...and live in a dream world. When they find the winds have already blown without them, companies then spend years and dollars in playing catch-up.

Of course, it would have been more expedient to spot the trends and benefit from change. Business rarely learns the lessons and changes with the marketplace later, rather than sooner.

Hollywood is no exception. The studios underestimated the impact and importance of TV. What they initially saw as a detriment ultimately became the savior of the Hollywood studios. The ultimate beneficiaries were the consuming public.

Most major studios avoided TV in the 1950s, as though it was the plague. They cited several reasons, which constituted their existing corporate agendas. Among the beliefs which they articulated into policies included:

- That TV was a threat to movie theatre attendances.
- That TV was lesser quality than movies and would always be a stepchild.
- That the only talents working in TV were because they could not cut it in movies.
- That the material pandered to the lowest common denominator.
- That TV was good as a showcase for promoting movies.
- That TV threatened to end the movie studio system.
- That a few grandiose movies could effectively compete with the TV invasion.
- That the TV threat would eventually go away and movies' status quo would return.
- That movies shown on TV hurt box office attendance.
- That movie palaces as we knew them would always remain the same.
- That movies could not play well on the small screen.
- That movies will never be shown directly on home TV sets.

Obviously, these flaws in the major studios' corporate thinking have mostly been proven to be untrue. Yet, many a studio executive went down in defeat proclaiming that things would return to what they once were in their glory days. This fallacy in mindset brings down most companies in most industries...Hollywood tends to stand on ceremony more than other industries.

Beginning in 1948, television was fertile new ground for independent producers based out of Hollywood. There was much available airtime to fill. It was a whole new ballgame, and the pioneers always get to invent as they go.

Audiences would not buy a steady diet of live New York originated programming forever. The major studios were decrying television as the biggest threat that had besieged theatre going. Radio whetted appetites for programming that could only be fulfilled with adding pictures to sounds.

The handwriting was on the wall for the two strongest bastions for independent movie producers: repeat-run movie houses and drive-in theatres. They would be replaced by television. This chain of events was the natural progression for the newly emerging medium.

Independent movie producers began looking toward television. So did radio producers. They saw filmed anthologies and series as vehicles to continue some semblance of the studio system. Indies wished to find employment for actors and crews who were acclimated to B-movies on scant budgets and quick production schedules. They wanted to showcase major stars whose heydays on the big screen had peaked, build their own stables of new talents and innovate techniques that they couldn't in the motion picture or radio forms.

The earliest series, independently produced, were transitioned from radio, or were close clones to radio shows. These included "Martin Kane, Private Eye," "Mr. and Mrs. North," "Suspense," "The Lone Ranger," "The Green Hornet," "Lux Playhouse," "Burns & Allen Show," "Sky King," "Adventures of Superman," "Death Valley Days," "Sergeant Preston of the Yukon," etc.

Others were reworked plots from movies. These included "The New Adventures of Charlie Chan," "The Third Man," "The Cisco Kid," "Boston Blackie," "How to Marry a Millionaire," etc. A few (such as "Playhouse 15," "The Gabby Hayes Show," "The Tim McCoy Show") were directly edited from B movies.

Very soon, a new breed of independent producers emerged. They had started in movies, acquired additional skills in radio and saw television as a blank slate on which to create. Rather than try to recreate what they did in other media, people like Dick Powell, Desi Arnaz and Frederick Ziv charted new ground. Ultimately, the major studios followed their leads.

Ziv

Frederick W. Ziv bought a radio transcription company and advanced it into television. Radio transcriptions were delayed-broadcasts for markets around the country. Some were original productions, and others were repeat broadcasts. This became the mold for Ziv Television.

In the 1950s, there was no inventory of reruns, other than old movies. Ziv produced low-budget, fast-paced programming that could run in fringe timeslots on local network-affiliated stations, as well as serving as mainstay programming for independent non-network stations. In time, Ziv also became a distributor for off-network programs, known as reruns.

Ziv aggressively sold programs to sponsors, who took packages directly to stations. The Ziv chain was like having another network. Stations bought new programs based upon Ziv's seamless concept of good programs, good selling potential and consistency in delivery.

For series stars, Ziv recruited bankable movie talents who also had the finesse of stage stars, since Take 1 was usually what you saw in the edited films. Great talents like Broderick Crawford, Macdonald Carey, Richard Carlson and Gene Barry possessed and utilized all the powers to draw out good performances from ensemble casts. Even actors blowing lines could gracefully recover and turn in consistently high performances.

Ziv had a repertory company of directors, producers and writers, who rotated the various series. Contract actors worked well on Ziv productions, some of whom (Leonard Nimoy, Stuart Whitman, Guy Williams) later propelling to stardom after cutting their teeth at Ziv.

Ziv shows had action, lots of outdoor sequences (to cut down studio rental time), easily followed plotlines and appeal to all members of the family. They had values, style and believability.

Ziv's TV Series:

Cisco Kid (Duncan Renaldo, Leo Carrillo)

Boston Blackie (Kent Taylor)

Your Favorite Story (anthology, hosted by Adolphe Menjou)

I Led Three Lives (Richard Carlson)

Mr. District Attorney (David Brian)

Meet Corliss Archer (Ann Maker, Mary Brian, Bobby Ellis, John Eldredge)

Science Fiction Theatre (anthology, hosted by Truman Bradley)

Highway Patrol (Broderick Crawford)

Dr. Christian (Macdonald Carey)

The Man Called X (Barry Sullivan)

Adventures at Scott Island (Barry Sullivan)

New Adventures of Martin Kane (William Gargan)

Sea Hunt (Lloyd Bridges)

Tombstone Territory (Pat Conway, Richard Eastham)

Harbor Command (Wendell Corey)

The Rough Riders (Kent Taylor, Jan Merlin, Peter Whitney)

Bat Masterson (Gene Barry)

MacKenzie's Readers (Richard Carlson)

This Man Dawson (Keith Andes)

Men Into Space (William Lundigan)

Lock Up (Macdonald Carey)

Bold Venture (Dane Clark)

Miami Undercover (Lee Bowman)

The Case of the Dangerous Robin (Rick Jason)

Klondike (Ralph Taeger)

King of Diamonds (Broderick Crawford)

The Everglades (Ron Hayes)

Ripcord (Larry Pennell, Ken Curtis)

Self-Produced TV Shows

Many stars from the movies and radio saw their future courses in the new medium of television. In the beginning, there was no studio, so they just formed their own production companies. The purpose was to produce and shepherd every aspect of their own starring shows.

Self-Produced TV Series. Included "The Adventures of Ozzie & Harriet," "I Married Joan," "Jack Benny Show," "Loretta Young Show" and "Roy Rogers Show" (his Frontier Productions also filming "Brave Eagle," a sympathetic portrayal of American Indians.)

Gene Autry saw the problems associated with distribution of his motion pictures and (like Walt Disney) formed his own company to produce shows directly for television. In addition to "The Gene Autry Show," his Flying A Productions also produced "The Range Rider," "Annie Oakley" and "Buffalo Bill Jr."

Two major independent producers started out as self-produced single series. Their talents, finesse and audience appeal were so vast that large production companies evolved. Their names were Desilu and Four Star.

Desilu

Much has been written about one of the great romances of the century. Lucille Ball and Desi Arnaz met on a movie set and soon married. Desi was constantly on the road with his band, and Lucy was a working actress in Hollywood. They yearned to spend more time together, and working together was the means to achieving their goal.

Over objections to casting Desi as her on-screen husband, "I Love Lucy" was born. Desi didn't know much about TV production. He assembled a team of experts and quickly mastered the process. They say that necessity is the mother of invention. Desi knew that Lucy worked best in front of a live audience, so he employed the three-camera filming technique that became industry standard.

The network assumed that Lucy and Desi would come to New York to do their show, as had George Burns and Gracie Allen. In order to stay in Hollywood with their new baby, Desilu Productions was formed. When Lucy got pregnant again in the second season, Desi filled some weeks by inventing a new TV concept...reruns.

When "I Love Lucy" became the medium's mega-hit, Desilu responded by pioneering other concepts, such as syndicating reruns while original episodes were still on the network and dubbing foreign-language episodes for the growing international marketplace.

What killed Desilu was its quest to become a major studio. This put strains on the Lucy-Desi marriage. Personal problems of Desi Arnaz kept him from taking care of business. Desilu coasted, then eroded and finally was acquired by Paramount.

Desilu's TV Series:

I Love Lucy (Lucille Ball, Desi Arnaz, Vivian Vance, William Frawley)

The Lineup/San Francisco Beat (Warner Anderson, Tom Tully)

Our Miss Brooks (Eve Arden, Gale Gordon, Richard Crenna, Robert Rockwell)

Life and Legend of Wyatt Earp (Hugh O'Brian)

December Bride (Spring Byington, Frances Rafferty, Harry Morgan, Verna Felton)

Adventures of Jim Bowie (Scott Forbes)

Gale Storm Show (Gale Storm, Zasu Pitts)

Sheriff of Cochise/U.S. Marshal (John Bromfield)

Official Detective Stories (anthology, hosted by Everett Sloane)

Walter Winchell File (anthology, hosted by Walter Winchell)

Grand Jury (Lyle Bettger, Harold J. Stone)

Desilu Playhouse (which spun off "The Untouchables" and "Twilight Zone")

Ann Sothern Show (Ann Sothern, Don Porter, Ernest Truex)

The Texan (Rory Calhoun)

The Californians (Richard Coogan)

The Untouchables (Robert Stack)

Barbara Stanwyck Show (anthology, hosted by Barbara Stanwyck)

Guestward Ho (Joanne Dru, Mark Miller, J. Carrol Naish, Flip Mark)

Harrigan and Son (Pat O'Brien, Roger Perry)

The Lucy Show (Lucille Ball, Vivian Vance, Gale Gordon)

The Mothers-in-Law (Eve Arden, Kaye Ballard)

Here's Lucy (Lucille Ball, Gale Gordon)

Star Trek (William Shatner, Leonard Nimoy, DeForest Kelley)

Mission: Impossible (Steven Hill, Peter Graves, Barbara Bain, Martin Landau, Greg Morris, Peter Lupus)

Four Star

Dick Powell was fresh from Arkansas when he became a juvenile player in Warner Brothers musicals of the 1930s. Seeking to change his image, Powell played in film noire mysteries. He was the first in Hollywood to "reinvent himself." He did many radio shows, notable "Richard Diamond, Private Detective."

The Powell style included staccato delivery of lines, sophisticated humor, wise cracks, plot ironies and "good guy wins out over evil" direction in storylines. Powell's shows were chocked full of wit, style, good writing, good acting and quality production. They had the components of an A picture and, thus, could be watched over and over again.

Powell formed Four Star Productions with good friends David Niven and Charles Boyer. They launched "Four Star Playhouse," an anthology dramatic series. The fourth star rotated, though it ultimately settled upon Ida Lupino.

Four Star then expanded into episodic television, beginning with "Richard Diamond, Private Detective," with Powell casting David Janssen in his former radio role. Four Star distinguished itself with cop shows and westerns. All had literate storylines, high production values and movie-quality acting. Thus, it is no wonder that stars of Four Star shows soon became superstars, including Steve McQueen, Robert Culp, Chuck Connors and David Janssen.

While the action genres flourished, Powell stuck with the playhouse format, as the jewel in Four Star's crown. After "Four Star Playhouse" went its course, Powell reinvented it in Western garb as "Zane Grey Theatre." In due course, that show was replaced by "The Dick Powell Show."

Niven and Boyer continued doing anthologies, via the Four Star-produced "Alcoa/Goodyear Theatre" and Niven's own series. The two later reteamed in "The Rogues." TV exposure rejuvenated Niven's movie career, winning him many coveted roles, box office popularity and an Oscar.

Four Star groomed independent producers who later struck gold on their own, notably Blake Edwards ("Peter Gunn," "Mr. Lucky" and the "Pink Panther" movies) and Aaron Spelling ("Charlie's Angels," " The Love Boat," "Fantasy Island," "Beverly Hills 90210," "Melrose Place"). Four Star joint-ventured on many projects, unlike the major studios, and created success via innovative approaches to business.

What led to Four Star scaling down was Powell's untimely death in 1963. Projects in the works ("Burke's Law," "The Rogues," "Honey West," "The Big Valley") saw fruition in the 60s, but the rudder to the ship was gone. Four Star and Desilu stand as monuments to strong talents, good teams and fulfillment of a niche in program production until such time as the major studios took over filmed TV.

Four Star's TV Series:

Four Star Playhouse (Dick Powell, David Niven, Charles Boyer, Ida Lupino)

Alcoa/Goodyear Theatre (anthology)

Richard Diamond, Private Detective (David Janssen)

Zane Grey Theatre (anthology, hosted by Dick Powell)

Dupont Theatre (anthology)

Trackdown (Robert Culp)

Wanted Dead or Alive (Steve McQueen)

The Rifleman (Chuck Connors, Johnny Crawford)

Black Saddle (Peter Breck)

Law of the Plainsman (Michael Ansara)

Johnny Ringo (Don Durant)

The Westerner (Brian Keith)

Michael Shayne (Richard Denning)

Stagecoach West (Robert Bray, Wayne Rogers)

The Detectives (Robert Taylor)

The Law and Mr. Jones (James Whitmore)

Dante (Howard Duff)

Ensign O'Toole (Dean Jones)

Dick Powell Show (anthology, hosted by Dick Powell)

June Allyson Show (anthology, hosted by June Allyson)

Target: The Corrupters (Stephen McNally, Robert Harland)

Burke's Law (Gene Barry)

The Rogues (David Niven, Charles Boyer, Gig Young)

Honey West (Anne Francis, John Ericson)

The Big Valley (Barbara Stanwyck, Richard Long, Peter Breck, Lee Majors, Linda Evans)

Disney

Walt Disney was a pioneering creative talent. He wasn't the strongest businessman. Driven by creativity, his studio was on the brink of financial disaster on more than one occasion. Eager to get money to build his amusement park, Disney partnered with the fledgling ABC-TV. "Disneyland" became a Hollywood showcase series...a potpourri of retreaded theatrical material, new features, documentaries and promotion of current Disney projects.

Through TV, Disney reached new generations of fans...those who are now parents and grandparents of current Disney consumers. The Disney organization of today is much more prolific and profitable than in Walt's time. Its success can be traced to the crossroads when Walt emerged from his creative environment and began a series of business collaborations that transformed his company.

Disney kept the creative product above par. Like Desi Arnaz and Dick Powell, Disney invested heavily in production...knowing that it would not pay for itself until reruns and syndication. Quality paid off at all stages...thus the foundation of the enduring Disney empire.

Disney's TV series:

"Disneyland...Walt Disney's Wonderful World of Color...Walt Disney Presents,"

"Mickey Mouse Club"

"Zorro" (Guy Williams).

McCadden

McCadden Productions started as another one-show company, but then it diversified. George Burns and Gracie Allen tired of commutes to New York to do their shows live. CBS then switched their base of operations to the West Coast, though the show remained live. Spawned by the success of "I Love Lucy," Burns and Allen switched to the filmed sitcom concept.

McCadden subsequently produced comedies for other stellar performers, plus one suspense anthology series, "Panic." These gave Burns' stable of writers the chance to diversify, though the emphasis remained on vaudeville comedy, lots of jokes, tricky-unbelievable plotlines and great joy for the viewers. Burns even championed the creation of "Mr. Ed," which became a Filmways production.

McCadden's TV series:

"Burns & Allen Show" (George Burns, Gracie Allen, Bea

Benaderet, Fred Clark, Larry Keating)

"Bob Cummings Show/Love That Bob" (Bob Cummings, Ann B. Davis, Rosemary DeCamp, Dwayne Hickman)

"The People's Choice" (Jackie Cooper)

"Panic" (anthology)

"George Burns Show" (George Burns)

"Wendy and Me" (George Burns, Connie Stevens).

Filmways

McCadden alumni and their compadres worked well at Filmways. The comedies were high-energy, vaudeville-like and were welcome fixtures in the homes of viewers. They have remained among the most popular reruns in TV history.

Filmways TV series:

"Mr. Ed" (Alan Young, Connie Hines, Larry Keating, Edna Skinner)

"The Beverly Hillbillies" (Buddy Ebsen, Irene Ryan, Donna Douglas, Max Baer, Raymond Bailey)

"Petticoat Junction" (Bea Benaderet, Edgar Buchanan, June Lockhart)

"Green Acres" (Eddie Albert, Eva Gabor).

Danny Thomas-Sheldon Leonard

Like Desi Arnaz, Danny Thomas had spent a disproportionate amount of time on the road working. The title "Make Room for Daddy" was actually uttered by his children. Thus, he got the idea of an autobiographical sitcom, with storylines, kids' anecdotes and realities just like his own.

Thomas formed Marterto Productions, named for his three children, Marlo, Terry and Tony. He leased space at Desilu Studios and collaborated with Sheldon Leonard, known to movie goers as an actor who specialized in playing gangsters. The Thomas-Leonard partnership endured and produced some of the most memorable TV series of the 50s and 60s.

Danny Thomas/Sheldon Leonard TV Series:

Make Room for Daddy (Danny Thomas, Jean Hagen, Marjorie Lord, Sherry Jackson, Rusty Hamer, Angela Cartwright, Sid Melton, Pat Carroll)

The Real McCoys (Walter Brennan, Richard Crenna, Kathy Nolan)

Andy Griffith Show (Andy Griffith, Don Knotts, Ronny Howard, Frances Bavier)

Dick Van Dyke Show (Dick Van Dyke, Mary Tyler Moore, Morey Amsterdam, Rose Marie, Carl Reiner, Richard Deacon, Jerry Paris, Ann Morgan Guilbert, Larry Matthews)

Joey Bishop Show (Joey Bishop)

Bill Dana Show (Bill Dana)

Gomer Pyle, USMC (Jim Nabors)

That Girl (Marlo Thomas)

I Spy (Robert Culp, Bill Cosby)

Aaron Spelling

Aaron Spelling acknowledges Dick Powell as his mentor. As an actor who switched to writing scripts, Spelling learned that becoming a producer was the best way to showcase his literary works. He began at Four Star by writing introductory lines for Dick Powell on "Zane Grey Theatre." At Four Star, he produced several series, including Powell's prestigious hour-long anthology. Based upon his Four Star experiences, Spelling continued to revere and champion the television forms of westerns, anthologies and crime dramas.

Spelling became the most commercially successful television producer and had collaborators at various times, including Danny Thomas and Leonard Goldberg.

Aaron Spelling's TV Series:

Guns of Will Sonnett (Walter Brennan, Dack Rambo)

Rango (Tim Conway)

The Mod Squad (Michael Cole, Peggy Lipton, Clarence Williams, Tige Andrews)

The New People

The Silent Force (Ed Nelson, Lynda Day George, Percy Rodriguez)

The Most Deadly Game (George Maharis, Yvette Mimieux, Ralph Bellamy)

The Rookies (Georg Stanford Brown, Michael Ontkean, Sam Melville, Kate Jackson)

Starsky and Hutch (David Soul, Paul Michael Glaser)

S.W.A.T. (Robert Urich, Steve Forrest, Rod Perry)

Family (James Broderick, Sada Thompson, Kristy McNichol, Gary Frank, Meredith Baxter)

Charlie's Angels (Farrah Fawcett, Jacklyn Smith, Kate Jackson, Cheryl Ladd, David Doyle)

The Love Boat (Gavin MacLeod, Bernie Kopell, Fred Grandy, Ted Lange, Lauren Tewes)

Fantasy Island (Ricardo Montalban, Herve Villechaize)

Vegas (Robert Urich, Phyllis Davis)

Hart to Hart (Robert Wagner, Stefanie Powers)

Dynasty (John Forsythe, Linda Evans, Joan Collins)

T.J. Hooker (William Shatner, Heather Locklear, Adrian Zmed)

Matt Houston (Lee Horsley)

Hotel (James Brolin, Connie Selleca, Shari Belafonte, Anne Baxter)

Beverly Hills 90210

Melrose Place

QM

Quinn Martin honed his talents, business finesse and knowledge of styles-trends by working for Ziv. He then joined Desilu, producing "Desilu Playhouse" and its spin-off series, "The Untouchables."

QM Productions series were stylistic, almost film noir in context. Each act and the closing Epilog were labeled, augmented by narration. The emphasis was upon characters interfacing, despite circumstances. Lead characters showcased the guest stars and their stories...setting the tone for subsequent Hollywood drama series.

QM's TV Series:

The Fugitive (David Janssen)

The FBI (Efrem Zimbalist Jr.)

The Invaders (Roy Thinnes)

Twelve O'Clock High (Robert Lansing, Paul Burke)

Barnaby Jones (Buddy Ebsen)

Cannon (William Conrad)

Streets of San Francisco (Karl Malden, Michael Douglas)

The Hunter (Ken Howard)

Sharpe-Lewis

Don W. Sharpe and Warren Lewis boasted successful partnerships with both Desilu and Four Star. They leased studio space from both and produced one-of-a-kind series that stand as all-time favorites to veteran TV collectors.

Sharpe-Lewis TV series:

"Meet McGraw" (Frank Lovejoy)

"Yancy Derringer" (Jock Mahoney)

"Man With a Camera" (Charles Bronson).

Hal Roach

Many of the early independent TV producers leased studio space with Hal Roach, just as had been done in movies since the 1920s. Roach studios released its movie catalog to TV, with "Our Gang Comedies" retitled "The Little Rascals" for the tube. Roach housed production of many TV commercials, as well as numerous independent producers.

Hal Roach's TV Series:

Amos n' Andy (Tim Moore, Spencer, Williams, Alvin Childress, Ernestine Wade, Johnny Lee)

My Little Margie (Gale Storm, Charles Farrell)

Screen Directors Playhouse (anthology)

Telephone Time (anthology)

Other 1950s Independent Producers

Here is a capsule example of early TV. Small independent producers created the first wave of filmed TV shows. They were successful and, thus, drew competition to their field. Second generation independents took the production market to dominate. Major studios, in turn, stole the major independents' domination. This was the genesis of Hollywood-produced TV programming in the 1950s and 1960s.

Roland Reed followed the Ziv formula with action-adventure shows. His biggest successes included "Racket Squad" (Reed Hadley), "Waterfront" (Preston Foster), "Public Defender" (Reed Hadley), "Code 3" (Richard Travis) and "Passport to Danger" (Cesar Romero).

An excellent producer in the first wave, the trail blazers, was Bernard L. Schubert. His series included "Topper" (Ann Jeffreys, Robert Sterling, Leo J. Carroll), "Adventures of the Falcon" (Charles McGraw) and "The Lone Wolf" (Louis Hayward).

Russell Hayden Productions specialized in Westerns aimed at

the youth market. Hayden was a former staple in B Westerns of the 1940s. On TV, he produced and starred in "Cowboy G-Men," along with Jackie Coogan. He also produced "Judge Roy Bean" and "26 Men."

Gross-Krasne produced "Big Town/Heart of the City" (Patrick McVey, Jane Nigh) (based upon a radio series) and "O. Henry Playhouse" (anthology, hosted by Thomas Mitchell).

Jack Webb's Mark VII Productions brought us "Dragnet" (from radio), "The D.A.'s Man" (John Compton), "Adam 12" (Martin Milner, Kent McCord). Jack Wrather Productions produced "The Lone Ranger" (Clayton Moore, Jay Silverheels) and "Lassie" (Jon Provost, June Lockhart, Hugh Reilly, George Chandler).

The kings of game show production, Mark Goodson and Bill Todman, entered the field of filmed dramatic series. Theirs included "The Rebel" (Nick Adams) and "Branded" (Chuck Connors).

TPA brought us "Fury" (Peter Graves, Bobby Diamond, William Fawcett), "The Count of Monte Cristo" (George Dolenz), "Hawkeye-Last of the Mohicans" (John Hart, Lon Chaney) and "The New Adventures of Charlie Chan" (J. Carrol Naish).

The studio system in television would not have emerged without early pioneering by independent production companies, who blazed the trails, took the chances and created the formulas. As is the case with big business, the larger players follow the pioneers, sand the rough edges, package the product glossier, create new revenue streams and dominate the marketplace.

The major studios dismissed TV in its infancy because they feared it. Given successes of the independent production companies, the major studios soon charted their own courses to conquer TV. Early attempts were lukewarm. By the end of the 1960s, major studios grabbed the stronghold from the independents, perfected the processes and reaped the rewards.

It's Channel 7 for...

New GRAND SLAM

"HALL of FAME"

BASEBALL'S GREATEST MOMENTS

with MARTY GLICKMAN

in *Interviews — Action*

Joe Di Maggio
Larry Doby
Bob Feller
Preacher Roe
Stan Musial
Yogi Berra
Pee Wee Reese
Warren Spahn
Monte Irvin
Marty Marion
Johnny Pesky

You'll relive unforgettable **PLAYS** of baseball history from All-Star and World Series games — and meet the **PLAYERS** who make the diamond sport America's favorite of exciting sports!

7:45 P.M. **WNAC-TV**

TUESDAY
WEDNESDAY
THURSDAY

6

Foreign Import Shows

Foreign television filmed productions made a big splash on the American airwaves in the 1950s and 1960s, for a variety of reasons. In television's first decade, the major Hollywood studios were not yet of the mind to cooperate with the fledgling medium, least of all produce all of the filmed programming that was needed. Thus, the networks and syndicators looked elsewhere for material.

After World War II, new themes and locales had begun appearing in mainstream movies. The realities of war brought us stories of international intrigue, rebuilding of societies, searches for lost families and the globalization of the world's business and culture. No longer were all films made on Hollywood backlots. In order to present modern stories effectively, location filming took viewers to every part of the world.

Film noir was revolutionizing the movies. Early TV series borrowed stylistically from this genre. European film techniques took the concept further. With a familiarity for certain storylines and locales, the audiences expressed a desire to see television series crafted after certain genres and specific concepts. American producers also went global to produce series with new settings, also avoiding union scales for crews.

Many former Hollywood producers and stars found new careers

by creating productions in heretofore uncharted territories. Former screen Tarzan and champion athlete Buster Crabbe took his own production company to French Morocco for the filming of "Captain Gallant of the Foreign Legion," which also starred Cuffy Crabbe (his son) and Fuzzy Knight.

Clint Eastwood's trek to Italy for a film during a hiatus on "Rawhide" proved to be the supercharge for his future movie career. After four hit American TV series, Gene Barry added a British show, "Adventurer" to his prestigious resume.

Following his Saturday morning series "Fury," Peter Graves starred in two American series which were filmed abroad, "Court-Martial" (England, with Bradford Dillman) and "Whiplash" (Australia). Both of these series expanded his TV body of work that made him more bankable in the Hollywood super-series with an international look, "Mission: Impossible."

There were espionage shows set against post-war reconstruction-era European motifs. Sheldon Reynolds went across Europe for "Foreign Intrigue," stories of post-war espionage through the eyes of three sub-series: "Dateline Europe" (Jerome Thor), "Overseas Adventure" (James Daly) and "Cross Current" (Gerald Mohr). Reynolds utilized actors and crews from Sweden and France, affording many talents their first U.S. exposure.

Another espionage show, "Secret File USA" (1953, starring Robert Alda), roved Europe with Danish casts and crews.

Hollywood subsequently copied and added its own production values to this concept, with series including "Dangerous Assignment" (1952, Brian Donlevy), "I Led Three Lives" (1953, Richard Carlson), "Lone Wolf" (1954, Louis Hayward), "Passport to Danger" (1954, Cesar Romero), "The Hunter" (1954, Barry Nelson), "Crusader" (1955, Brian Keith), "I Spy" (1955, Raymond Massey), "The Man Called X" (1956, Barry Sullivan), "China Smith" (1956, Dan Duryea), "Behind Closed Doors" (1958, Bruce Gordon), "International Detective" (1959, Art Fleming), "Five Fingers" (1959, David Hedison, Luciana Paluzzi, Paul Burke) and "The Third Man" (1960, Michael Rennie, Jonathan Harris).

Great Britain exported the largest number of series to the United

States and, thus, the rest of the world. The first wave centered around costume dramas based upon English legends previously romanticized in books and movies.

The first period piece was "The Adventures of Robin Hood" in 1955. Richard Greene had been acting in America but returned home to his native England to don Lincoln Green and lead the merry band in Sherwood Forest. His Robin Hood characterization is more imbued in the consciousness of baby boomers than that of Errol Flynn in the movies. Greene's ensemble cast set the precedent for other British costume dramas.

Other period-piece historical adventures which subsequently hit on U.S. television included "Adventures of Sir Francis Drake" (1962, Terence Morgan), "Adventures of Sir Lancelot" (1956, William Russell), "Adventures of William Tell" (1957, Conrad Phillips), "The Buccaneers" (1956, Robert Shaw) and "Long John Silver" (1956, Robert Newton).

A Hollywood attempt to copy this trend was "Ivanhoe," produced by Columbia/Screen Gems. It marked the series debut of Roger Moore, who would subsequently have two more American series ("The Alaskans," "Maverick") and two British series ("The Saint," "The Persuaders") before succeeding Sean Connery as James Bond in several 007 films.

Next came the wave of British adventure, suspense, drama and mystery series, including "Scotland Yard" (1956), "African Patrol" (1957, John Bentley), "Colonel March of Scotland Yard" (1954, Boris Karloff), "The Invisible Man" (1958), "The Man from Interpol" (1960, Richard Wyler, John Longden), "Mark Saber of London" (1957, Donald Gray), "The White Hunter" (1957, Rhodes Reason), "The Pursuers" (1960, Louis Hayward) and "The Cheaters" (1960, John Ireland).

London super-sleuth Sherlock Holmes surfaced periodically on TV series. The first was in 1954, produced by Sheldon Reynolds at the same time that he was traveling Europe to film "Foreign Intrigue." Reynolds starred Ronald Howard in the 1954 series and Geoffrey Whitehead in the 1968 color series. A 1980s and 90s Sherlock Holmes (for Granada, British TV) starred Jeremy Brett.

British-produced anthology series brought a variety of stories, stars and styles into the world's living rooms. Such series of the 1950s and 60s included "The Veil" (1957, Boris Karloff), "The Vise" (1958, Ron Randell), "Mystery and Imagination," "Hammer House of Horrors" and "Edgar Wallace Mysteries."

The year 1960 marked the start of two series that spawned an entire spy show genre for British and later American television. Both predated the James Bond craze and, though compatible with it, were mystery-espionage shows all their own. "Danger Man" starred Patrick McGoohan as an international detective named John Drake, who aided various law enforcement agencies with his super-sleuthing. The series was a half-hour when first broadcast in the U.S. in 1961. Then, it expanded to an hour, with the "Danger Man" title remaining. In 1965, the hour-long episodes were again tele-vised in the U.S., under the title "Secret Agent" and with an American theme song recorded by Johnny Rivers.

When John Drake left the intelligence corps, his character was whisked off to a Utopian community and exposed to a variety of mind games and struggles to retain his own self-sufficiency. Patrick McGoohan helped create and starred in this landmark series, "The Prisoner." In the U.S., "The Prisoner" first appeared as a summer replacement for Jackie Gleason. It subsequently gravitated to pub-lic television and video cassette classic status.

"Police Surgeon" began Sept. 10, 1960, as a live mystery series starring Ian Hendry. Its premiere show, "Easy Money," marked one of the earliest guest-starring roles for Michael Crawford, later to become the singing sensation of "Phantom of the Opera." In order to bolster the show, Patrick Macnee was added in the character of detective John Steed. By season's end, the title had been changed to "The Avengers," and Macnee emerged as the star.

"The Avengers" was sophisticated, witty, fast-paced and cere-bral in its solutions to complex mysteries. Macnee boasted a series of charismatic leading ladies to assist him in solving crimes, includ-ing Julie Stevens, Honor Blackman, Diana Rigg, Linda Thorson and Joanna Lumley. During the Blackman seasons, the show switched from live-on-tape to a filmed format, employing more action, country sides and more locations. These shows paralleled the James Bond movies, collectively popularizing spy films and secret agent dramas.

Other 1960s British shows which were syndicated to U.S. stations included "Glencannon" (1957, Thomas Mitchell), "Adventures of a Jungle Boy" (1957, Michael Carr Hartley), "O.S.S." (1957, Ron Randell), "Interpol Calling" (1959, Charles Korvin) "The Flying Doctor" (1959, Richard Denning), "The Four Just Men" (1959, Dan Dailey, Jack Hawkins, Richard Conte, Vittoria DeSica), "Ghost Squad" (1961, Donald Wolfit), "Zero One" (1962, Nigel Patrick), "Man of the World" (1962, Craig Stevens), "The Sentimental Agent" (1963, Carlos Thompson), "Gideon's Way" (1964, John Gregson) and "The Human Jungle" (1964, Herbert Lom).

With the success of 1960s British spy shows, Hollywood studios produced their own versions. Some of the most memorable American counterparts included "The Man from UNCLE" (1964, Robert Vaughn, David McCallum, Leo G. Carroll), "I Spy" (1965, Robert Culp, Bill Cosby), "Get Smart" (1965, Don Adams, Barbara Feldon), "Blue Light" (1966, Robert Goulet), "Mission: Impossible" (1966, Peter Graves, Martin Landau, Barbara Bain, Greg Morris, Peter Lupus, Leonard Nimoy, Lesley Ann Warren), "The Girl from UNCLE" (1966, Stefanie Powers, Noel Harrison, Leo G. Carroll), "Most Deadly Game" (1970, George Maharis, Yvette Mimieux, Ralph Bellamy) and "Silent Force" (1970, Ed Nelson, Lynda Day George, Percy Rodrigues).

The next wave of filmed British intrigue shows often featured stars who were well-known from hit American TV shows. They included "The Saint" (1963, Roger Moore), "The Adventurer" (1972, Gene Barry), "The Persuaders" (1971, Roger Moore, Tony Curtis, Laurence Naismith), "Man in a Suitcase" (1967, Richard Bradford), "The Protectors" (1972, Robert Vaughn), "Department S" (1970, Peter Wyngarde, Joel Fabiani, Rosemary Nicols, Dennis Alaba Peters) and "The Thunderbirds" (1965).

The British continued to supply the world with quality live-on-tape series for each decade since the 1950s. Such shows included

"Hancock's Half Hour," "Doctor Who," "Monty Python's Flying Circus," "The Benny Hill Show," "Quartermass and the Pit" and "Masterpiece Theatre." And there were the British influences upon American TV. "Till Death Do Us Part" inspired "All in the Family" (1971, Carroll O'Connor, Jean Stapleton, Rob Reiner, Sally Struthers). "Steptoe and Son" inspired "Sanford and Son" (1972, Redd Foxx, Demond Wilson).

Australian television brought us such series as "Whiplash" (1961, Peter Graves)," "Riptide" (1968, Ty Hardin), "Chopper Squad" (1971, Dennis Christopher), "Spyforce" (1970, Jack Thompson) and "Skippy the Bush Kangaroo (1966, Ed Devereaux, Tony Bonner, Garry Pankhurst, Liza Goddard).

Canadian television brought us such series as "Salty" (1972, Mark Slade), "Forest Rangers" (1965), "Quentin Durgens, M.P." (1968, Gordon Pinsent), "R.C.M.P./Royal Canadian Mounted Police" (1959, Gilles Pelletier, John Perkins) and "Wojeck" (1968, John Vernon).

American television suppliers began producing series in Europe. Shows produced in England included "The New Adventures of Charlie Chan" (1957, J. Carrol Naish) and "The New Adventures of Martin Kane, Private Eye" (1957, William Gargan). Shows produced in France included "The Count of Monte Cristo" (1955, George Dolenz) and "Paris Precinct" (1956, Louis Jourdan, Claude Dauphin). Shows produced in Canada included "Last of the Mohicans" (1957, John Hart, Lon Chaney) and "Hudson's Bay" (1958, Barry Nelson, George Tobias). Shows produced in Sweden included "13 Demon Street" (1960, Lon Chaney).

7

Emergence of the Studio System

Case Studies of Hollywood Adapting to Television.

History has shown that the independent TV producers carved a niche in the 1950s. The New York TV establishment had a vested interest in keeping TV there. Live dramas, variety shows and game shows had a New York emphasis.

The first wave of filmed Hollywood productions consisted of small independent companies who produced a variety of shows in the movie serial feature style. Other independents transferred their winning formulas from radio to the TV screen.

The second wave of TV independents were the innovators: Frederick Ziv, Desi Arnaz and Dick Powell. They created quality productions for the TV culture and banked on reruns to bring back their investments. They created the basis for filmed TV...which the major Hollywood studios followed, tried to duplicate and built upon.

By the 1970s, Hollywood studios learned how to creatively join in and dominate TV production. It recreated its own studio system. Many majors didn't learn the lessons that had benefited the independents in the 50s.

By the 1990s, more independents spun off the studio bureaucracies to create a domination of independent producers. History is indeed very cyclical.

This is a review of how each major Hollywood studio climbed on board the TV gravy train, their creative output and their contributions to the body of classic TV work.

Revue-Universal

Revue thought and behaved like an independent and successfully became the dominant studio in filmed television.

Universal was known for its "program pictures," B movies, horror series and low-budget westerns. It didn't have the luster of MGM and 20th Century-Fox, nor the stock company of Warner Brothers, nor the theatrical distribution network of Paramount. It was a second-tier studio, and it tried harder all the time.

While the major studios scoffed at TV in the late 40s, Universal got into TV first. It established Revue Productions. Revue produced anthologies, often lifting material from their old movies. Revue soon developed a dominance for theatrical-looking stories with mystery and suspense emphasis.

By the end of the 50s, Revue outdistanced the two major independents, Desilu and Four Star. Its success made Revue the cash cow for parent company MCA. Revue bought Universal International Pictures and in 1964 changed its name to Universal. Film lot tours started as a bread-and-butter necessity (just like TV production) and evolved Revue-Universal into a major tourist attraction.

Revue's high production values were enhanced by an excellent music program. Under the direction of Stanley Wilson, original scores were introduced to the studio's series, such as "Wagon Train." Previously, TV series (independent and major studios) used canned music. Wilson developed a stable of composers and arrangers, notably John Williams, Elmer Bernstein, Laurindo Almeida, Skip Martin and Jack Marshall.

To this day, the Revue theme song is still used at the end of Universal productions. It was written by Juan Esquivel in 1959, when he was scoring two popular Revue series, "Markham" and "The Tall Man."

Revue-Universal invented the made-for-TV movie. This carried forward the studio's program of anthology series, which were great proving grounds for former stars, up-and-coming stars and behind-the-scenes experts. To this day, made-for-TV movies are the closest thing to dramatic anthology series on the tube.

The studio groomed directors such as Steven Spielberg...who cut his teeth by directing TV episodes of "Columbo," "Name of the Game," "Rod Serling's Night Gallery," "Marcus Welby, M.D.," "Owen Marshall, Counselor at Law," "The Psychiatrist." He also directed such TV movies as "Something Evil," "Savage" and "Duel." Spielberg's Universal product for TV was just as high in quality as the feature films...thus ushering in the hybrid philosophy.

Thanks in large part to Universal, TV does not have to take a backseat to movies and, given the constraints, evolves many fine examples of the film art form.

Here are groupings of the memorable Revue-Universal shows from the 1950s, 1960s and 1970s...collectively establishing the largest Body of Work in classic television.

Revue-Universal Anthologies:

Alcoa Premiere/Fred Astaire Presents

Alfred Hitchcock Presents/Alfred Hitchcock Hour

Bob Hope Chrysler Theatre

Campbell Soundstage

Chevron Theatre

Fireside Theatre/Jane Wyman Presents (hosted by Jane Wyman)

General Electric Theatre (hosted by Ronald Reagan)

Kraft Suspense Theatre

Lux Playhouse

The Millionaire (hosted by Marvin Miller)

Night Gallery (hosted by Rod Serling)

Pepsi-Cola Playhouse

Schlitz Playhouse

Studio 57

Suspense (produced by Alfred Hitchcock)

Thriller (hosted by Boris Karloff)

Revue-Universal Crime-Mystery-Detective Shows:

Adam-12 (Martin Milner, Kent McCord)

Arrest and Trial (Ben Gazzara, Chuck Connors)

Baretta (Robert Blake)

Biff Baker, U.S.A. (Alan Hale, Randy Stuart)

Checkmate (Anthony George, Doug McClure, Sebastian Cabot)

City Detective, State Trooper, Coronado 9 (Rod Cameron series)

Columbo (Peter Falk)

The Crusader (Brian Keith)

Dragnet (Jack Webb, Harry Morgan)

87th Precinct (Robert Lansing)

Emergency (Robert Fuller, Julie London, Bobby Troup)

Hec Ramsey (Richard Boone)

Ironside (Raymond Burr)

It Takes a Thief (Robert Wagner, Malachi Throne)

Johnny Midnight (Edmond O'Brien)

Johnny Staccato (John Cassavetes)

M Squad (Lee Marvin)

Man Against Crime/Follow That Man (Ralph Bellamy, filmed in New York)

Markham (Ray Milland)

McCloud (Dennis Weaver)

McMillan and Wife (Rock Hudson, Susan Saint James)

Mike Hammer (Darren McGavin)

Quincy, M.E. (Jack Klugman)

Rockford Files (James Garner, Noah Beery)

Special Agent 7 (Lloyd Nolan)

Treasury Men/Federal Men (case dramatization, Walter Greaza)

Revue-Universal Westerns:

Adventures of Kit Carson (Bill Williams, Don Diamond)

Alias Smith and Jones (Pete Duel, Ben Murphy, Roger Davis)

The Deputy (Henry Fonda, Allen Case)

Frontier Circus (Chill Wills, John Derek, Richard Jaeckel)

Laramie (Robert Fuller, John Smith, Spring Byington, Hoagy Carmichael)

Laredo (Neville Brand, Peter Brown, Philip Carey, William Smith)

Overland Trail (William Bendix, Doug McClure)

The Restless Gun (John Payne)

Riverboat (Darren McGavin, Burt Reynolds)

Shotgun Slade (Scott Brady)

Tales of Wells Fargo (Dale Robertson)

The Tall Man (Barry Sullivan, Clu Gulager)

The Virginian (James Drury, Doug McClure, Lee J. Cobb, Charles Bickford, Roberta Shore)

Wagon Train (Ward Bond, Robert Horton, John McIntire, Frank McGrath, Terry Wilson)

Revue-Universal Dramatic Series:

The Bold Ones (E.G. Marshall, John Saxon, David Hartman, Hal Holbrook, Leslie Nielsen, Burl Ives, James Farentino, Joseph Campanella)

Channing (Henry Jones, Jason Evers)

The Incredible Hulk (Bill Bixby, Lou Ferigno)

Matt Lincoln (Vince Edwards)

Owen Marshall, Counselor at Law (Arthur Hill, Lee Majors)

Ramar of the Jungle (Jon Hall)

Run For Your Life (Ben Gazzara)

The Sixth Sense (Gary Collins)

Soldiers of Fortune (John Russell, Chick Chandler)

Wide Country (Earl Holliman, Andrew Prine)

Revue-Universal Comedies:

Bachelor Father, The John Forsythe Show (John Forsythe series)

Jack Benny Show (Jack Benny, Don Wilson, Eddie Anderson, Dennis Day, Mel Blanc)

Karen (Debbie Watson, Richard Denning)

Leave It To Beaver (Jerry Mathers, Barbara Billingsley, Hugh Beaumont, Tony Dow)

McHale's Navy (Ernest Borgnine, Joe Flynn, Tim Conway)

The Munsters (Fred Gwynne, Yvonne DeCarlo, Al Lewis)

Pistols 'n' Petticoats (Ann Sheridan, Douglas Fowley, Ruth McDevitt, Carole Wells)

Ray Milland Show/Meet Mr. McNutley (Ray Milland)

Tammy (Debbie Watson, Denver Pyle, Donald Woods, Frank McGrath)

Yes, Yes, Nanette (Nanette Fabray, Wendell Corey, Bobby Diamond)

Screen Gems-Columbia

Like Universal, Columbia Pictures was a B-movie studio. Under the management of Harry Cohn, it took risks, tried new things and basically tried harder. Out of necessity, Columbia learned how to film economically and get great work on tight production schedules and small budgets.

Columbia was the first major studio to piece together packages of its films for late shows. Columbia was the first major studio to get into television production, forming its Screen Gems subsidiary in 1949. Like Revue-Universal (which got into TV in 1950), Columbia adapted well to TV, reinventing its B-picture schedules and processes.

Screen Gems had a sitcom output that rivaled industry leader Desilu. It is for sitcoms that Screen Gems is best known today. However, in the 1950s, Columbia created several of its own TV specialty program niches for Screen Gems, including children's series such as "Tales of the Texas Rangers," "Captain Midnight" and "Circus Boy."

Screen Gems had the distinction of producing the first filmed movie for TV (1 hour) in 1951, an adaptation of "The Three Musketeers." The studio procuded filmed episodes for CBS's "Playhouse 90," a live series. The studio pioneered in producing filmed syndicated variety shows, from "Tex Ritter's Ranch Party" to "The Patti Page Show."

Screen Gems developed directors, producers, writers and performers who were versatile and developed staying power. Its proteges and alumni included Herbert B. Leonard, Harry Ackerman, Sally Field, Larry Hagman, Barbara Eden, Elizabeth Montgomery, Michael Nesmith, Paul Lynde and Monte Markham.

Classic Screen Gems Shows:

Ford Theatre (anthology)

Father Knows Best (Robert Young, Jane Wyatt, Elinor Donahue, Billy Gray, Lauren Chapin)

Adventures of Rin Tin Tin (Lee Aaker, James L. Brown)

Captain Midnight (Richard Webb, Sid Melton, Olan Soule)

Tales of the Texas Rangers (Willard Parker, Harry Lauter)

Circus Boy (Mickey Dolenz, Robert Karnes, Noah Beery)

Casey Jones (Alan Hale)

Syndicated music variety series, starring Tex Ritter, Patti Page, etc.

Donna Reed Show (Donna Reed, Carl Betz, Shelley Fabares, Paul Petersen)

Shirley Temple's Storybook (anthology, hosted by Shirley Temple)

Alcoa Theatre/Goodyear TV Playhouse

Rescue 8 (Jim Davis, Lang Jeffries)

Filmed episodes of "Playhouse 90"

Hotel de Paree (Earl Holliman, Jeanette Nolan, Strother Martin)

Tightrope (Mike Connors)

Manhunt (Victor Jory, Patrick McVey)

U.S. Border Patrol (Richard Webb)

Tallahassee 7000 (Walter Matthau)

Dennis the Menace (Jay North, Joseph Kearns, Herbert Anderson, Gloria Henry)

Route 66 (Martin Milner, George Maharis, Glenn Corbett)

Naked City (James Franciscus in 30-min. version, Paul Burke in one-hour form)

Shannon (George Nader, Regis Toomey)

Dan Raven (Skip Homeier)

Hazel (Shirley Booth, Don DeFore, Whitney Blake, Bobby Buntrock)

Empire/Redigo (Richard Egan, Ryan O'Neal)

Bewitched (Elizabeth Montgomery, Dick York, Agnes Moorehead, David White, Dick Sargent)

The Farmer's Daughter (William Windom, Inger Stevens)

I Dream of Jeannie (Barbara Eden, Larry Hagman, Bill Daily, Hayden Rorke)

Gidget (Sally Field, Don Porter, Pete Duel)

The Monkees (Mike Nesmith, Mickey Dolenz, Davy Jones, Peter Tork)

The Flying Nun (Sally Field, Alejandro Rey)

Love on a Rooftop (Pete Duel, Judy Carne)

Mr. Deeds Goes to Town (Monte Markham)

The Second Hundred Years (Arthur O'Connell, Monte Markham)

My World and Welcome To It (William Windom, Joan Hotchkis, Lisa Gerritsen)

The Partridge Family (Shirley Jones, David Cassidy, Susan Dey)

The Interns (Broderick Crawford, Mike Farrell)

The Good Life (Larry Hagman, Donna Mills)

Getting Together (Bobby Sherman)

Paul Lynde Show (Paul Lynde, Elizabeth Allen)

Temperatures Rising (Cleavon Little, James Whitmore, Joan Van Ark)

The Girl With Something Extra (John Davidson, Sally Field)

Republic

Republic Pictures dominated movie theatres in the 1930s and 1940s with its own brand of B-Westerns and serial thrillers. Their primary constituency was young people.

Its Western heyday spawned the careers of Gene Autry, Roy Rogers and John Wayne, plus a couple more tiers of favorite performers. Cliff-hanger serials balanced theatrical bills and served as the prototype for what later came to be known as episodic television.

Sadly, the Republic magic in movie theatres (especially small town arcades) did not translate into television. Republic's zenith had passed by the dawning of the TV age. Trying to compete, Republic had a few series that were draped around old footage from its serials. After a few attempts at TV, Republic sold its lot to Four Star, which later sold to CBS.

Republic maintained its distribution company and continues to reissue old movie and serial products on video tape. Republic also serves as the video distrubutor for TV shows that it did not produce, from "Bonanza" to "Car 54, Where Are You?"

Classic Republic Shows:

Stories of the Century (Jim Davis)

Frontier Doctor (Rex Allen)

Adventures of Dr. Fu Manchu

Disney

Disney was the first major Hollywood studio to make a major commitment to television. They had begun with specials in 1950. By 1954, they were cash-poor and needed an infusion of capital to build Disneyland, their first theme park. Out of desperation, they went to ABC-TV and offered major interest in the park, with the reciprocal being their commitment to produce quality TV shows for the network.

"Disneyland" was a cornucopia of cartoons, documentaries, adventure segments and Westerns (which Walt Disney hated). Some segments were recut from old feature films and shorts. Other segments were specially filmed, such as the trend-setting "Davy Crockett" sub-series. There were lots of documentaries and retrospectives that set the tone for future TV specials.

Walt Disney hosted himself, added credibility to the program and became everyone's surrogate uncle. Nobody seemed to balk at the obvious commercialism...in the context of the show, all the promos were part of the mosaic.

Walt Disney was a creative genius and spent far more on each show than first-run network TV budgets could afford. Like independent producers Dick Powell and Desi Arnaz, he exceeded budgets, knowing that the quality would bode well in endless TV reruns, the real cash-cow market. He filmed everything in color, though the first six years of "Disneyland" were shown in black and white.

In later years, Disney became more of a corporate success, grew its scope of operation and eventually purchased the TV network to whom it went hat in hand back in 1954.

Classic Disney Shows:

Disneyland/Walt Disney's Wonderful World of Color/Walt Disney Presents

Mickey Mouse Club

Zorro

Sub-series within Disneyland: Davy Crockett, Andy Burnett, The Swamp Fox, Elfego Baca

Warner Brothers

On the opposite end of the spectrum was Warner Brothers. Jack Warner, head of the studio, believed and was vocal in expressing the following commonly held views of television by the Hollywood establishment:

- That TV was a threat to movie theatre attendances.
- That TV was lesser quality than movies and would always be a stepchild.
- That the only talents working in TV were because they could not cut it in movies.
- That the material pandered to the lowest common denominator.
- That TV was good as a showcase for promoting movies.
- That TV threatened to end the movie studio system.
- That a few grandiose movies could effectively compete with the TV invasion.
- That the TV threat would eventually go away and movies' status quo would return.
- That movies shown on TV hurt box office attendance.
- That movie palaces as we knew them would always remain

the same as we knew them when we grew up.

• That movies could not play well on the small screen.

• That movies will never be shown directly on home TV sets.

Warner and the others were subsequently proven to be wrong on every count and did not fully understand the impact of TV upon Hollywood...until they had departed their studios.

Impressed by and envious of Disney's success entering television, Warner Bros. grudgingly committed to a showcase series, comprised of TV remakes of three of its classic movies ("Casablanca," "King's Row" and "Cheyenne") and a segment to promote its current movies. Jack Warner wouldn't go on TV, instead relegating host chores to actor Gig Young. Neither "Casablanca" nor "King's Row" translated well to the medium. "Cheyenne" emerged as its own hit TV series.

After trying one more unsuccessful anthology series, Warner Bros. committed to episodic TV series. They did it to keep the studio busy, provide work and training ground for fledgling movie artists.

Warner Bros. had a knack for getting creative ideas, milking them dry and chasing off the ideas' originators (notably Roy Huggins, creator of "Maverick" and "77 Sunset Strip"). Actors were low-paid and, when they asked for more money, were simply replaced. The only performer who successfully sued the studio to achieve equity was James Garner. Others' careers were significantly damaged for having fought the power structure.

Warner Bros. had a bean counter mentality, that every episode must make a profit. Thus, the product got repetitive, monotonous and did not hold up well in reruns. Scripts from old movies were notoriously recycled from series to series, with writing credit "W. Hermanos" (Spanish for Warner Bros.) suggested by the lawyers to avoid paying royalties.

Warner Bros. saw TV as an attempt to recreate the old days of the studio system...years after the fact. They put all their shows on network, the lowest-rated ABC. In 1960, Warner Bros. shows constituted one-third of ABC's schedule...by 1964, none.

Warner Bros. didn't diversify, change strategy or develop relationships with independent producers and other distributors. They never realized the value of TV syndication. Thus, the studio missed every mark, and their day in the sun was very short (five years). Thereafter, Warner Bros. (now known as The Burbank Studios) became space and talent for rent by independent producers and directors.

Classic Warner Brothers Shows:

Warner Brothers Presents (anthology)

Crisis (anthology)

Cheyenne (Clint Walker)

Lawman (John Russell, Peter Brown)

Maverick (James Garner, Jack Kelly)

Colt 45 (Wayde Preston, Donald May)

77 Sunset Strip (Efrem Zimbalist Jr., Roger Smith, Edd Byrnes, Richard Long)

Sugarfoot (Will Hutchins)

Bronco (Ty Hardin)

The Alaskans (Roger Moore, Jeff York, Dorothy Provine)

Hawaiian Eye (Anthony Eisley, Robert Conrad, Grant Williams, Troy Donahue, Connie Stevens)

Bourbon Street Beat (Richard Long, Andrew Duggan, Arlene Howell, Van Williams)

Surfside Six (Van Williams, Troy Donahue, Lee Patterson, Diane McBain)

The Roaring 20s (Donald May, Rex Reason, Dorothy Provine, Gary Vinson, Mike Road)

The Dakotas (Chad Everett, Larry Ward, Jack Elam, Mike Greene)

The Gallant Men (Robert McQueeney, William Reynolds)

General Electric True (anthology, hosted by Jack Webb)

Room for One More (Andrew Duggan, Peggy McCay)

Mr. Roberts (Roger Smith, Steve Harmon, Richard X. Slattery, George Ives)

F Troop (Ken Berry, Forrest Tucker, Larry Storch)

Nichols (James Garner)

Paramount

In a circuitous way, Paramount led the way for the packaging of Hollywood filmed product on television. Paramount owned a large stable of movie theatres up through the 1940s. Its forced breakup, due to anti-trust violation suits, paved the way for independent TV producers, Hollywood's first wave.

Leonard Goldensen, the man in charge of Paramount's theatre chain, subsequently took the helm of ABC-TV and guided it to major network status. Goldensen was the first network executive to court, recruit and embrace Hollywood studios as constant suppliers of TV programming...knowing well the values of film distribution and marketing.

In the 1950s, Paramount focused on wide-screen color movies and did little TV production. It hit dominance in 1967, with the acquisition of kingpin independent production company Desilu. Lucille Ball had personally championed the last stable of Desilu shows (Star Trek, Mission: Impossible and Mannix)...she saw them become the cornerstones in Paramount's TV empire of the 1970s.

Classic Paramount Shows:

Police Station

The Outlaws (Barton MacLane, Don Collier, Jock Gaynor, Bruce Yarnell, Slim Pickens)

Star Trek (William Shatner, Leonard Nimoy, DeForest Kelley)

Mission: Impossible (Steven Hill, Peter Graves, Martin Landau, Barbara Bain, Greg Morris, Peter Lupus, Leonard Nimoy, Lee Meriwether, Lesley Ann Warren, Sam Elliott)

Mannix (Mike Connors, Gail Fisher)

Love American Style (comedy anthology)

The Brady Bunch (Robert Reed, Florence Henderson, Ann B. Davis)

The Odd Couple (Tony Randall, Jack Klugman)

Barefoot in the Park (Scoey Mitchell, Tracy Reed, Thelma Carpenter, Nipsey Russell)

The Immortal (Christopher George, Don Knight, David Brian)

Longstreet (James Franciscus, Peter Mark Richman, Marlyn Mason, Bruce Lee)

MGM

Louis B. Mayer's rein as the kingmaker of elite Hollywood had ended when television came along in the 1950s. Out of economic necessity and as a corporate culture statement, the new reign dared to change and take chances.

MGM's first show (as was Warner Brothers Presents) was a clone of Walt Disney's TV entry. George Murphy (later to become Senator from California) hosted a cornucopia of clips from classic MGM features and short subjects and interviewed stars of the studio's latest movies.

Next, MGM experimented in producing video programming, adapting the famous "Thin Man" series for TV. Next came one of the medium's first color series, "Northwest Passage," based upon MGM's 1940 movie. The studio adhered to MGM production values, albeit on television budgets. Nonetheless, their series had the feel of theatre-quality programs. Alas, MGM became better known as the home base for independent productions.

Classic MGM Shows:

MGM Parade (George Murphy)

The Thin Man (Peter Lawford, Phyllis Kirk)

Northwest Passage (Keith Larsen, Buddy Ebsen, Don Burnett)

Lawless Years (James Gregory)

Not For Hire (Ralph Meeker)

One Step Beyond (John Newland)

National Velvet (Lori Martin, Arthur Space, Ann Doran, Carole Wells, Joseph Scott)

The Islanders (William Reynolds, James Philbrook)

Asphalt Jungle (Jack Warden, Arch Johnson, Bill Smith)

Dr. Kildare (Richard Chamberlain, Raymond Massey)

Cain's Hundred (Mark Richman)

Mr. Novak (James Franciscus, Dean Jagger, Burgess Meredith)

Jericho (Don Francks, Marino Mase, John Leyton)

Tales of Jamie McPheeters (Kirk Russell)

The Man from UNCLE (Robert Vaughn, David McCallum, Leo G. Carroll)

The Girl from UNCLE (Stefanie Powers, Noel Harrison, Leo G. Carroll)

Many Happy Returns (John McGiver, Elinor Donahue, Mark Goddard, Mickey Manners)

A Man Called Shennandoah (Robert Horton)

The Rounders (Chill Wills, Ron Hayes, Patrick Wayne)

The Courtship of Eddie's Father (Bill Bixby, Brandon Cruz, James Komack)

Medical Center (Chad Everett, James Daly)

United Artists

United Artists was the first alliance of independent Hollywood filmmakers (Douglas Fairbanks, Mary Pickford, Charles Chaplin). It continued over the years to foster creative, breakthrough productions. United Artists was not so much a "bricks and mortar" studio...it was an ideology of renting facilities and utilizing top-flight freelance talent, including those loaned out by major studios.

In 1960, United Artists acquired TV's pioneering independent program producer, Ziv. During the 1960-61 season, Ziv shows (Bat Masterson, Lock Up, Sea Hunt) carried the joint "Ziv-United Artists" logo. United Artists shows hence had more of a Hollywood major studio look, though it was clear that they were fostering independent projects.

Classic United Artists Shows:

Stoney Burke (Jack Lord, Bruce Dern, Warren Oates)

The Outer Limits (anthology)

Patty Duke Show (Patty Duke, William Schallert, Jean Byron)

20th Century-Fox

After MGM and Warner Brothers, the other upholder of the Hollywood studio system was 20th Century-Fox.

The studio's first series, "The 20th Century-Fox Hour," consisted of TV-movie remakes of classic Fox films. Next, for series material, Fox (like MGM) adapted feature films to the TV medium...with comparable major-studio feel to the productions. Fox too became the rented home to independent producers in the 1960s and 1970s.

Classic 20th Century-Fox Shows:

Many of their TV series were based upon many of their hit movies.

The 20th Century-Fox Hour (anthology)

My Friend Flicka (Johnny Washbrook, Gene Evans, Anita Louise, Frank Ferguson)

Broken Arrow (John Lupton, Michael Ansara)

How to Marry a Millionaire (Barbara Eden, Lori Nelson, Merry Anders)

Adventures in Paradise (Gardner McKay)

Hong Kong (Rod Taylor, Lloyd Bochner, Jack Kruschen)

The Many Loves of Dobie Gillis (Dwayne Hickman, Bob Denver, Frank Faylen, Florida Friebus, Sheila James) (launched careers for Warren Beatty and Tuesday Weld)

Margie (Cynthia Pepper, Penney Parker, Wesley Tackitt, Tommy Ivo)

Bus Stop (Marilyn Maxwell, Rhodes Reason, Richard Anderson)

Five Fingers (David Hedison, Luciana Paluzzi, Paul Burke)

Follow the Sun (Brett Halsey, Barry Coe)

Daniel Boone (Fess Parker, Patricia Blair, Ed Ames, Veronica Cartwright, Darby Hinton)

Peyton Place (Dorothy Malone, Ed Nelson, Ryan O'Neal, Mia Farrow, Barbara Parkins)

Lancer (Andrew Duggan, James Stacy, Wayne Maunder, Elizabeth Baur)

Lost in Space (Guy Williams, June Lockhart, Billy Mumy, Angela Cartwright, Jonathan Harris, Mark Goddard, Marta Kristen)

Batman (Adam West, Burt Ward)

The Green Hornet (Van Williams, Bruce Lee)

The Long Hot Summer (Roy Thinnes)

Judd for the Defense (Carl Betz, Stephen Young)

The Time Tunnel (James Darren, Robert Colbert)

Voyage to the Bottom of the Sea (Richard Basehart, David Hedison)

Room 222 (Lloyd Haynes, Denise Nicholas, Michael Constantine, Karen Valentine)

Julia (Diahann Carroll, Lurene Tuttle, Lloyd Nolan, Betty Beaird, Marc Copage, Michael J. Link)

Nanny and the Professor (Richard Long, Juliet Mills)

Anna and the King (Yul Brynner, Samantha Eggar, Keye Luke)

What started out as a misunderstood rivalry blossomed into a good collaboration. Hollywood studios quickly saw television as innovative new ground for different production modes.

The creative process brought forth new stars, writers, producers, directors and other talents.

Some aspects of the old movie studio system were kept. Others proved to be obsolete. Touches from Broadway, radio and live TV were added. The mixture became the definitive formula for series television.

Given technological advances and a growing audience for its product, Hollywood embraced television, which subsequently embraced Hollywood movies, which (through videotape distribution) expanded markets for Hollywood movie product forever.

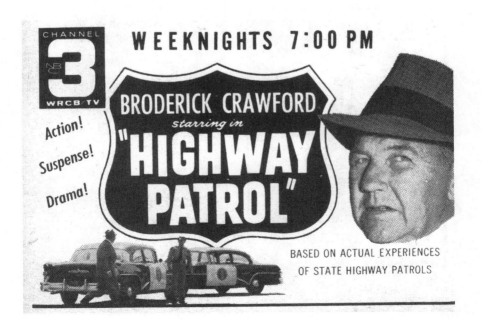

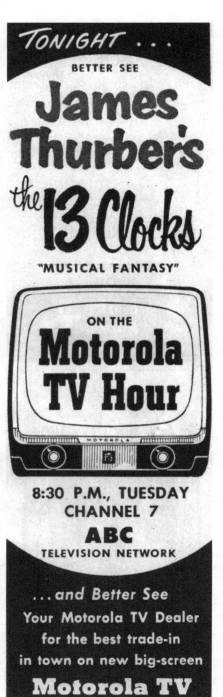

8

Timeline, Chronology and Factors Influencing the Development of Classic Television

1898

First suggestions made that pictures with sound could be carried across large distances. Movies were introduced in European arcades in 1895. Within three years, research was begun to carry the moving pictures to distant locations. This actually proceeded the development of radio.

1920

First radio sets sold by Westinghouse to promote its first station, 8XK in Pittsburgh, PA.

1926

NBC Radio signed on the air.

Congress created the Federal Radio Commission, later the Federal Communications Commission, as regulatory entity.

1927

CBS Radio signed on the air.

First test television pictures sent.

1928

First American home gets a TV set.

First regularly scheduled TV programs, over WGY-TV and WRNY-TV.

First trans-oceanic TV signal sent, from London to New York.

1929

First public demonstration of a color TV model.

1930

First closed-circuit TV projected on a big screen in a theatre.

1931

CBS-TV and NBC-TV signed on the air. CBS' first station, W2XAB (later WCBS-TV) began regular daily programming. RCA and NBC put a TV transmitter atop the Empire State Building.

1937

"The Guiding Light" premiered on CBS radio. This is the longest-running series and the longest-running soap opera, having gone from radio to TV in 1952. It is still on the air.

1938

NBC covered the first live, breaking TV news story (a fire).

1939

This year stands as the movies' Golden Year and the peak of

Hollywood's Golden Age.

NBC covered the opening of the World's Fair.

First football game, baseball game and prize fight were broadcast.

1940

First basketball game and hockey match were broadcast.

First coverage of political conventions.

1941

First licensed commercial television station (WNBT-TV) went on the air. The first commercial cost sponsor Bulova Watches a total of nine dollars.

1944

First boxing and wrestling matches broadcast.

CBS began its first evening news show, hosted by Ned Calmer. NBC began TV news the next year.

Premieres: "Gillette Cavalcade of Sports," "Missus Goes a' Shopping."

1945

First public demonstration of a TV set in a department store, 25,000 watching.

At this point, nine commercial TV stations were in operation.

Premieres: "Magic Carpet," "Thanks for Looking," "World in Home," "Photocrime," King's Record Shop," "Magazine of the Air."

1946

Audio tape introduced to American network radio. Bing Crosby brought the BASF process from Europe, so he could pre-tape his radio shows and spend more time on the golf course. Soon, most other network radio shows went to tape. This ultimately spelled the beginning of the end of network radio as a primary family entertainment medium.

First televised heavyweight boxing title championship.

First hour-long musical variety show broadcast by NBC (whose network consisted of three stations).

Premieres: "Play the Game," "See What You Know," "Choreotones," "Famous Jury Trials," "Ladies Be Seated," "Right or Rewrite," "Draw Another," "King's Party Line," "Serving Through Science," "Cash and Carry," "Here's Morgan," "Your ESSO Report," "Charm School," "You Are an Artist," "Broadway Previews," "Let's Rhumba."

1947

44,000 TV sets in use. 40 million radios in use. First mass production of television receivers.

Dumont Network signed on the air. It was conceived as a vehicle for selling Dumont TV sets. Named for founder Abner B. Dumont. Its flagship station was Channel 5, WABD in New York, and other affiliates provided programming to the network.

First broadcast of a joint session of Congress.

First broadcast of a World Series baseball championship. CBS, NBC and Dumont pooled their resources to jointly telecast. It was seen by 4 million people.

First kinescopes created. NBC and Eastman Kodak devised a process for recording programs off a TV monitor and distributing for later broadcast.

TV's first syndicator, Ziv, enters the medium, with its first series, "The Cisco Kid," shot in color as an investment toward longer-term residuals. Ziv had created a niche as a radio syndicator. It's hit TV series included "Boston Blackie," "I Led Three Lives," "Highway Patrol," "Sea Hunt," "Science Fiction Theatre," "The Man Called X" and "Lock Up."

Premieres: "Kraft Television Theatre" (first commercial dramatic series), "Howdy Doody" (first major children's program), "Meet the Press" (first current events and newsmaker talk show),

"Borden Variety Show," "Juvenile Jury," "To the Queen's Taste," "Campus Hoopla," "Author Meets the Critics," "Musical Merry-Go-Round," "Charade Quiz."

1948

One million TV sets in use, 36 TV stations in 19 cities, able to reach one-third of the U.S. population.

ABC-TV signed on the air.

Columbia Records first issued long-playing record albums on the market. This changed the packaging and distribution of popular music, which gave the rise to a broader audience and music variety shows on television.

"Ed Sullivan Show/Toast of the Town" premiered on CBS. This became the longest-running variety show, lasting 1974 and syndicated thereafter.

"Milton Berle Show/Texaco Star Theatre" premiered on NBC. Berle commanded the highest rating for a single time period, up to 92%. As a show of support, in 1951, NBC signed Berle to an exclusive 30-year contract, which it fully honored.

First Academy Awards ceremonies on TV. As an equivalent venue for recognizing its own excellence, the Television Academy of Arts and Sciences was founded, subsequently bestowing its Emmy Awards.

"Ted Mack's Original Amateur" hour premiered. During its 22 years, it discovered thousands of talented performers and ran on all four networks.

CBS began the first nightly news broadcast, hosted by Douglas Edwards.

The first game show transitioned from radio to TV. It was "Winner Take All" on CBS, hosted by Bud Collyer. This was the first quiz show developed by Mark Goodson and Bill Todman, who subsequently produced the most game shows.

Premieres: "Westinghouse Studio One" (with live commercials by Betty Furness), "Arthur Godfrey's Talent Scouts," ," "Philco

Television Playhouse," "Hollywood Screen Test," "Barney Blake, Police Reporter," "Broadway Jamboree," "Stop Me If You've Heard This One," "Lamp Unto My Feet," "We the People," "Dennis James Carnival."

1949

2,150,000 TV sets in use (720,000 in New York City alone).

Sid Caesar entered TV. His second series, "Your Show of Shows" ranked right behind Milton Berle as TV's variety show ratings leader. It set the vanguard for sketch comedy that all other shows copied. Its stable of writers included Mel Brooks, Neil Simon, Selma Diamond, Danny Simon, Carl Reiner and Woody Allen. It later served as the inspiration for the "Dick Van Dyke Show."

Columbia Pictures was the first major Hollywood studio to enter TV production. Its Screen Gems subsidiary was prolific throughout the 1950s, 1960s and 1970s.

RCA Victor Columbia Records first issued 45-RPM singles on the market. This changed the packaging and distribution of popular music, which gave the rise to a broader audience and music variety shows on television.

Laws are passed enabling TV aerials to be perched atop buildings to improve signals.

Premieres: "The Lone Ranger," "Kukla, Fran & Ollie," "I Remember Mama," "Hopalong Cassidy," "Ed Wynn Show," "Voice of Firestone," "The Goldbergs," "Morey Amsterdam Show," "Front Row Center," "Fred Waring Show," "Ed Wynn Show," "Starring Boris Karloff," "The Life of Riley," "Pantomime Quiz," "Paul Whiteman's TV Teen Club," "Martin Kane, Private Eye," Twenty Questions," "Hank McCune Show," "Dave Garroway at Large," "It Pays to Be Ignorant," "Cross Question," "Johns Hopkins Science Review," "Draw Me a Laugh," "Bowling Headliners," "Academy Theatre," "Science Circus," "Hotel Broadway."

1950

5,343,000 TV sets in use.

Jack Benny, Burns & Allen, Bob Hope, Groucho Marx, Frank Sinatra, Vaughn Monroe, Art Linkletter and Gene Autry entered television. This procession of well-regarded radio stars into regular TV shows brought built-in audiences and legitimized the infant video medium.

Revue Productions entered television, taking over Universal Studios in the 1960's and becoming the most prolific supplier of filmed programming to television.

The Korean War became the first living room war, via film footage sent back to networks.

Premieres: "Your Hit Parade," "Robert Montgomery Presents," "Truth or Consequences," "What's My Line?," "Ken Murray Show," "Kay Kyser's College of Musical Knowledge," "Dick Tracy," "Horace Heidt Show," "Colgate Comedy Hour," "Beulah," "Prudential Family Theatre," "Treasury Men in Action," "Paul Winchell & Jerry Mahoney Show," "Big Town," "Nash Airflyte Theatre," "Hold That Camera," "Stars Over Hollywood," "Lux Video Theatre," "Magnavox Theatre," "Life with the Erwins," "Danger," "The College Bowl," "Pulitzer Prize Playhouse," "Adventures of Ellery Queen," "Jack Carter Show," "Cavalcade of Stars," "Broadway Open House," "Garry Moore Show," "Arthur Murray Show," "Alan Young Show," "My True Story," "Robert Q. Lewis Show," "Hawkins Falls," "Easy Aces," "NBC Opera Theatre," "Escape," "The Show Goes On," "Marshall Plan in Action," "Detective's Wife," "Windy City Jamboree."

1951

13 million TV sets in use.

RCA unveiled the first community TV antenna system (forerunner of cable TV).

Desilu Productions formed. Its first series, "I Love Lucy," was the first to be filmed in front of a live audience. A ratings hit, it set the pace for TV reruns. Desilu's prolific output over the next 16 years included "Our Miss Brooks," "December Bride," "The Lucy Show," "The Untouchables," "Star Trek," "Mannix" and "Mission: Impossible."

"Hallmark Hall of Fame" premiered on NBC. Its first production was "Amahl and the Night Visitors." This became the longest-running series of specials and cultural arts show.

NAACP first protested "Amos n' Andy" as a distorted picture of black life.

Premieres: "Watch Mr. Wizard," "Search for Tomorrow," "Dragnet," "Love of Life," "Dinah Shore Show," "Roy Rogers Show," "Adventures of Superman," "See It Now" (first TV newsmagazine, hosted by Edward R. Murrow), "Racket Squad," You Asked For It," "Schlitz Playhouse," "Mark Saber Mystery Theatre," "Red Skelton Show," "Ford Festival," "Mr. District Attorney," "Crime Syndicated," "Gruen Guild Theatre," "Faye Emerson Show," "It's News to Me," "Sam Levinson Show," "Steve Allen Show," "March of Time," "Henry Morgan's Great Talent Hunt," "Hollywood Adventure Time," "Music from Chicago," "Peter Lind Hayes Show," "Strike It Rich," "Sky King," "The Amazing Mr. Malone," "Rootie Kazootie," "Cosmopolitan Theatre," "Sound-Off Time."

1952

15 million TV sets in use.

Coaxial cable was laid, facilitating national broadcast transmissions.

Four Star productions formed by Dick Powell and partners, premiering with "Four Star Playhouse." Its prolific output over the next 14 years included "Zane Grey Theatre," "The Rifleman," "Dick Powell Show," "Burke's Law," "Honey West" and "The Big Valley."

Premieres: "Jackie Gleason Show," "Adventures of Ozzie and Harriet," "Ford Theatre," "My Little Margie," "I've Got a Secret,"

"This Is Your Life," "I Married Joan," "Death Valley Days," "The Today Show," "Our Miss Brooks," "Omnibus," "Mr. and Mrs. North," "My Hero," "Biff Baker, U.S.A.," "Red Buttons Show," "Life with Luigi," "Mr. Peepers," "Victory at Sea," "Masquerade Party," "Life is Worth Living," "Heaven for Betsy," "Hollywood Off-Beat," "Jane Froman Show," "Meet Millie," "The Name's the Same," "Art Linkletter's House Party," "Liberace Show," "Campbell Playhouse," "Eddy Arnold Show," "Bob and Ray Show," "My Friend Irma," "The Hunter," "Quick on the Draw," "Dagmar's Canteen," "All Star Venue."

1953

25 million TV sets in use.

First live coast-to-coast broadcast: the inauguration of President Dwight D. Eisenhower.

First worldwide event coverage: the coronation of Queen Elizabeth (film flown from England).

Highest rated TV event: the birth of Little Ricky on "I Love Lucy."

First educational TV station (KUHT-TV, Houston, TX) signed on the air.

TV Guide began publication.

Arthur Godfrey fired Julius La Rosa on the air, saying that La Rosa lacked humility.

Leonard Goldenson takes over ABC-TV from previous owners...launches long journey to make the fledgling network a contender to giants CBS and NBC. It took until 1976 for ABC to become #1 in the overall ratings. The network focused upon young viewers, who matured and remained loyal to the network of their youth.

RCA tested compatible color TV system on the air for the first time.

Premieres: "General Electric Theatre" (hosted by Ronald Reagan), "Name That Tune," "Loretta Young Show," "Make Room for

Daddy," "Person to Person," "You Are There," "Ding Dong School," "Private Secretary-Ann Sothern Show," "Ernie Kovacs Show," "U.S. Steel Hour," "The Big Picture," "My Favorite Husband," "Revlon Mirror Theatre," "Life with Father," "Meet Mr. McNulty," "Pepsi-Cola Playhouse," "Where's Raymond?," "Coke Time with Eddie Fisher," "Col. Humphrey Flack," "Winky Dink and You," "Bob Crosby Show," "Anyone Can Win," "Bank on the Stars," "Pride of the Family," "Old American Barn Dance," "Johnny Jupiter," "What's Your Bid?" "Lash of the West," "Eddie Albert Show."

1954

This year stands as television's Golden Year and the peak of its Golden Age.

First color TV show transmissions: "Climax/Shower of Stars" on CBS.

Walt Disney entered TV, hosting Disneyland and promoting his theme park concept. His first major mini-series hit was "Davy Crockett," launching a commercial merchandising tradition.

Premieres: "The Tonight Show," "Miss America Pageant," "Medic," "Father Knows Best," "December Bride," "Lassie," "Lux Video Theatre," "People Are Funny," "Adventures of Rin Tin Tin," "Studio 57," "Halls of Ivy," "The Lineup," "The Vise," "Best of Broadway," "Caesar's Hour," "Producer's Showcase," "Spike Jones Show," "George Gobel Show," "Dear Phoebe," "Captain Midnight," "That's My Boy," "Jack Paar Show," "Hey Mulligan," "It's a Great Life," "Stage Show," "Pinky Lee Show," "Face the Nation," "The Secret Storm," "Tony Martin Show," "Rocky Jones, Space Ranger," "Portia Faces Life," "Happy Felton's Spotlight Gang."

1955

Warner Brothers and 20th Century-Fox both entered TV with anthology series, subsequently getting into episodic series production.

Premieres: "Alfred Hitchcock Presents," "Gunsmoke," "The Life and Legend of Wyatt Earp," "Phil Silvers Show/You'll Never Get Rich/Sgt. Bilko," "$64,000 Question," "Bob Cummings Show/Love That Bob," "Mickey Mouse Club," "Captain Kangaroo," "The Millionaire," "The People's Choice," "Tales of the Texas Rangers," "MGM Parade," "Adventures of Robin Hood," "Brave Eagle," "The Honeymooners," "Frontier," "Sgt. Preston of the Yukon," "Screen Director's Playhouse," "20th Century-Fox Hour," "Ford Star Revue," "It's Always Jan," ""Playwrights '56," "The Crusader," "Grand Ole Opry," "The Big Surprise," "Crossroads," "Adventures of Champion," "Navy Log," "NBC Matinee Theatre," "Tennessee Ernie Ford Show," "TV Reader's Digest," "Julius Larosa Show," "Those Whiting Girls," "Johnny Carson Show," "The Soldiers," "Soupy Sales Show," "Damon Runyon Theatre," "Ozark Jubilee," "Wide Wide World," "Jan Murray Show," "Commando Cody," "So This is Hollywood."

1956

The year's top ratings phenomenon was Elvis Presley on the "Ed Sullivan Show."

Video tape was first used on television production. Originally, tape was used for commercials and portions of programs. By 1958, entire programs were taped and edited for later broadcast. This ultimately spelled the beginning of the end of live television (except for news shows).

Desilu Productions acquired the RKO Pictures lot (later selling to Paramount in 1967).

"The Wizard of Oz" was broadcast for the first time on TV. This becomes an annual holiday theme event.

MGM entered TV with series based upon some of its movies: "Dr. Kildare," "The Thin Man," "Asphalt Jungle," "Northwest Passage." "As the World Turns" and "The Edge of Night" became TV's first home-grown expanded length soap operas. Their predecessors were 15 minutes long and transitioned from radio.

Premieres: "Huntley-Brinkley News," "Steve Allen Show,"

"Playhouse 90," "My Friend Flicka," "Oh, Susanna," "Wire Service," "Lawrence Welk Show," "Ray Anthony Show," "Broken Arrow," "Adventures of Sir Lancelot," "Dick Powell's Zane Grey Theatre," "Circus Time," "Hey, Jeannie," "Twenty-One," "The $64,000 Challenge," "Patti Page Show," "Tales of the 77th Bengal Lancers," "West Point Story," "Walter Winchell Show," "Adventures of Jim Bowie," "The Buccaneers," "Do You Trust Your Wife?," "To Tell the Truth," "Adventures of Hiram Holiday," "Noah's Ark," "Treasure Hunt," "Mighty Mouse Playhouse," "Tic Tac Dough," "Queen for a Day," "Gabby Hayes Show," "Washington Square," "The Price Is Right," "Jonathan Winters Show," "Kaiser Aluminum Hour," "Herb Shriner Show," "Nat 'King' Cole Show," "Combat Sergeant," "Joe and Mabel," "It Could Be You," "Bold Journey," "Charles Farrell Show," "Stand Up and Be Counted."

1957

40 million TV sets in use.

Jack Paar took over as host of "The Tonight Show" on NBC.

First coverage of the space exploration program.

Premieres: "American Bandstand," "Maverick," "Perry Mason," "Wagon Train," "Have Gun, Will Travel," "Bachelor Father," "Zorro," "The Real McCoys," "Leave It to Beaver," "Mr. Adams and Eve," "Panic," "Tales of Wells Fargo," "Blondie," "Meet McGraw," "Tombstone Territory," "Club Oasis," "The Big Record," "The Californians," "Date with the Angels," "Richard Diamond, Private Detective," "Eve Arden Show," "Harbourmaster," "M Squad," "The Thin Man," "Trackdown," "Court of Last Resort," "Walter Winchell File," "Scotland Yard," "The Veil," "Pat Boone Chevy Showroom," "Lux Show with Rosemary Clooney," "Alcoa-Goodyear Theatre: Turn of Fate," "Sugarfoot," "Restless Gun," "Gumby Show," "Keep It in the Family," "The Verdict is Yours," "Andy's Gang."

1958

Dumont Network signed off the air...is merged into ABC-TV.

The first Aaron Spelling-produced TV series, as he takes over "Zane Grey Theatre." He stands as TV's most prolific producer, including Dick Powell Theatre," "Mod Squad," "Charlie's Angels," "Love Boat," "Fantasy Island," "Dynasty" and "Melrose Place."

Four Star Productions acquires the Republic Pictures lot (later selling to CBS in 1965).

Premieres: "77 Sunset Strip," "Concentration," "Peter Gunn," "Donna Reed Show," "Wanted: Dead or Alive," "Bat Masterson," "The Rifleman," "Ann Sothern Show," "The Texan," "Cimarron City," "Steve Canyon," "Man with a Camera," "Yancy Derringer," "Bronco," "Pursuit," "Naked City," "George Burns Show," "Lawman," "The Rough Riders," "Kraft Music Hall with Milton Berle," "Desilu Playhouse," "Ruff and Reddy," "Play Your Hunch" (first of Merv Griffin's game shows), "Dick Clark Beechnut Show," "Jefferson Drum," "Decision," "Andy Williams Chevy Showroom," "Brains and Brawn," "MacKenzie's Raiders," "Behind Closed Doors," "Love That Jill," "Make Me Laugh," "Haggis Baggis," "From These Roots," "Encounter," "Music from Manhattan," "Day in Court."

1959

Paola investigations into rock n' roll music, the recording industry and plugging of records on radio and television.

Premieres: "Bonanza," "Twilight Zone," "G.E. College Bowl," "Rawhide," "Rocky and His Friends," "CBS Reports," "The Untouchables," "Markham," "One Step Beyond," "Dennis the Menace," "Riverboat," "Bourbon Street Beat," "Adventures in Paradise," "Dupont Show with June Allyson," "The Detectives," "The Man from Blackhawk," "Mr. Lucky," "Five Fingers," "Betty Hutton Show," "Johnny Staccato," "The Man and the Challenge," "The Deputy," "The Alaskans," "The Rebel," "Laramie," "Hennesey," "Fibber McGee and Molly," "Men into Space,"

"Johnny Ringo," "Brenner," "Take a Good Look," "Hawaiian Eye," "The Lawless Years," "Hotel de Paree," "Dennis O'Keefe Show," "The Big Party," "Law of the Plainsman," "Ford Startime," "Tightrope," "Philip Marlowe," "David Niven Show," "21 Beacon Street," "Matty's Funday Funnies," "The Invisible Man," "Jackpot Bowling," "Love and Marriage," "Wichita Town," "Young Doctor Malone," "Pete Kelly's Blues," "Black Saddle," "The D.A.'s Man," "John Gunther's High Road," "The Troubleshooters," "Accused," "For Better or Worse."

1960

90% of all U.S. households now have TV.

An overhead blimp was utilized for the first time in live sports coverage.

First Olympics marathon coverage, originating from Rome.

The Kennedy-Nixon debates set ratings and precedent for election coverage.

Premieres: "My Three Sons," "Route 66," "Andy Griffith Show," "The Flintstones," "Pete and Gladys," "The Outlaws," "The Tall Man," "The Roaring Twenties," "The Law and Mr. Jones," "Hong Kong," "Checkmate," "Stagecoach West," "Barbara Stanwyck Show," "Michael Shayne," "Harrigan and Son," "Guestward Ho," "The Islanders," "My Sister Eileen," "The Aquanauts," "Peter Loves Mary," "The Westerner," "Dan Raven," "National Velvet," "Tab Hunter Show," "Bugs Bunny Show," "Klondike," "Bringing Up Buddy," "Thriller," "Tom Ewell Show," "Angel," "Surfside Six," "Mr. Garlund," "Candid Camera," "The Man from Interpol," "Overland Trail," "Video Village," "Silents Please," "Shari Lewis Show," "Magic Land of Allakazam," "About Faces."

1961

The last live TV drama program. Shows had gone to tape and film. There would not be another live TV drama until "Fail Safe" in 2000 and "On Golden Pond" in 2001.

NBC premiered "Saturday Night at the Movies," launching prime-time telecasts of top films. Due to heavy demand on recent theatrical inventory, NBC began running made-for-TV movies in 1964.

Premieres: "Dick Van Dyke Show," "Dr. Kildare," "Ben Casey," "Password," "Hazel," "The Defenders," "Mister Ed," "ABC'S Wide World of Sports," "Sing Along with Mitch," "Car 54: Where Are You?," "Joey Bishop Show," "Top Cat," "Nanette Fabray Show," "Dick Powell Show," "Bus Stop," "Follow the Sun," "Alvin Show," "Asphalt Jungle," "The New Breed," "Ichabod and Me," "Window on Main Street," "Alcoa Premiere," "Target: The Corrupters," "Margie," "New Bob Cummings Show," "Straightaway," "The Americans," "The Investigators," Bob Newhart Show," "Mrs. G. Goes to College," "Cain's Hundred," "David Brinkley's Journal," "Father of the Bride," "Danger Man," "Walt Disney's Wonderful World of Color," "87th Precinct," "Frontier Circus," "The Hathaways," "Calvin and the Colonel," "The Gunslinger," "Way Out," "Holiday Lodge," "You're in the Picture," Say When," "Issues and Answers," "Frank McGee's Here and Now," "College of the Air."

1962

Johnny Carson took over as host of "The Tonight Show" on NBC.

Walter Cronkite took over as anchor of the CBS Evening News.

Premieres: "The Beverly Hillbillies," "The Lucy Show," "Merv Griffin Show," "Saints and Sinners," "Wide Country," "The Eleventh Hour," "Lloyd Bridges Show," "Combat," "I'm Dickens, He's Fenster," "Empire," "Andy Williams Show," "The Gallant Men," "Fair Exchange," "McHale's Navy," "New Loretta Young Show," "Ensign O'Toole," "Jack Paar Show," "The Nurses," "Jackie Gleason Show," "Going My Way," "Our Man Higgins," "The Virginian," "Mr. Smith Goes to Washington," "Roy Rogers & Dave Evans Variety Show," "It's a Man's World," "Sam Benedict," "Don't Call Me Charlie," "The Jetsons," Pro Bowlers Tour," "Oh Those Bells," "Tell It to Groucho," "The Lively Ones," "Sir Francis Drake."

1963

Coverage of the Civil Rights movement became a staple of daily TV news coverage.

Major news event: the assassination of President John F. Kennedy.

Premieres: "The Fugitive," "General Hospital," "The Outer Limits," "Petticoat Junction," "Patty Duke Show," "Phil Donahue Show" (as a local; talk show in Ohio), "East Side, West Side," "The Breaking Point," "My Favorite Martian," "Burke's Law," "Bob Hope Chrysler Theatre," "Arrest and Trial," "The Lieutenant," "Mr. Novak," "Richard Boone Show," "Greatest Show on Earth," "Judy Garland Show," "Bill Dana Show," "The Farmer's Daughter," "Kraft Suspense Theatre," "Channing," "Hollywood and the Stars," "Danny Kaye Show," "Harry's Girls," "Grindl," "New Phil Silvers Show," "Jerry Lewis Show," "Travels of Jaimie McPheeters, "Temple Houston," "Espionage," "Glynis," "Tennessee Tuxedo," "Fireball XL-5," "Hootenanny," "As Caesar Sees It," "The Dakotas," "The Match Game," "You Don't Say," "Keefe Brasselle Show," "Picture This," "Edie Adams Show," "Laughs for Sale," "Wild Kingdom," "The Doctors."

1964

The year's top ratings phenomenon was The Beatles on the "Ed Sullivan Show."

Dick Clark moved his base of operations from Philadelphia to Hollywood.

Major news and cultural icon: the British Invasion (rock music, fashions, fads).

ABC pitted Les Crane against Johnny Carson in the late-night TV derby.

Premieres: "Green Acres," "Gilligan's Island," "Another World," "Voyage to the Bottom of the Sea," "Hollywood Palace," "That Was the Week That Was," "Peyton Place," "Gomer Pyle, USMC," "The Man from UNCLE," "Another World," "Bewitched," "The Addams Family," "The Munsters," "Shindig," "Slattery's People,"

"90 Bristol Court," "Daniel Boone," "Destry," "Let's Make a Deal," "Twelve O'Clock High," "Flipper," "Mr. Broadway," "Profiles in Courage," "The Tycoon," "Bing Crosby Show," "Wendy and Me," "Many Happy Returns," "No Time for Sergeants," "The Reporter," "Valentine's Day," "Jonny Quest," "The Entertainers," "Baileys of Balboa," "Kentucky Jones," "Broadside," "Cara Williams Show," "Mickey," "World War One," "On Broadway Tonight," "Shenanigans," "Linus the Lionhearted," "The NFL Today," "Famous Adventures of Mr. Magoo," "Tell It to the Camera."

1965

Coverage of the Vietnam War became a staple of daily TV news coverage.

The advent of audio cassette tapes.

Premieres: "The F.B.I.," "Days of Our Lives," "Hogan's Heroes," "Run for Your Life," "Hullabaloo," "The Wild, Wild West," "I Dream of Jeannie," "Green Acres," "The Big Valley," "Dean Martin Show," "The Long Hot Summer," "Lost in Space," "Gidget," "Tammy," "Mr. Roberts," "Convoy," "Get Smart," "I Spy," "Branded," "King Family Show," "Where the Action Is," "Smothers Brothers Show," "F Troop," "Please Don't Eat the Daisies," "Trials of O'Brien," "Steve Lawrence Show," "Honey West," "A Man Called Shenandoah," "Hank," "Laredo," "The Loner," "Camp Runamuck," "The Wackiest Ship in the Army," "My Mother the Car," "The American Sportsman," "Mona McCluskey," Atom Ant," "Legend of Jesse James," "John Forsythe Show," "Our Private World," "Supermarket Sweep."

1966

Premieres: "Dark Shadows," "Batman," "The Green Hornet," "Family Affair," "That Girl," "Mission: Impossible," "Star Trek," "Hollywood Squares," "The Dating Game," "The Newlywed Game," "T.H.E. Cat," "Pistols n' Petticoats," "It's About Time," ""Love on a Rooftop," "The Rounders," "The Pruitts of

Southampton," "The Iron Horse," "Run, Buddy, Run," "The Time Tunnel," "Felony Squad," "The Rat Patrol," "Tarzan," "Hawk," "Tammy Grimes Show," "The Monkees," "The Monroes," "The Man Who Never Was," "ABC Stage '67," "How the Grinch Stole Christmas," "Sammy Davis Jr. Show," "Shane," "Occasional Wife," "Jericho," "The Double Life of Henry Phyffe," "Kraft Music Hall," "The Face is Familiar," "Blue Light," "The Avengers," "Daktari," "The Baron," "Magilla Gorilla," "The Hero," "Peter Potamus," "Hey Landlord," "Cool McCool."

1967

Super Bowl #1 was seen by 51 million viewers.

Final episode of "The Fugitive" ranked next to the birth of Little Ricky as TV's highest ratings getter.

National Educational Television hence became known as the Public Broadcasting System.

ABC pitted Joey Bishop against Johnny Carson in the late-night TV derby.

Ted Turner bought WTCG-TV, a UHF independent station in Atlanta and began programming TV series reruns, movies and sports. WTBS became the flagship for his broadcasting empire.

Premieres: "Rowan & Martin's Laugh-In," "Ironside," "Carol Burnett Show," "Mannix," "60 Minutes," "The Saint," "The Flying Nun," "Smothers Brothers Comedy Hour," "The Invaders," "Judd for the Defense," "Gentle Ben," "Cimarron Strip," "Garrison's Gorillas," "Good Morning World," "He and She," "Hondo," "The Guns of Will Sonnett," "NYPD," "Cowboy in Africa," "Maya," "The Mothers-in-Law," "The High Chaparral," "Custer," "The Second Hundred Years," "Dundee and the Culhane," "Captain Nice," "Coronet Blue," "Away We Go," "Love Is a Many Splendored Thing," "Danny Thomas Hour," "Rango," "Mr. Terrific," "Good Company," "Off to See the Wizard," "Aquaman," "Accidental Family," "The Family Game," "Coliseum," Malibu U."

1968

Major news events: assassinations of Martin Luther King and Robert F. Kennedy, plus rioting in the Chicago streets during the Democratic National Convention.

The advent of eight-track tapes.

ABC pitted Dick Cavett against Johnny Carson in the late-night TV derby.

Premieres: "Rowan & Martin's Laugh-In," "Mod Squad," "Julia," "Here's Lucy," "It Takes a Thief," "Hawaii 5-O," "Adam-12," "The Prisoner," "One Life to Live," "Happening '68," "Here Come the Brides," "The Ghost and Mrs. Muir," "Name of the Game," "The Ugliest Girl in Town," "Land of the Giants," "The Good Guys," "Doris Day Show," "The Outsider," "Lancer," "That's Life," "The Outcasts," "Don Rickles Show," "Man in a Suitcase," "Dean Martin Presents the Golddiggers," "Journey to the Unknown," "New Adventures of Huckleberry Finn," "Phyllis Diller Show," "Of Black America," "Dom Deluise Show," "The Baby Game," "The Champions," "Funny You Should Ask," "Mayberry RFD," "Banana Splits Adventure Hour," "The Archie Show," "Dream House."

1969

ABC innovated the first weekly series of made-for-TV movies.

Major news event: landing on the moon.

CBS pitted Merv Griffin against Johnny Carson in the late-night TV derby.

Premieres: "The Brady Bunch," "My World and Welcome To It," "Hee Haw," "Glen Campbell Goodtime Hour," "Sesame Street," "Medical Center," "Marcus Welby, M.D.," "Room 222," "Then Came Bronson," "Bill Cosby Show," "Scooby-Doo, Where Are You?," "The Governor and J.J.," "Bracken's World," "Mr. Deeds Goes to Town," "The Bold Ones," "To Rome with Love," "Johnny Cash Show," "Hee-Haw," "The Courtship of Eddie's Father," "Love American Style," "The Survivors," "Jim Nabors Hour,"

"Jimmy Durante Presents the Lennon Sisters Hour," "Debbie Reynolds Show," "The Music Scene," "The New People," "Hot Wheels," "Fat Albert and the Cosby Kids," "It Takes Two," "What's It All About, World?," "Leslie Uggams Show," "My Friend Tony," "Bright Promise," "Tom Jones Show," "Dudley Do-Right Show," "Generation Gap," "Turn-On."

1970

This was the last year for cigarette advertising on television.

Satellite, cable and pay TV systems started their aggressive growth. In the beginning, they carried clear reception for out-of-town channels.

Classic radio shows from the 1930s, 1940s and 1950s began to be marketed on vinyl LP records and audio cassette tapes.

Premieres: "All My Children," "Flip Wilson Show," "The Partridge Family," "Masterpiece Theatre," "NFL Monday Night Football," "Mary Tyler Moore Show," "The Odd Couple," "The Young Lawyers," "Nanny and the Professor," "Dan August," "The Young Rebels," "Matt Lincoln," "The Immortal," "Arnie," "Nancy," "Don Knotts Show," "Tim Conway Show," "Most Deadly Game," "The Silent Force," "Barefoot in the Park," "Dinah's Place," "Another World-Somerset," "Make Room for Granddaddy," "Hot Dog," "Lancelot Link, Secret Chimp," "Josie and the Pussycats," "The Bugaloos," "McCloud," "Engelbert Humperdinck Show," "Paris 7000," "Headmaster."

1971

Barter syndication strip series concept introduced.

Premieres: "All in the Family," "Columbo," "McMillan and Wife," "The Electric Company," "Sonny & Cher Comedy Hour," "Owen Marshall, Counselor at Law," "Cannon," "Funny Face," "New Dick Van Dyke Show," "Cade's County," "Columbo," "McMillan and Wife," "Sarge," "Man and the City," "Shirley's World," "The Good Life," "The Partners," "O'Hara, U.S. Treasury," "The Persuaders," "Getting Together," "Alias Smith

and Jones," "New Andy Griffith Show," "The Smith Family,"
"The D.A.," "Bearcats," "Chicago Teddy Bears," "Nichols,"
"Jimmy Stewart Show," "The Funny Side," "Pearl Bailey Show,"
"Three on a Match," "Pebbles and Bamm Bamm," "Lidsville,"
"Curiosity Shop."

1972

Major news event: tragedy at the Olympics games, as sports and
news coverage melded.

Premieres: "The Waltons," "Sanford and Son," "Maude," "The
Price Is Right" (with Bob Barker as host), "MASH," "Bob
Newhart Show," "Streets of San Francisco," "Kung-Fu," "Bridget
Loves Bernie," "Ghost Story," "Banyon," "The Rookies," "New
Bill Cosby Show," "Temperature's Rising," "Emergency," "The
Sixth Sense," "Hec Ramsey," "Anna and the King," "Banacek,"
"The Delphi Bureau," "Little People," "Cool Million,"
"Madigan," "Marty Feldman Show," "Me and the Chimp," "Paul
Lynde Show," "Julie Andrews Hour," "ABC Afterschool
Specials," "Midnight Special," "In Concert," "The Super,"
"Jigsaw," "Assignment: Vienna," "John Byner Comedy Hour,"
"The Osmonds," "The Joker's Wild," "Kid Power," "Brady Kids,"
"Return to Peyton Place," "Search for the Nile," "Don Rickles
Show."

1973

Premieres: "Police Story," "Kojack," "$10,000 Pyramid," "The
Six Million Dollar Man," "Police Story," "Barnaby Jones,"
"Alistair Cooke's America," "ABC's Wide World of
Entertainment," "Goodnight America with Geraldo Rivera,"
"Chase," "Adam's Rib," "Doc Elliot," "The Snoop Sisters,"
"Toma," "New Adventures of Perry Mason," "Diana," "The
Magician," "Love Story," "Needles and Pins," "The Tomorrow
Show with Tom Snyder," "The Young and the Restless," "The Girl
with Something Extra," "Lotsa Luck," "Thicker than Water,"
"Sigmund and the Sea Monsters," "Calucci's Department," "Roll
Out," "NBC Follies," "Hawkins," "Tenafly," "Faraday and Co.,"

"Bob and Carol and Ted and Alice," "Yogi's Gang," "The Wizard of Odds."

1974

Roone Arledge, head of ABC Sports, also took over as head of ABC News.

Premieres: "Happy Days," "Six Million Dollar Man," "Little House on the Prairie," "The Rockford Files," "Chico and the Man," "Good Times," "Apple's Way," "Police Woman," "Kolchak: The Night Stalker," "Rhoda," "Born Free," "Petrocelli," "Lucas Tanner," "That's My Mama," "Harry O," "Nakia," "Manhunter," "Amy Prentiss," "Friends and Lovers," "Tattletales," "Get Christie Love," "Planet of the Apes," "The Texas Wheelers," "Movin' On," "Kodiak," "The New Land," "Sons and Daughters," "Dirty Sally," "Chopper One," "Firehouse," "The Cowboys," "High Rollers," "Mac Davis Show," "Shazam."

1975

Premieres: "Saturday Night Live," "The Jeffersons," "Barney Miller," "Welcome Back Kotter," "Starsky and Hutch," "Wheel of Fortune," "Good Morning America," "One Day at a Time," "Baretta," "S.W.A.T.," "The Muppet Show," "Beacon Hill," "Bronk," "Matt Helm," "Joe Forrester," "Phyllis," "Saturday Night with Howard Cosell," "Mobile One," "Ellery Queen," "When Things Were Rotten," "The Family Holvak," "Three for the Road," "Barbary Coast," "The Invisible Man," "Doc, "Switch," "Karen," "Sunshine," "Hot L Baltimore," "Khan," "Bob Crane Show," "Swiss Family Robinson," "Kate McShane," "The Blankety Blanks," "Karibe," "Doctors' Hospital," "The Law," "Big Eddie," "Fay," "The Montefuscos," "On the Rocks," "Medical Story," "Archer," "Musical Chairs."

1976

The cable TV era began. Ted Turner's WTCG-TV in Atlanta became cable TV's first Superstation and changed its call letters to

WTBS, the flagship for his broadcasting empire.

Barbara Walters moved from NBC over to ABC. Her first stint was as cohost of the ABC Evening News with Harry Reasoner.

Premieres: "The Bionic Woman," "Laverne and Shirley," "Rich Man, Poor Man," "Alice," "Quincy, M.E.," "Charlie's Angels," "Donny & Marie Show," "Family," "The Blue Knight," "One Day at a Time," "Most Wanted," "Gemini Man," "Gibbsville," "Baa Baa Blacksheep," "Wonder Woman," "What's Happening," "Family Feud," "The Dumplings," "Good Heavens," "The Quest," "All's Fair," "Executive Suite," "Spencer's Pilots," "The Big Event," "Holmes and Yo Yo," "Mr. T. and Tina," "Bert D'Angelo-Superstar," "Sara," "Cop and the Kid," "Grady," "Tony Randall Show," "Nancy Walker Show," "Van Dyke and Company," "Best Sellers," "Ball Four," "McNaughton's Daughter, "Cos," "The Practice," "Jigsaw John," "Popi."

1977

97% of all U.S. households now have TV.

ABC-TV finally hit #1 overall in the ratings.

The first home video cassette recorders went on the marketing, selling at $1,700 each.

Blank video tapes were selling for $30.00 each.

Premieres: "Roots," "Soap," "Lou Grant," "Three's Company," "The Love Boat," "Fish," "Brady Bunch Variety Hour," "Grizzly Adams," "Eight Is Enough," "Busting Loose," "The Hardy Boys," "Nancy Drew Mysteries," "Dog and Cat," "Tales of the Unexpected," "Hunter," "Feather and Father Gang," "Man from Atlantis," "Logan's Run," "Tabitha," "James at 15," "Keane Brothers Show," "On Our Own," "CPO Sharkey," "Chips," "McLean Stevenson Show," "We've Got Each Other," "Operation Petticoat," "Rosetti and Ryan," "Young Dan'l Boone," "San Pedro Beach Bums," "Betty White Show," "Rafferty," "The Oregon Trail," "Big Hawaii," "Langan's Rabbi," "Blanskey's Beauties," "Fantastic Journey," "Sirota's Court," "Loves Me, Loves Me Not,"

"The Andros Targets," "Who's Who," "Nashville 99," "Code R."

1978

Home Box Office premiered.

Premieres: "Dallas," "Fantasy Island," "Taxi," "Mork & Mindy," "Centennial," "WKRP in Cincinnati," "Quark," "How the West Was Won," "Baby, I'm Back," "Flying High," "The Incredible Hulk," "The Amazing Spider-Man," "The White Shadow," "Battlestar Gallactica," "Mork & Mindy," "Julie Farr, M.D.," "Sam," "Quark," "Roller Girls," "Project U.F.O.," "Dick Clark's Live Wednesday," "Mary," "Ted Knight Show," "David Cassidy-Man Undercover," "Eddie Capra Mysteries," "The Waverly Wonders," "Grandpa Goes to Washington," "American Girls," "Sword of Justice," "Apple Pie," "In the Beginning," "People," "Who's Watching the Kids," "Kaz," "Lifeline," "W.E.B.," "For Richer, For Poorer."

1979

Premieres: "This Old House," "The Facts of Life," "Diff'rent Strokes," "The Dukes of Hazzard," "B.J. and the Bear," "Hello, Larry," "The Ropers," "Salvage-1," "Trapper John, M.D.," "Benson," "Real People," "Buck Rogers in the 25th Century," "Working Stiffs," "Hart to Hart," "Makin' It," "Mrs. Columbo," "Super Train," "The Mackenzies of Paradise Cove," "13 Queens Blvd.," "The Bad News Bears," "The Associates," "California Fever," "240-Robert," "Doctors' Private Lives," "Lazarus Syndrome," "Eischeid," "Shirley," "Little Women," "Time Express," "The Chisholms," Billy," "Flatbush," "Turnabout," "Dear Detective," "Sweepstakes," "Struck by Lightning," "The Last Resort," "The Duke."

1980

The concept of videotape rentals was first introduced.

The retail cost of VCRs went below $1,000 for the first time.

Black Entertainment Television (BET) premiered.

Showtime premiered.

Ted Turner's Cable News Network (CNN) premiered.

Premieres: "ABC News Nightline," "David Letterman Daytime Show," "Magnum, P.I.," "Palmerstown, USA," "That's Incredible," "B.A.D. Cats," "Too Close for Comfort," "Knots Landing," "Flo," "House Calls," "Bosom Buddies," "It's a Living," "Breaking Away," "Young Maverick," "Beyond Westworld," "Tenspeed and Brownshoe," "Tim Conway Show," "Pink Lady," "Skag," "Goodtime Girls," "Those Amazing Animals," "I'm a Girl Now," "Freebie and the Bean," "Secrets of Midland Heights," "The Big Show," "Me and Maxx," "One in a Million," "Texas," "Ends," "Games People Play," "Ladies' Man" "Marie," "Number 96," "Barbara Mandrell & the Mandrell Sisters Show," "Here's Boomer," "When the Whistle Blows," "The Contender," "United States."

1981

MTV premiered.

USA Network premiered.

CBS premiered its Signature cable channel (which ceased after 14 months' operation)..

Dan Rather took over as anchor of the CBS Evening News.

Classic television shows from the 1950s and 1960s began to be marketed on video cassette tapes.

Premieres: "Knots Landing," "Dynasty," "Hill Street Blues," "The Greatest American Hero," "Nero Wolfe," "Flamingo Road," "The Two of Us," "SCTV," "Simon and Simon," "Gimme a Break," "Jessica Novak," "Father Murphy," "Smurfs," "Strike Force," "The Fall Guy," "Love, Sidney," "Darkroom," "This Week with David Brinkley," "Ritchie Rich," "Harper Valley PTA," "Aloha Paradise," "Shannon," "Lewis and Clark," "American Dream," "Private Benjamin," "The Krypton Factor," "Maggie," "Walking Tall," "McClain's Law," "Fitz and Bones," "Open All Night," "The Gangster Chronicles," "Riker," "Concrete Cowboys,"

"Checking In," "Park Place," "Nurse," "Mr. Merlin," "Best of the West," "Today's F.B.I.," "Code Red."

1982

The cost of blank videotapes dropped below $20.00 for the first time.

The Arts Network and The Entertainment Channel (later becoming A&E) premiered.

TNN (The Nashville Network) premiered.

Premieres: "Family Ties," "Cheers," "Newhart," "Late Night with David Letterman," "Regis Philbin Show," "St. Elsewhere," "Cagney and Lacey," "T.J. Hooker," "Making the Grade," "Police Squad," Falcon Crest," "Teachers Only," "Bring 'Em Back Alive," "Matt Houston," "9 to 5," "Powers of Matthew Star," "Remington Steele," "Joanie Loves Chachi," "Tucker's Witch," "The Book of Lists," "King's Crossing," "Pac Man," "Square Pegs," "Silver Spoons," "One of the Boys," "Counterattack," "Baker's Dozen," "Knight Rider," "The Phoenix," "Tales of the Gold Monkey," "Star of the Family," "It Takes Two," "Ripley's Believe It or Not," "Billy Crystal Comedy Hour," "Cassie and Company," "Q.E.D.," "Filthy Rich," "Seven Brides for Seven Brothers," "Gloria," "Gavilan," "Voyagers."

1983

Broadcast of the final episode of "Mash" became TV's highest ratings getter. It knocked the birth of Little Ricky and the final episode of "The Fugitive" to second and third place.

Home shopping channels debuted.

The Disney Channel premiered.

Premieres: "Mama's Family," "The A-Team," "Ace Crawford," "Goodnight Beantown," "Webster," "Hardcastle & McCormick," "Baby Makes Five," "Wizards and Warriors," "Scarecrow & Mrs. King," "AfterMASH," "Emerald Point N.A.S.," "Yellow Rose," "The Rousters," "Whiz Kids," "Condo," "Mr. Smith," "Jennifer

Slept Here," "Zorro & Son," "Bay City Blues," "Oh, Madeline," "Boone," "Ryan's Four," "Base Essence," "Just Our Luck," "Casablanca," "High Performance," "Lottery," Foot in the Door," "Gun Shy," "Call to Glory," "For Love and Honor," "The Renegades," "Small and Frye."

1984

The retail cost of VCRs went below $500 for the first time.

Premieres: "Murder, She Wrote," "The Cosby Show," "Kate & Allie," "Night Court," "Miami Vice," "Highway to Heaven," "Airwolf," "Who's the Boss," "Mickey Spillane's Mike Hammer," "Hawaiian Heat," "Riptide," "Punky Brewster," "Glitter," "People Do the Craziest Things," "Brothers."

1985

The cost of blank videotapes dropped below $10.00 for the first time.

VH-1 premiered.

Premieres: "Moonlighting," "The Golden Girls," "Spenser: For Hire," "Lime Street," "MacGyver," "The Equalizer," "New Twilight Zone," "New Alfred Hitchcock Presents," "Hollywood Beat," "Misfits of Science," "Amazing Stories," "Stir Crazy," "George Burns Comedy Week," "Growing Pains," "Charlie & Company," "Insiders," "227," "Lady Blue."

1986

Compact discs introduced as the newest technology for record albums, with laser discs playing at 78 RPM (the original phonograph speed). CDs eclipsed vinyl records within the next five years and became the preferred source for music, over cassette tapes. This trend also spelled the beginning of the end for the Top 40 singles market.

ABC cancelled "American Bandstand," ending its 39-year run on the network.

Premieres: "Designing Women," "L.A. Law," "Perfect Strangers,"

"Paper Chase," "Oprah Winfrey Show" (going syndicated from local), "Life with Lucy," "Our House,""Matlock," "The Colbys," "Alf, "My Sister Sam," "Sledge Hammer," "Crime Story," "Sidekicks," "Amen," "Ellen Burstyn Show," "Head of the Class," "Easy Street," "Valerie," "Downtown," "Better Days," "Together We Stand," "Jack and Mike," "You Again," "Heart of the City."

1987

Fox Network signed on the air, with its first two series, "Married...with Children" and "The Tracey Ullman Show."

Premieres: "Star Trek, the Next Generation," "Beauty and the Beast," "thirtysomething," "Full House," "Houston Knights," "21 Jump Street," "Tour of Duty," "Wiseguy," "Highway to Heaven," "Jake and the Fatman," "The Law and Harry McGraw," "Beauty and the Beast," "West 57th Street," "Once a Hero," "A Year in the Life," "Hooperman," "Slap Maxwell Story," "Werewolf," "Duet," "My Two Dads," "Frank's Place," "Max Headroom," "The Charmings," "Sledge Hammer," "A Different World," "I Married Dora," "Everything's Relative," "Mr. President," "Second Chance," "Rags to Riches," "Oldest Rookie," "Women in Prison," "New Adventures of Beans Baxter."

1988

Premieres: "Murphy Brown," "The Wonder Years," "China Beach," "48 Hours," "Unsolved Mysteries," "Roseanne," "Dear John," "In the Heat of the Night," "Midnight Caller," "Hogan Family," "It's Garry Shandling's Show," "Knightwatch," "America's Most Wanted," "The Reporters," "Paradise," "Beyond Tomorrow," "New Mission: Impossible," "Tattingers," "Coming of Age," "Day by Day, "Baby Boom," "Raising Miranda," "Dirty Dancing," "Empty Nest," "Sonny Spoon," "Something is Out There," "Annie McGuire," "High Risk."

1989

Premieres: "Lonesome Dove," "Rescue 911," "Wolf," "Island Son," "Mr. Belvedere," "Quantum Leap," "Young Riders," "In

Living Color," "Twin Peaks," "Doogie Howser, M.D.," "Anything But Love," "Life Goes On," "Sister Kate," "Major Dad," "Fabulous Teddy Z," "Peaceable Kingdom," "Evening Shade," "Family Matters," "The People Next Door," "Mancuso, F.B.I.," "Midnight Caller," "Living Dolls," "Free Spirit," "Homeroom," "Top of the Hill," "Totally Hidden Video," "Booker," "Open House, "Alien Nation," "Chicken Soup."

1990

The cost of blank videotapes dropped below $5.00 for the first time.

The retail cost of VCRs went below $250 for the first time.

Premieres: "Seinfeld," "Northern Exposure," "America's Funniest Home Videos," "The Simpsons," "Wings," "Beverly Hills 9020," "Law and Order," "Uncle Buck," "True Colors," "Parker Lewis Can't Lose," "America's Funniest People," "Coach," "Fresh Prince of Bel Air," "Trials of Rosie O'Neill," "Get a Life," "Father Dowling Mysteries," "Ferris Beuller," "Parenthood," "Doctor, Doctor," "Fanelli Boys," "Bagdad Cafe," "Over My Dead Body," "Cops," "American Chronicles," "Haywire," "Cop Rock," "Lenny," "Family Man," "E.A.R.T.H. Force," "The Flash," "Good Grief," "Against the Law," "Going Places."

1991

Courtroom Television Network premiered.

Major news events: end of the Soviet Union and the Gulf War.

Premieres: "I'll Fly Away," "Brooklyn Bridge," "Home Improvement," "The Commish," "Sisters," "The Torkelsons," "Eerie, Indiana," "Top Cops," "Royal Family," "Teech," "Baby Talk," "Step by Step," "Carol Burnett Show," "Palace Guard," "Drexell's Class," "Blossom," "ROC," "Herman's Head," "Adventures of Mark and Brian," "Good & Evil," "Dinosaurs," "Pros and Cons," "Flesh n' Blood, "P.S. I Luv U," "FBI: The Untold Stories," "American Detective," "Princesses," "Palace Guard," "Sibs," "Real Life with Jane Pauley," "Best of the Worst."

1992

Jay Leno took over as host of "The Tonight Show" on NBC.

1997

With the advent of the Internet, Classic television shows from the 1950s,1960s, 1970s and 1980s began to be marketed on video cassette tapes.

2000

With the advent of the Direct Video Discs, Classic television shows from the 1950s,1960s, 1970s and 1980s began to be marketed on DVDs.

2002

Satellite radio was introduced.

New and creative ways of re-packaging and marketing classic TV shows continued to develop.

9

You Must Remember This

In my 35+ years of advising senior management of business organizations, I have found it clear that executives and leaders are more products of pop culture than formal business training.

Subsequent efforts to change or modify are often met with resistance. I realized that presenting organizational strategies as an extension of previously-held pop-culture values gets more support.

Most leaders of today's corporations grew up in the 1950s and 1960s. I have conducted countless strategy meetings where leaders cannot articulate business philosophies, but they can accurately recite lyrics from "golden oldie" song hits or TV trivia.

Being one of the rare senior business advisors who is equally versed in pop culture, I found that bridging known avenues with current realities resulted in fully articulated corporate visions. Many a Strategic Plan was written by piecing together song fragments, nostalgic remembrances and movie scenarios...then were aptly converted into contemporary corporate nomenclature.

There have been many books on business philosophies and strategy. There have been many books on the entertainment industry. This one is likely the first to combine the two phenomena and look at business executives' development through their own nostalgic eyes in pop culture.

When we recall the messages of the songs and books, today's adults were formerly taught to:

- Think Big Picture.
- Conceptualize your own personal goals.
- Understand conflicting societal goals.
- Fit your dreams into the necessities and realities of the real world.
- Find your own niche...do your thing.
- Get satisfactions from doing something well and committing to long-term excellence.
- Seek truths in unusual and unexpected sources.
- Share your knowledge, and learn further by virtue of mentoring others.

How individuals and organizations start out and what they become are different concepts. Mistakes, niche orientation and lack of planning lead businesses to failure. Processes, trends, fads, perceived stresses and "the system" force adults to make compromises in order to proceed. Often, a fresh look at previous knowledge gives renewed insight.

I developed the concept of integrating **Pop Culture Wisdom** with management strategy, raining and business planning over the last 25 years, applying it to many of my 2,000 clients (from small businesses to Fortune 500 corporations to the public sector). All agreed that no road map was laid out for them. Executives amassed knowledge "in the streets," through non-traditional sources.

Few lessons made sense at the time and, thus, did not sink in. When repackaged years later, executives vigorously enjoyed the rediscovery process. The previously overlooked became sage wisdom. Knowledge they were not ready to receive before became crystal clear in later times. Executives and companies, in these troubled times, seek reflection and redirection. The anticipated benefits of this book include:

1. Understanding how and why we change and evolve.

2. Inspiring executives to think holistically about each component of the business in terms of the Big Picture, master change and take companies to new tiers.

3. Fresh approaches toward re-applying past knowledge and experiences.

Wisdom from the Golden Oldie Files and Classic TV Memories

They won't always be kids."
Elvis Presley, 1956 (philosophizing upon what came to be known as The Baby Boom)

"As for the future, remember this. There'll always be quiz shows."
Jack Barry, 1958 (His scandal-riden "Twenty One" inspired the movie "Quiz Show.")

"I can't think of an innocent person that I have ravaged."
Mike Wallace

"It's good to know that if you ever have a flat tire anywhere, someone might recognize you and help."
David Nelson (son of Ozzie & Harriet, brother of Ricky)

"If you don't have a girl on the show, you don't have to shave so often." Broderick Crawford, 1956

"Let's hear it for the Lord's Prayer." Ed Sullivan, 1965

"The finest display of Levi's we have ever seen."
Executive of Levi Strauss & Co. (commenting on Elly Mae Clampett, character on "The Beverly Hillbillies," as played by Donna Douglas)

"I was a has-been. Now, I'm an am-is," Micky Dolenz to gangster, on "The Monkees."
Gangster's comment: "There have been some changes since you've been away."
Dolenz's retort: "Change them back!"

"It is so simple. The obvious often appears simple. One must adapt to the tools at hand." Sherlock Holmes

"Books are the best of things when used and the worst when abused." Ralph Waldo Emerson

"We live in a sick civilization. The well people are the exception. With talent goes responsibility. Have you been responsible? The reprimand, if there is one, comes from your own conscience." Testimony-theatrical dialog from "The Caine Mutiny Court Martial"

"Never turn away a scoundrel. They seldom call without good reason." The Sheriff of Nottingham, "Robin Hood"

"In order to prove his worth, a sheriff needs an outlaw." Maid Marian to the Sheriff of Nottingham, "Robin Hood"

"The best place to hide something is where everyone can see it." Edgar Allen Poe

"An army marches on its stomach." Napoleon

"There are 6 ways to roll a 7 with a pair of dice. It's amazing how they don't come when you want them." The Falcon (undercover espionage agent)

"The hardest part about being champion is that you have to prove it all the time." John L. Sullivan, prize fighter

"To really understand the most insignificant thing is to understand the universe." Alfred Lord Tennyson

"It's a funny thing about greed. It sorta grows on you. It starts out when you're young, wanting someone's baseball bat or a football that doesn't belong to you. Then, later on, wanting somebody's job. First thing you know, you're wanting everything in sight." Roy Rogers

Observations from Mickey Spillane's detective, Mike Hammer (character portrayed by Darren McGavin):

- "Never kick a man when he's down. You never know when he will get up on his feet."

- "There's a lot of detail work in this business. You ask a lot of questions. If you get the right answers, you start over again. It's just a matter of questions and legwork. Sooner or later, you get the right answers."

Wisdom from Jim Newton, on "Fury" (character portrayed by Peter Graves):

- "A man can run away from everything...but not from himself."

- "Learn to like people for what they are, not what they've been. Figure a person for what he is, not for something that happened before."

- "Some people ridicule what they cannot understand. The sad part is if they start thinking that way when they are kids, sometimes the thinking never gets straightened out."

- "I'm just a man trying to do a job for people he serves...a human being with my share of faults."

- "You never really forget words of wisdom. You had them in the back of your head all the time. We all just sort of sidetrack them for a spell."

From the journal of Dr. Jekyll:

- "It is possible to produce a monster and an angel in the same man."

- "The journey is into the soul itself. One way to define the soul is to dissect it the way you would any other organ."

- "None of us is very good or very bad...just a mixture. Mr. Hyde had become a disease which I could no longer control. Every man has a Hyde within him."

- "My life is now a battleground where good and evil are at war. It was an unholy thing to separate the beast and the angel, but only the good remains."

Wisdom from the Brady Bunch:

- "Nobody has smooth sailing all the time."

- "Some of us are good at one thing. Others are good at another."
- "If you keep your eyes open, opportunities will present themselves."
- "Sometimes, when we lose, we win."
- "When it's time to change, you've got to rearrange."

Wisdom from Indian chief Cochise, on "Broken Arrow" (portrayed by Michael Ansara):

- "A man fears a trick more than a wound because it injures his pride."
- "Man learns that the ideas of a few are not as powerful as the consensus of many."
- "Friendship cannot live without trust."
- "When wise men speak, who knows what they will say or how long it will take them to say it."
- "A bruise carried a few days is a great lesson."

Narratives from dramas directed by Alfred Hitchcock:

- "We're always taught that it didn't matter what happened inside the house, as long as the neighbors didn't know about it. I used to wonder if all families were like that, if they only pretended to be happy and love each other, when other people were watching."
- "Loving someone is one thing. To stop loving because you lose them is not living. It's sickness."

Wisdom from Charlie Chan:

- "Knowledge is the only medicine to cure the itch of curiosity."
- "Walk in fresh air helps clear mind, particularly if walk is in right direction."
- "Men are never strong enough to fight the fate their own evil

has created."
- "When the trap is baited, there is no need for the hunter to hasten to spring same."
- "The smoke of sincerity in your belief indicates the fire of truth."
- "Journey of life is like tether of a stream...must continue with current."
- "Waiting for tomorrow is waste of today."
- "Theories like mist on eyeglasses...obscure facts."
- "Drops of water on parched tongue worth more than gold in purse."
- "Inconspicuous molehill sometimes more important than conspicuous mountain."
- "If you want wild bird to sing, do not put him in a cage."
- "Pleasant company turn lonely sandwich into rich banquet."
- "When looking for needle in haystack, most sensible location is haystack."
- "Question without answer like faraway water...not good for fire."
- "Very wise to know way out before going in."
- "Too soon to count chickens until eggs in nest."
- "One grain of luck sometimes worth more than a rice field of wisdom."
- "Men who seek trouble never find it far off."
- "Frightened bird difficult to catch."
- "Guilty conscience only enemy to peace and rest."
- "To understand men, study women."
- "Grain of sand in eye may hide mountain."
- "Size of package does not indicate quality within."
- "Wise precaution to accept applesauce with large pinch of salt."

- "Curiosity responsible for cat needing nine lives."
- "Kindness in heart more valuable than gold in bank."
- "Perfect case like donut...has a hole. Optimist sees donut. Pessimist sees hole. Very typical to explain hole in donut, but hole always there."
- "Silence is big sister to wisdom."
- "Good tools shorten labor."
- "Inquisitive person like bear after honey...sometimes find hornet's nest."
- "Not always wise to accept simplest solution. Mind like parachute...only function when open."
- "He who requests fiddler must be willing to share tune."
- "Great happiness follows great pain."

Wisdom from Annie Oakley (character portrayed by Gail Davis):

- "You cannot judge a man by his appearance. Sometimes, a man is not as he seems."
- "There are some people with silly fears about people who don't live as they do. If they don't know why, they don't take the trouble to understand."
- "Your attention is like a gun. Aim it and hold it there. And don't think of anything else."

Wisdom from Peter Gunn (character portrayed by Craig Stevens):

- "In the case of murder, I always try to keep an open mind."
- "Compulsive talkers are usually insecure."
- "There never was a blackmailer that quit at the first touch."

Commentary from Dr. Richard Kimble, The Fugitive (character portrayed by David Janssen):

- "People have always been sure. Sure they could make gold out of lead, sure the world was flat, sure that if a mad dog bit them, they would die. Being sure does not make you right."

From the writings of William Shakespeare:

- "There are more things in heaven and earth than are dreamt of in your philosophy."

- "The quality of mercy is not strained, it droppeth as the gentle rain from heaven

upon the place beneath. It blesseth him that gives and him that takes."

Narratives from Rod Serling, on "The Twilight Zone":

- "Some people possess talent. Others are possessed by it. When that happens, a talent becomes a curse"

- "To most people, but not all, time is an enemy. A dream takes only a second or so, and yet, in that second, a man can live a lifetime."

- "The tools of conquest do not necessarily come with bombs and explosions and fallout. There are weapons that are simply thoughts, attitudes, prejudices—to be found only in the minds of men. Prejudices can kill and suspicion can destroy, and a thoughtless, frightened search for a scapegoat has a fallout all its own. And the pity of it is that these things cannot be confined to The Twilight Zone."

- "Odd how the real consorts with the shadows, how the present fuses with the past."

- "Sometimes, the product of man's talent and genius can walk amongst us untouched by the normal ravages of time. Perfection is relative."

- "Any state, any entity, any ideology that fails to recognize the worth, the dignity, the rights of man, that state is obsolete."

- "There was nothing in the dark that wasn't there when the lights were on."

- "For civilization to survive, the human race has to remain civilized."

- "Some superstitions, kept alive by the long night of igno-
  rance, have their own special power."
- "Childhood, maturity and old age are curiously intertwined
  and not separate."
- "The major ingredient of any recipe for fear is the unknown.
  Fear is extremely relative. It depends on who can look down
  and who must look up. It depends on other vagaries, like the
  time, the mood, the darkness."
- "The subject: fear. The cure: a little more faith."
- "You can't out-punch machinery. No matter what else the
  future brings, man's capacity to rise to the occasion will
  remain unaltered. His potential for tenacity and optimism
  continues, as always, to outfight, outpoint and outlive any
  and all changes made by his society."

"Things are never quite the same when you try to go back to the
past. That's like when you leave gum on the window sill overnight
and try to chew it the next morning."
Beaver Cleaver, "Leave It To Beaver"

"If you want to call me that, smile!" The Virginian

"Every member of the Hall of Fame had one thing in common.
They were always trying to improve."
Red Barber, baseball Hall of Fame member

"Who can explain it? Who can tell you why? Fools give you rea-
sons. Wise men never try."
Richard Rodgers & Oscar Hammerstein, "Some Enchanted
Evening," from "South Pacific"

"A man is like a rope. He's only as strong as the thinnest part."
Dale Robertson, "Tales of Wells Fargo"

"When there's a smile in your heart, there's no better time to
start." Peter Pan

"Never drink with strangers. But, if you do, don't enjoy it. A
woman would much rather forgive you than believe you"
Willie Dante, "Dante's Inferno"

"There are two occasions in a man's life when he shouldn't speculate...when he can afford it and when he cannot." Mark Twain

"If you cannot find a man, you must arrange for the man to find you." Zorro

"You've got to learn to play the other man's game."
Hopalong Cassidy

"Only a fool becomes angry. An angry man loses the choice of weapons. And an angry man cannot shoot very straight."
Yancy Derringer (character portrayed by Jock Mahoney)

"There's a little bit of failure in every success and a little bit of success in every failure."
O. Henry (short story writer)

"The round burner still cooks a good square meal."
Kitchen promo film in the 1930's

"You don't know what it's like being a newcomer in town. It's all politics. People are afraid that someone will take what's theirs."
Detective Stu Bailey, "77 Sunset Strip"

"Enjoy yourself. It's later than you think." World War II song

"It's always later than you think."
Herb Philbrick, FBI counterspy on "I Led Three Lives"

"You always hurt the one you love."
Song by The Mills Brothers

"Funny thing about trouble. The more you worry about it, the bigger it gets." Sheriff Pat Garrett, who stalked outlaw Billy the Kid

"When my bankroll is getting small, I think of when I had none at all. And I fall asleep, counting my blessings." Irving Berlin

"It takes a lot of man to walk away from a challenge."
The Rifleman (character portrayed by Chuck Connors)

"Fear is a delayed reaction. So is guilt."
Johnny Staccato (portrayed by John Cassavetes)

"To pre-judge guilt is the highest form of injustice."
Oliver Wendell Holmes, U.S. Supreme Court justice

"We will get a car someday...when they get perfected. They're still too dangerous!"
The Kingfish, on "Amos n' Andy"

"It's a wonderful system. The men run the country, and women run the family. They don't know we're running it. Welcome to a higher form of civilization."
Gladys Porter, on "Pete & Gladys" (character portrayed by Cara Williams)

"When you wish upon a star. Makes no difference who you are. Your dreams will come true."
Jiminy Crickett, in the Disney movie classic "Pinnochio" (1941)

Wisdom of Benjamin Franklin:

- "In this world, nothing can be said to be certain except death and taxes."

- "God grant that not only the love of liberty but a thorough knowledge of the rights of man may pervade all the nations of the earth, so that a philosopher may set his foot anywhere on its surface and say: This is my country."

- "He who multiplies riches multiplies cares."

- "Laziness travels so slowly that poverty soon overtakes him."

- "Men and melons are hard to know."

- "He that lives upon hope will die fasting."

- "There is no kind of dishonesty into which otherwise good people more easily and frequently fall than that of defrauding the government."

- "A little neglect may breed great mischief. For the want of a nail, the shoe was lost. For the want of a shoe, the horse was lost. For the want of a horse, the rider was lost."

- "No nation was ever ruined by trade."

- "At 20 years of age, the will reigns; at 30, the wit; and at 40, the judgment."

The Hits Just Keep Rolling.....

Music lyrics and expressions are imbedded in our psyches, reflecting all aspects of our lives, including business. Here are some, by subject area:

Poems, Prayers and Promises

"Big girls don't cry. That's just an alibi."

"Walk like a man. Fast as you can. Walk like a man, my son."
The Four Seasons (1962)

Business Lessons for Today:

- Good intentions do not substitute for careful planning and benchmarking achievements.
- Companies that talk in generalities do not become specifically successful.

Letters, We Get Letters

"A line a day when you're far away. Little things mean a lot. Give me your heart to rely on." Kitty Kallen (1954)

Business Lessons for Today:

- Keep lines of communication open.
- Put more emphasis upon customer service.

We'll Remember Always

"Freedom's just another word for nothing left to lose."
Kris Kristofferson (1967)

"When you move real slow, it seems like mo', cause it's alright."
Curtis Mayfield (1963)

"The Ballroom prize we almost won. We will have these moments to remember." The Four Lads (1955)

"Diamonds, diamonds, pearls galore. She buys them at the five and ten cent store. She wants to be just like Zsa Zsa Gabor. Even though she's the girl next door." Dion (1963)

Business Lessons for Today:

- Memories and their recollections are good teaching tools and preparers for tomorrow.
- One learns three times more from failure than success.
- Changing perspectives opens up new opportunities.
- Standing still and living in the past represents lost ground and missed opportunities.

The Old Ways Don't Work Anymore

"Keep movin', movin', movin. Though they're disapprovin'. Keep them doggies rolling. Soon we'll be livin' high and wide." "Rawhide" theme, 1958.

Business Lessons for Today:

- Dysfunctional corporate culture must be corrected and dismantled.
- Executives who are rigid and controlling in their approach will become dinosaurs.
- The old, regimented ways will no longer be observed...the marketplace won't allow it.

Human Potential

"You could have been anything that you wanted to. And I can tell...the way you do the things you do." Smokey Robinson (1964)

"It's your thing, Do what you want to do." The Isley Brothers (1969)

"When there's a smile in your heart, there's no better time to start."Peter Pan

Business Lessons for Today:

- Each organization's best and most under-utilized resource is its people.
- Team members with focus and dedication perform best.
- People are motivated to achieve by things other than money.

Missed Opportunities

"It's too late, baby, now it's too late. Though we really did try to make it. Something inside has died and I can't hide. There'll be good times again for me and you."
Carole King (1971)

Business Lessons for Today:

- Celebrate successes, and learn from failures...both as valuable experiences.
- Glitz and hype do not substitute for a poorly run company.
- Planning is a road map to success...otherwise your journey tends to meander.

People Skills—Team Power

"Picking up a passenger in every town. Wondring if he's ever gonna shoot you down. Sittin' on a board eying in the weather. Prayin' to the Lord...keep us together. Side by side on the Wagon Train." "Wagon Train" second theme song, 1958.

Business Lessons for Today:

- Embrace the concepts of Empowerment.
- We are all in this together.
- When people face adversity, they rise to the occasion.
- You don't always know, going in, who your enemies are. Some who you branded as negative charges will become positive charges.

Focus—Organizational Responsibility

"When you wish upon a star. Makes no difference who you are. Your dreams will come true."
Jiminy Crickett, in the Disney movie classic "Pinnochio" (1941)

Business Lessons for Today:

- We make our own futures and cannot abdicate to others.
- Putting our future is someone else's hands spells failure for every organization.

Thinking & Reasoning Skills

"Who can explain it? Who can tell you why? Fools give you reasons. Wise men never try."
Richard Rodgers & Oscar Hammerstein, "Some Enchanted Evening," from "South Pacific"

Business Lessons for Today:

- Thinking-reasoning skills must be developed steadily and are more important than technology.

Planning and Anticipation

"And in the end, the love you take is equal to the love you make."The Beatles (1969)

"Enjoy yourself. It's later than you think."World War II song

Business Lessons for Today:

- Investments pay off.

- Community, professional and personal goodwill, if strategic, are bankable for the future.

- Mentor others to cast bread on the water.

- When you give for the right reasons, the paybacks are exponentially high.

Respect

"You always hurt the one you love."
Song by The Mills Brothers

"There ain't no good guys. There ain't no bad guys. There's only you and me, and we just disagree." Dave Mason

Business Lessons for Today:

- Workforce diversity and commitment toward excellence begins and ends with respect.

- Respect is shown when earned by the exhibitor.

Ethics and Values

"When my bankroll is getting small, I think of when I had none at

all. And I fall asleep, counting my blessings."
Irving Berlin

Business Lessons for Today:

- Core values are grown, believed and communicated.
- It takes more than a Mission Statement to achieve true organizational Vision.
- One must walk the talk, or else the value systems are not valid.

Enlightenment and the Potentiality to Achieve

"Happy days are here again. The skies above are clear again. Altogether shout it now. There's no one who can doubt it now. So let's tell the world about it now. Happy days are here again."
Composed by Benny Meroff (1930)

Business Lessons for Today:

- The best time to plan is when things are great, when times are terrible and everytime in between.

Youthful Perspective

- "Life goes on...after the thrill of living is gone."
- John Mellencamp, song lyric, "Jack and Diane," 1982

Communicating

"Oh what I'd give for that wonderful phrase, to hear those three little words that's all I'd live for the rest of my days. And what I feel in my heart, they tell sincerely. No other words can tell it half so clearly. Three little words, eight little letters which simply mean I love you."
Burt Kalmar & Harry Ruby (1930)

10

Theme Songs and Slogans

Music from the Back of the Mind.

We sing and whistle them. We remember them. The fine art of television theme song writing links bonds to viewers. Themes set the instrumental moods for TV show storylines. Vocal themes tell stories which set up premises of the series:

"Keep movin', movin', movin. Though they're disapprovin'. Keep them doggies rolling. Soon we'll be livin' high and wide."
"Rawhide" theme, 1958.

"People yakkety yak a streak and waste your time of day. But Mr. Ed will never speak unless he has something to say. A horse is a horse, of course, of course."
"Mr. Ed" theme, 1960.

"Beware of pretty faces you may find. A pretty face may hide an evil mind. Careful what you say. Don't give yourself away. Odds are you won't live to see tomorrow."
"Secret Agent" theme, 1965.

"From West Virginia they came to stay in sunny California."
"Real McCoys" theme, 1957.

"Picking up a passenger in every town. Wondering if he's ever gonna shoot you down. Sittin' on a board eying the weather. Prayin' to the Lord...keep us together. Side by side on the Wagon Train." "Wagon Train" second theme song, 1958.

"So get a witch's shawl on, a broomstick you can crawl on. We're gonna pay a call on the Addams Family."
"Addams Family" theme, 1964.

"Where love and adventure await, this is your fate. And you cannot stray from...you can't run away from the Hawaiian Eye."
"Hawaiian Eye" theme, 1959.

"You might just make it after all."
Mary Tyler Moore Show theme, 1970.

"A knight without armor in a savage land. A soldier of fortune is the man called Paladin."
"Have Gun, Will Travel" second theme song, 1958.

"New York is where I'd rather stay. I get allergic smelling hay."
"Green Acres" theme, 1965.

"One for four. Four for one. This we guarantee. We got a right to pick a little fight, Bonanza. If anyone fights any one of us, he's gotta fight with me." "Bonanza" theme, 1959.

"We're the young generation. And we got something to say."
"Monkees" theme, 1966.

Discography Listings

Though certainly not complete, here is an annotated reference listing of vocal television theme songs that were released on records, most becoming hits during the heydays of their respective series:

ADVENTURES OF ROBIN HOOD — "Robin Hood" (1956) Nelson Riddle

ALL IN THE FAMILY — "Those Were the Days" (1972) Carroll O'Connor & Jean Stapleton

ANDY GRIFFITH SHOW — "The Fishing Hole" (1961)
Andy Griffith

ANDY WILLIAMS SHOW — "Moon River" (1962)
Andy Williams

ANGIE — "Different Worlds" (1979) Maureen McGovern

BARETTA — "Keep Your Eye On the Sparrow" (1975)
Merry Clayton

BATMAN — "Batman Theme" (1966) Neal Hefti

THE BEVERLY HILLBILLIES — "The Ballad of Jed Clampett"
(1963) Lester Flatt and Earl Scruggs

THE BIG RECORD - PATTI PAGE SHOW — "This Is My Song"
(1952) Patti Page

BILL COSBY SHOW — "Hikky Burr" (1969) Bill Cosby

CHICO AND THE MAN — "Chico and the Man" (1974)
Jose Feliciano

CHINA BEACH — "Reflections" (1967)
Diana Ross and The Supremes

COCA-COLA COMMERCIALS — "I'd Like to Teach the World
to Sing" (1971) The New Seekers

COSBY SHOW — "A House Full of Love" (1986) Grover
Washington, Jr.—Lori Fulton

THE COURTSHIP OF EDDIE'S FATHER — "My Best Friend"
(1969) Harry Nilsson

DANIEL BOONE — "Daniel Boone" (1965) Fess Parker

DEAN MARTIN SHOW — "Everybody Loves Somebody"
(1964) Dean Martin

DISNEYLAND — "The Ballad Of Davy Crockett" (1955) Fess
Parker/Bill Hayes

DR. KILDARE — "Three Stars Will Shine Tonight" (1962)
Richard Chamberlain

THE DUKES OF HAZZARD — "Good Ol' Boys" (1980)
Waylon Jennings

THE FACTS OF LIFE — "The Facts of Life" (1982)
Gloria Loring

FAMILY LAW — "War" (1970) Edwin Starr

FAMILY TIES — "Without Us" (1982) Johnny Mathis and
Deniece Williams

THE FLYING NUN — "Who Needs Wings To Fly?" (1967)
Sally Field

GENE AUTRY SHOW — "Back in the Saddle Again" (1939)
Gene Autry

GETTING TOGETHER — "Getting Together" (1971)
Bobby Sherman

GIDGET — "Wait Till You See My Gidget" (1966)
Johnny Tillotson

THE GOLDEN GIRLS — "Thank You For Being A Friend"
(1978) Andrew Gold

THE GREATEST AMERICAN HERO — "Believe It Or Not"
(1981) Joey Scarbury

GREEN ACRES — "Green Acres" (1966) Eddie Albert

GROWING PAINS — "Long as We Got Each Other" (1988)
B.J. Thomas & Dusty Springfield

HAPPENING '68 — "Happening '68" (1968)
Paul Revere & the Raiders

HAPPY DAYS — "Happy Days" (1976) Pratt & McClain

HAVE GUN, WILL TRAVEL — "The Ballad of Paladin" (1959)
Johnny Western

HEC RAMSEY — "Where Did He Come From?" (1972)
Jerry Wallace

HERE COME THE BRIDES — "Seattle" (1969) Perry Como

HOWDY DOODY — "It's Howdy Doody Time" (1954) Buffalo
Bob Smith

I LOVE LUCY — "I Love Lucy—Babalu" (1951) Desi Arnaz

JUDY GARLAND SHOW — "Maybe I'll Come Back" (closing theme) (1963) Judy Garland

JUST THE TEN OF US — "Doin' It the Best I Can" (1988) Bill Medley

LAVERNE AND SHIRLEY — "Making Our Dreams Come True" (1976) Cyndi Grecco

LOEWENBRAU COMMERCIALS — "Here's To Good Friends" (1978) Arthur Prysock

LOVE AMERICAN STYLE — "Love American Style" (1969) The Cowsills

THE LOVE BOAT — "Love Boat Theme" (1979) Jack Jones

MAKIN' IT — "Makin' It" (1979) David Naughton

MARRIED WITH CHILDREN — "Love and Marriage" (1955) Frank Sinatra

MARY TYLER MOORE SHOW — "Love Is All Around" (1980) Sonny Curtis

MICKEY MOUSE CLUB — "Mickey Mouse March (Alma Mater Theme)" (1956) Jimmy Dodd and the Mouseketeers

MISTER ROGERS' NEIGHBORHOOD — "It's a Lovely Day in the Neighborhood" (1973) Fred Rogers

THE MONKEES — "Monkees Theme" (1966) The Monkees

MOONLIGHTING — "Moonlighting Theme" (1987) Al Jarreau

MOVIN' ON — "Movin' On" (1975) Merle Haggard

ON BROADWAY TONIGHT — "On Broadway Tonight" (1965) Frankie Valli & Four Seasons

OZARK JUBILEE — "Sugarfoot Rag" (1957) Bob Wills

PARTRIDGE FAMILY — "Come On, Get Happy" (1970) The Partridge Family

PERRY COMO SHOW — "Dream Along With Me" (1956) Perry Como

PETTICOAT JUNCTION — "Petticoat Junction" (1964)
Curt Massey

RAWHIDE — "Rawhide" (1958) Frankie Laine

THE REBEL — "The Rebel—Johnny Yuma" (1961) Johnny Cash

THE ROARING 20's — "The Roaring 20's" (1960)
Dorothy Provine

SECRET AGENT—DANGER MAN — "Secret Agent Man"
(1966) Johnny Rivers

SING ALONG WITH MITCH — "Sing Along" (1957)
Mitch Miller

SONNY & CHER COMEDY HOUR — "The Beat Goes On"
(1967) Sonny & Cher

THEN CAME BRONSON — "Long Lonesome Highway" (1969)
Michael Parks

WHERE THE ACTION IS — "Action" (1965) Freddy Cannon

WOODY WOODPECKER SHOW — "Woody Woodpecker"
(1948) Kay Kyser

WYATT EARP — "The Legend of Wyatt Earp" (1956)
Hugh O'Brian

ZORRO — "Zorro" (1958) The Chordettes

In addition to the numerous soundtrack albumns and compilations of television theme music, here is an annotated reference listing of instrumental television theme songs that were released on records, most becoming hits during the heydays of their respective series:

THE ADDAMS FAMILY — "Theme from 'The Addams Family'"
(1965) Vic Mizzy

ALFRED HITCHCOCK PRESENTS — "Funeral March of a
Marionette" (classical)

ALKA SELTZER COMMERCIALS — "No Matter What Shape"
(1966) The T-Bones

AMERICAN BANDSTAND — "Bandstand Boogie" (1954)
Les Elgart

BEECHNUT COMMERCIALS — "Mexican Shuffle" (1964)
Herb Alpert & Tijuana Brass

BENSON & HEDGES COMMERCIALS — "The Disadvantages
of You" (1966) Brass Ring

BONANZA — "Theme from 'Bonanza'" (1962) David Rose

CADE'S COUNTY — "Theme from 'Cade's County'" (1971)
Henry Mancini

DARK SHADOWS — "Dark Shadows Theme/Collinwood"
(1969) Robert Cobert

DRAGNET — "Dragnet" (1953) Ray Anthony

ERNIE KOVACS SHOW — "Song of the Nairobi Trio
(Solfeggio)" (1965) Robert Maxwell

GENERAL ELECTRIC THEATER — "Emblem" (opening
theme) and "Progress" (closing theme) (1958) Elmer Bernstein

GEORGE GOBEL SHOW — "Gobelues" (1955)
Richard Hayman

GILLETTE FRIDAY NIGHT FIGHTS — "Look Sharp—Be
Sharp" (1956) Arthur Fiedler and the Boston Pops Orchestra

THE GREEN HORNET — "Green Hornet Theme" (1966) Al Hirt

GUNSMOKE — "Gunsmoke Trails" (1955) Rex Koury

HAGGIS BAGGIS (game show) — "Haggis Baggis" (1959)
Billy Mure

HAVE GUN, WILL TRAVEL — "The Ballad of Paladin" (1962)
Duane Eddy

HAWAII FIVE-0 — "Hawaii Five-0" (1969) The Ventures

HIGH CHAPARRAL — "High Chaparral Theme" (1968)
David Rose

HIGHWAY PATROL — "Highway Patrol" (1958) Cyril Stapleton

HONG KONG — "Evans Theme" (1960) Lionel Newman

I SPY — "I Spy Theme" (1968) Earl Hagen

I'VE GOT A SECRET — "Plink, Plank Plunk" (1951)
Leroy Anderson

IRONSIDE — "Theme from 'Ironside'" (1972) Quincy Jones

JACKIE GLEASON SHOW — "Melancholy Serenade" (1953)
Jackie Gleason

L.A. LAW — "Theme from 'L.A. Law'" (1988) Mike Post

LAWRENCE WELK SHOW — "Bubbles In the Wine" (1954)
Lawrence Welk

THE LONE RANGER — "William Tell Overture: Finale"
(classical piece by Rossini)

MAGNUM P.I. — "Theme from 'Magnum P.I.'" (1982)
Mike Post

MARKHAM — "The Markham Theme" (1959) Nelson Riddle

MARTIN KANE, PRIVATE EYE — "Martin Kane Theme"
(1954) Nelson Riddle

M*A*S*H — "Song From M*A*S*H" (1970) Al De Lory

THE MATCH GAME — "A Swingin' Safari" (1962)
Bert Kaempfert

MEDIC — "Blue Star" (1955) Les Baxter

MISSION: IMPOSSIBLE — "Mission: Impossible" (1968)
Lalo Schifrin

MR. LUCKY — "Mr. Lucky" (1960) Henry Mancini

MR. PEEPERS — "Mr. Peepers" (1954) Tex Beneke

THE MUNSTERS — "Theme from 'The Munsters'" (1964)
Billy Strange

MURPHY BROWN — "Like the Whole World's Watching"
(1988) Steve Dorff

MY THREE SONS — "Theme from 'My Three Sons'" (1961)
Spencer Ross

NBC MYSTERY MOVIE — "Mystery Movie Theme" (1971)
Henry Mancini

PEANUTS SPECIALS — "Charlie Brown Theme" (1965) Vince
Guaraldi Trio

PEPSI COLA COMMERCIALS — "Music To Watch Girls By"
(1966) Bob Crewe Generation

PERRY MASON — "Park Avenue Beat, Theme from 'Perry
Mason'" (1957) Ray Conniff

PETER GUNN — "Peter Gunn" (1958) Henry Mancini/Ray
Anthony/Duane Eddy

RED SKELTON SHOW — "Holiday for Strings" (1942)
David Rose

RICHARD BOONE SHOW — "How Soon" (1963)
Henry Mancini

RICHARD DIAMOND, PRIVATE DETECTIVE — "Richard
Diamond Theme" (1959) Pete Rugulo

ROCKFORD FILES — "The Rockford Files" (1975) Mike Post

ROOTS — "Theme from 'Roots'" (1977) Quincy Jones

ROUTE 66 — "Route 66 Theme" (1962) Nelson Riddle

SANFORD AND SON — "Theme from 'Sanford and Son'"
(1973) Quincy Jones

SOUL TRAIN — "TSOP (The Sound of Philadelphia" (1974)
MFSB

SPENSER: FOR HIRE — "Theme from 'Spencer: For Hire'"
(1988) Steve Dorff

ST. ELSEWHERE — "Theme from 'St. Elsewhere'" (1984)
Dave Grusin

STARSKY & HUTCH — "Theme from 'Starsky & Hutch'"
(1976) The Rhythm Heritage

THIS IS YOUR LIFE — "This Is Your Life" (1959) Von Dexter

TONIGHT SHOW STARRING JOHNNY CARSON — "Johnny's
Theme" (1986) Doc Severinsen

TWILIGHT ZONE — "Theme from 'The Twilight Zone'" (1959)
Marius Constant

THE UNTOUCHABLES — "Theme from 'The Untouchables'"
(1960) Nelson Riddle

VICTORY AT SEA — "Song of the Seas" (1955)
Robert Russell Bennett

THE VIRGINIAN — "The Virginian" (1963) Percy Faith

WAGON TRAIN — "Wagons Ho!" (1960) Stanley Wilson

YOUNG AND THE RESTLESS — "Nadia's Theme" (1976)
Barry De Vorzon—Perry Botkin Jr.

Original TV soundtrack albumns were released on records for such series as, The Addams Family, The Big Valley, Bonanza, Bourbon Street Beat, General Electric Theatre, Hogan's Heroes, Hollywood Squares, Honey West, Hong Kong, Howdy Doody, Johnny Staccato, M Squad, The Man from UNCLE, Mission: Impossible, Mr. Lucky, Mr. Novak, One Step Beyond, Pete Kelly's Blues, Peter Gunn, Richard Diamond, The Roaring 20's, The Rogues, 77 Sunset Strip, Shotgun Slade, This Is Your Life, The Twilight Zone, Victory at Sea, Wagon Train, The Wonder Years and The Young and the Restless.

Messages for All-Time

Slogans, taglines and signoff messages give memorable reasons for viewers to tune in again and support show concepts:

"A day like all days, filled with the events that alter and illuminate our times, and you were there."   Walter Cronkite narrative, 1953.

"Faster than a speeding bullet. More powerful than a locomotive. Look, up in the sky. It's a bird, it's a plane. It's Superman."
Superman opening, 1952.

"Fury, the story of a horse and the boy who loved him."
Fury opening, 1955.

"Goodbye, good luck, and may the good lord take a likin' to you." Roy Rogers.

"Be very kind to each other." Garry Moore.

"Space, the final frontier." Star Trek opening, 1966.

"Right here on our stage, a really big shew." Ed Sullivan.

"This is the city. The stories are true. The names were changed to protect the innocent." Dragnet, 1952.

"A friend to those who have no friends." Boston Blackie.

"You're travelling through another dimension, a dimension not only of sight and sound but of mind; a journey into a wondrous land whose boundaries are that of imagination. That's the signpost up ahead...your next stop, the Twilight Zone." Rod Serling, 1959.

11

Advertising Slogans

Texture for Perspectives on Life.
The Witty, the Glib and the Pertinent.

Advertising jingles exist in our psyche. We recall them at a moment's notice. We quote them to our kids. We use them in memos and meetings. They are the brain waves for our lives. Thus, they were effective in creating recall value.

Advertising jingles are more than cute lyrics and catchy tunes. They are designed to market the worth of the sponsoring organization and its products. By hearing a jingle at least seven times, we have a familiarity of the product. Through repetition, we increase loyalty to the point that buying patterns commence.

Commercial messages weave into the fabric of classic television. Where such mini-songs are as vital as TV themes, promotional slogans and programming strategies in developing and exploiting public tastes, preferences and behaviors.

"Good for life," Dr. Pepper. The American Medical Association sued Dr. Pepper, charging that the slogan wrongly promoted the product as a health remedy. The case went all the way to the U.S. Supreme Court. Dr. Pepper lost and had to remove the slogan from public consumption. It replaced "Good for life" with "10-2-4."

"When you're Number Two, you try harder...or else," Avis Rent-a-Car. This campaign pulled the company out of the red and subsequently set the tone for customer-friendly campaigns by other emerging car rental companies.

"The end of the plain plane," Braniff Airways. This campaign utilized a fashion designer motif to catapult a regional airline from Dallas, Texas, into a national air carrier.

"Take it off. Take it all off," Noxema shaving cream. This campaign helped triple Noxema's business.

"I hate Qantas for bringing so many people to Australia," Qantas koala bear. During the ad's first eight years, airline sales tripled.

"To look sharp every time you shave. To feel sharp and be on the ball. Just be sharp...use Gillette Blue Blades for the quickest slickest shaves of all." This jingle was written in 1953 by Mahlon Merrick, who was Jack Benny's television conductor.

Burma-Shave created a unique form of advertising in the 1930s to appeal to highway motorists. Every few miles, a placard carried clever phrases, often plays on words. The aim was to intrigue viewers and keep them anticipating more. By recognizing the concept, audiences often created slogans of their own and submitted them to a willing company. Some of the classic Burma-Shave slogans included:

- "Half a pound for half a dollar. Spread on thin above the collar."

- "We can't provide you with a date. But we do supply the best darn bait."

- "His tomato was the mushy type...until his beard grew over-ripe."

- "Better try less speed per mile. That car may have to last a while."

- "To steal a kiss, he had the knack...but lacked the cheek to get one back."

- "It gave McDonald that needed charm. Hello Hollywood. Good-by farm."

- "Around the curve...lickety-split. It's a beautiful car...wasn't it?"

- "If Crusoe'd kept his chin more tidy, he might have found a lady Friday."

- "If anything will please your Jill, a little jack for this jar will."

- "That barefoot chap with cheeks of tan...won't let 'em chap when he's a man."

Creative Forces

Advertising is a profession that encompasses several specialties, including campaign strategy, planning, buying, specialties, point-of-purchase and sub-specialties per media.

Composers of advertising jingles are a rare breed. Pop music superstar Barry Manilow cut his teeth on ad jingles (State Farm Insurance, Band-Aid, McDonald's, etc.) in the early 1970s. Manilow ably learned the secrets of commercial hit records as having comparable traits as commercial jingles, including clever slogans, sense of humor, pertinence to the product, musical hooks, sing-a-long potential, memorability and mass-market appeal.

I worked in the 1980s with two of the best jingle creators. Dick Marx (father of rock star Richard Marx) had created jingles for hundreds of products, including Kellogg's ('best to you") and Malboro. Larry Sachnowitz was a master of the retail psyche, the intellect and the heart...all combining fuel for his potent lyrics.

Our client was a troubled city with an unemployment rate of 28%. On the U.S. side of the Mexican border, they were devastated by devaluation of the peso, energy woes and ranching downturns. Communitywide mistrust and a sense of hopelessness existed. My long-term recommendation was that the community actively solicit manufacturing operations to bolster the economy. The Maquiladora program did indeed drop the unemployment rate from 28% to 13% in three years.

But, for the moment, hope needed to be restored. A bank commissioned Marx and Sachnowitz to write a song of encouragement, "You Can Believe/Puede Creer." In what came to be the city song, these excerpts said it all: "If you believe in the brotherhood of people. If you believe in a strong and helping hand. If you believe in warm and friendly faces. If you believe in the better side of man. You can believe...you can be sure. You can be certain and secure. You Can Believe/Puede Creer."

I personally observed the team's genius with other local advertising campaigns, including Star Furniture, Elliott's Men & Boys Shops, Broadway National Bank ("what do ya' say, the Broadway") and others. Great advertising is not just national in scope. Every community creates memorable and effective advertising. The national jingle writers assist talents in every locality to meet the marks, exceed the goals and weave some art into a business format.

Some of the Best Ad Slogans
of the 20th Century

"You never outgrow your need for milk."
American Dairy Association

"We make money the old fashioned way...we earn it."
Smith Barney

"Please be kind...rewind." video rental stores

"Which twin has the Toni?" Toni home permanent

"They're G-R-E-A-T." (Tony the Tiger) Kellogg's Frosted Flakes

"The beer that made Milwaukee famous." Schlitz Beer

"A little dab'll do you. Use more...only if you dare. The girls will all pursue you. They love to get their fingers in your hair."
Brylcreem

"You deserve a break today." McDonald's

"50 million times a day...at home, at work or on the way. There's nothing like a Coca-Cola."

"I'd like to teach the world to sing in perfect harmony." Coca-Cola

"It's the real thing...in the back of your mind...like you're hoping to find." Coca-Cola

"Things go better with Coca-Cola."

"Raid kills bugs dead." S.C. Johnson Co.

"If you've got the time, we've got the beer." Miller High Life

"When you care enough to send the very best." Hallmark Cards

"I can't believe I ate the whole thing. Try it...you'll like it." Alka-Seltzer

"Let's get Mikey. He won't eat it. He hates everything. He likes it." Quaker Oats

"The milk from contented cows." Carnation

"See the USA in your Chevrolet. America is asking you to call. Drive the USA in your Chevrolet. America...the greatest land of all." Chevrolet

"Better things for better living through chemistry." Dupont

"The disadvantages of length. A silly millimeter longer." Benson & Hedges cigarettes

"You'll wonder where the yellow went when you brush your teeth with Pepsodent."

"Look mom, no cavities." Crest toothpaste

"You're in good hands with Allstate." Allstate Insurance Co.

"Like a good neighbor, State Farm is there." State Farm Insurance Co.

"Now it's Pepsi, for those who think young." Pepsi-Cola

"Wet and wild. Seven Up is first against thirst. So crisp, so smooth."

"How about a nice Hawaiian punch?"

"Hey, big spender, spend a little dime on me." Muriel Cigars

"You meet the nicest people on a Honda." Honda motorcycles

"The closer you get...the better you look." Clairol car coloring

"No matter what shape your stomach is in." Alka-Seltzer

"Takes a licking and keeps on ticking." Timex Watches

"Look sharp. Feel sharp. Be sharp." Gillette razors and blades

"Good to the last drop." Maxwell House Coffee

"When you say Bud, you've said it all. The King of Beers."
Budweiser Beer

"Everything you ever wanted in a beer...and less."
Miller Lite Beer

"Makes hamburgers taste more like steak." A-1 Steak Sauce

"Have it your way." Burger King

"I'd walk a mile for a Camel." Camel cigarettes

"Soup is good food." Campbell's Soup

"It cleans your breath while it cleans your teeth."
Colgate Toothpaste

"Is it true that Blondes have more fun?" Clairol car coloring

"Diamonds are forever." De Beer Consolidated Mines Ltd.

"Aren't you glad you use Dial? Don't you wish everybody did?"
Dial Soap

"Plop, plop, fizz, fizz. Oh, what a relief it is!" Alka-Seltzer

"Grapes, like children, need love and affection." Almaden

"I'd rather fight than switch." Herbert Tareyton cigarettes

"Tobacco is our middle name." American Brands

"Do you remember me? Don't leave home without it." American
Express card

"Reach out and touch someone." AT&T

"Come alive. You're in the Pepsi generation." Pepsi-Cola

"No bottles to break - just hearts. Promise her anything, but give her Arpege." Arpege Perfume

"The Greatest Show on Earth." Ringling Bros., Barnum & Bailey Circus

"Nothin' says lovin' like somethin' from the oven." Pillsbury

"Victory won't wait for the nation that's late." Big Bend Clocks

"When you've got it, flaunt it." Braniff Airlines

"The cereal that's shot from guns!" Quaker Puffed Wheat

"Equal Pay, Equal Time." Bulova Watches

"Quality is Job One." Ford Motor Company

"We will sell no wine before its time." Paul Masson Wines

"All you add is love." Ralston Purina pet food

"When there's no tomorrow." Federal Express

"You've come a long way, baby." Virginia Slims cigarettes

"Progress is our most important product. We bring good things to life." General Electric

"The greatest name in rubber." B.F. Goodrich

"Celebrate the moments of your life." General Foods

"For the times of your lives. America's storyteller." Kodak cameras and film

"The best to you each morning." Kellogg's cereals

"The milk chocolate that melts in your mouth, not in your hands." M&M's

"Betcha can't eat just one." Lay's Potato Chips

"All the news that's fit to print." The New York Times

"Tastes so good cats ask for it by name." Meow Mix catfood

"A child is someone who passes through your life and then disappears into an adult." Metropolitan Life Insurance

"Fly the friendly skies of United." United Airlines

"You can trust your car to the man who wears the star." Texaco

"The breakfast of Champions." Wheaties cereal

"My wife...I think I'll keep her." Geritol

"Enquiring minds want to know." The National Enquirer

"Opportunity can't knock unless it's on your doorstep."
The Wall Street Journal

"His master's voice." (dog named Little Nipper) RCA

"Mother made chicken with Shake & Bake. And I helped."

"New Ajax laundry detergent is stronger than dirt."

"I just called to say I love you." AT&T

"Ring around the collar." Wisk Laundry Detergent

"Let your fingers do the walking." Yellow Pages

"You never get a second chance to make a first impression."
Head and Shoulders shampoo

"Double your pleasure. Double your fun...with Doublemint Gum."

"For people who can't brush after every meal." Gleem toothpaste

"The real you coming through. Your true voice." AT&T

Public Service Campaigns

"Crime does not pay." Public service adage

"Only you can prevent forest fires." U.S. Forestry Service

"Thanks to you, it's working." United Way

"What this commercial is trying to sell you won't make your
breath any sweeter, your clothes any whiter or your acid indiges-
tion any better. It'll just make you more human." Business
Committee for the Arts

"Extinct is forever." Friends of Animals

"Be all that you can be." U.S. Army

"Just say no." Drug abuse prevention

Advertising Icons

Speedy, for Alka-Seltzer, introduced in 1958.

Mr. Clean, introduced in 1958.

Choo-Choo Charlie, for Good & Plenty Candy, introduced in 1959.

Charlie the Tuna, for Star Kist Tuna, introduced in 1962.

Ronald McDonald, introduced in 1963, becoming the official company spokesman in 1967.

Mr. Whipple (played by actor Dick Wilson), for Charmin, introduced in 1965.

Josephine the Plumber (played by actress Jane Withers), for Comet, introduced in 1965.

The Malboro Man, introduced in 1965.

The Pillsbury dough boy, introduced in 1966.

Madge the Manicurist (played by actress Jan Miner), for Palmolive, introduced in 1966.

The Maytag Repairman (played by actor Jesse White), introduced in 1967.

O.J. Simpson racing through an airport, demonstrating speed of service for Hertz Rent-a-Car.

Joe Namath wearing Beautymist Panty Hose.

Brother Dominic, the monk who photocopies his manuscripts, for Xerox.

Clara Peller as the "Where's the beef?" lady, for Wendy's, introduced in 1980.

The Energizer Bunny, for Eveready Batteries, introduced in 1980.

Ones That Didn't Quite Ring True

"We remain sincerely yours, the Bell System." AT&T

"LSMFT. Lucky Strike means fine tobacco."
Lucky Strike cigarettes

"Are you smoking more now but enjoying it less?" Pall Mall

"Come up, come up, come all the up." Kool cigarettes

"Are you man enough to try it?" Brylcreem

"Winston tastes good like a cigarette should." Winston cigarettes

"Don't hate me because I'm beautiful." Pantene Shampoo

"Move over bacon, here comes something leaner!" Sizzilean

"Hefty Hefty Hefty wimpy wimpy wimpy." Glad storage bags

Chapter 12

Show Genres

They rounded out popular TV schedules.

Live Television

In the early days of television, the programming was live and originated principally from New York City. It was an extension of radio, much of whose programming had already relocated to Hollywood for creative origination.

East coast fare included variety shows, game shows, soap operas and news programs. The earliest variety shows were 15 minutes in length and were hosted by singers such as Eddie Fisher, Dinah Shore, Perry Como, Patti Page, Jane Froman, The Ames Brothers, Gordon MacRae and Jo Stafford. The Ed Sullivan Show and the Milton Berle Show were the earliest hour-long variety shows. Producer Max Leibman then created the variety spectaculars running 90 minutes, notably Your Show of Shows with Sid Caesar and Imogene Coca.

The first game shows were called "panel shows," running 30 minutes in length and at night. What's My Line spawned a vast game show empire for producers Mark Goodson and Bill Todman.

Soon, game shows were running in the daytime too. Many of the most popular game shows had both nighttime and daytime versions.

The earliest news programs were panel shows. That genre (Meet the Press, Face the Nation, etc.) still reigns on Sunday mornings, though in early TV they ran weekday evenings.

Live dramas originating from New York City were plentiful. They drew plays and actors from Broadway. Studio One ran for 10 successful years. During much of its 11-year run, Kraft Television Theatre ran twice per week.

Many plays had their off-Broadway try-outs on live TV. The U.S. Steel Hour premiered "No Time For Sergeants," starring Andy Griffith. Then, it went to Broadway and later to the movies.

Other live dramas to premiere first on television and then proceed on to Broadway and the movies included "Requiem For a Heavyweight" and "The Miracle Worker." Others to premiere first on TV and then go to the movies included "Judgment at Nuremberg" and "Twelve Angry Men."

Live TV drama anthologies were good venues for restagings of popular Broadway shows and movies. Often, the original stars reprised their famous roles on TV. Humphrey Bogart appeared in the Producer's Showcase TV version of "The Petrified Forest" 19 years after the movie, which in turn was two years after he played the role of Duke Mantee on Broadway. Television restagings by Mary Martin served to create a long-running second career for her in TV musical-comedy specials.

Just as had occurred with radio, live drama program production began appearing from Hollywood. CBS-TV brought viewers two of the best theatrical series, Climax and Playhouse 90. As with the radio playhouse shows, these West Coast anthologies brought us movie stars who normally did not appear on television. Stars appeared on the live dramas in order to promote their latest movies and to fulfill the kinds of roles that they might not otherwise play on film.

Filmed Dramas...Heyday of the Playhouse Shows

As with radio, tin addition to the live hour-long plays on television, and there also flourished a series of half-hour filmed "playhouse" shows.

These 30-minute anthologies also brought viewers an array of top talent from Broadway and later Hollywood. These series included Schlitz Playhouse, Lux Playhouse, Pepsi-Cola Playhouse, Dupont Cavalcade Theatre, Rheingold Playhouse, Douglas Fairbanks Presents, Chevron Theatre, Ford Theatre, Errol Flynn Theatre, Damon Runyon Playhouse, The Visitor, O. Henry Playhouse and others.

Dramatic anthology shows created second careers for many Hollywood performers whose movie tenures had past. Tired of playing juvenile roles in film musical-comedies, Dick Powell became a film noir star, both in the movies and on radio. He took that same genre to television, creating "Four Star Playhouse," in which he hosted and alternated as occasional episodic star with Charles Boyer, David Niven and Ida Lupino. This success spawned Four Star Productions, which created many other anthology shows, westerns and sitcoms.

The Oscar winner for Best Actress of 1947, Loretta Young, moved to television in 1952. Her long-running "Loretta Young Show" featured her playing lead in most of the weekly plays.

Hot on the heels of "Bedtime For Bonzo" being a movie hit, Ronald Reagan came to television as the host of General Electric Theatre. Every few weeks, Reagan also starred in episodes, sometimes accompanied by his wife, Nancy Davis Reagan. The 10 years spent on G.E. Theatre gave Reagan the platform as a great communicator, from which he followed with a political career.

Even Ronald Reagan's ex-wife, Jane Wyman, the Oscar winner for Best Actress of 1948, hosted her own half-hour dramatic anthology, "Fireside Theatre." Other movie stars hosting dramatic anthologies included June Allyson, Ethel Barrymore, Joseph

Cotten, David Niven, Ray Milland, Rory Calhoun, Will Rogers Jr., Charles Boyer and Orson Welles.

Many of the halfd-hour dramatic anthologies gave birth to other TV series. Dick Powell's Zane Grey Theatre spawned Trackdown (which in turn spawned Wanted: Dead or Alive), The Westerner, Johnny Ringo and The Rifleman (which in turn spawned Law of the Plainsman).

In the second generation of TV came the hour-long dramatic anthology series, hosted by such luminaries as Dick Powell, Bob Hope, Fred Astaire, Danny Thomas and Desi Arnaz. Among the weekly series spinning off these anthologies were Burke's Law, The Untouchables, Court Martial, Run For Your Life and Stoney Burke.

By the late 1950s, the bulk of filmed production had shifted to Hollywood. Then, a wave of New York filmed series emerged. Some of the best included:

- Phil Silvers Show/Sgt. Bilko (Phil Silvers, Harvey Lembeck, Allan Melvin)
- The Big Story (hosted by Burgess Meredith)
- Decoy (Beverly Garland)
- The Defenders (E.G. Marshall, Robert Reed)
- Car 54, Where Are You? (Joe E. Ross, Fred Gwynne)
- East Side, West Side (George C. Scott)
- The Nurses/The Doctors and the Nurses
- NYPD (Jack Warden, Robert Hooks, Frank Converse)
- For the People (William Shatner)
- The Trials of O'Brien (Peter Falk)
- Coronet Blue (Frank Converse)
- NYPD Blue (Dennis Franz)
- Law and Order (Jerry Orbach, Sam Waterston, Steven Hill)

Specials and Events

By 1953, the television panorama had settled into a full-scope schedule, encompassing live and filmed programming of multiple genres.

As had been the case with radio, the TV programmers began seeking one-time programs to bring extra-special performers, programs and ratings opportunities to the tube. The first official "spectacular" was the Ford 50th Anniversary Show, featuring Mary Martin and Ethel Merman.

Inspired by huge ratings, the networks and sponsors began mounting many headliner specials. Top stars came to TV, appearing periodically in specials, including Bob Hope, Bing Crosby, Doris Day and Fred Astaire.

Some of these specials became series unto themselves. Hallmark Hall of Fame began in 1951 by staging a Christmas opera, "Amahl and the Night Visitors." Subsequently, its holiday timed offerings largely consisted of live restagings of Broadway plays and musicals.

CBS-TV created Shower of Stars, a potpourri of musical specials that alternated with its live dramatic series, Climax. Major sponsors such as Dupont, Ford, Coca-Cola, General Motors and Procter & Gamble bankrolled TV specials, which led to their subsequent sponsorships of regular TV series.

Documentaries

Television news divisions brought viewers various documentaries and specials that covered news events, features and lifestyles of the day in the hour-long format. Some appeared regularly under such banners as CBS Reports and NBC Project 20. Others appeared as events warranted. During the early years of the space program, there was widespread coverage. Every U.S. Presidential election was accompanied by documentary coverage.

Independent producers also brought viewers the best in documentaries. The most prolific was David L. Wolper, who created the original half-hour Biography series, hosted by Mike Wallace.

Made-for-TV Movies

With the advent of television, the motion picture studios found a willing and profitable after-market by licensing its inventories of old films. Networks and syndicators paid handsome sums for packages, which filled TV airwaves at all hours of the day and night.

The oldest film products had been gobbled up by local stations for daytime and late-night airings. In the early 1960s, the major networks began airing the most recent movies in prime-time. The blockbusters acquired such huge ratings that nightly "at the movies" segments appeared.

By 1964, the inventories of available movies had shrunk. Thus, the practice of developing original; movies for television began in earnest. TV had produced various filmed special in previous years, though the formalized TV movie genre began in the mid-60s.

In reality, TV movies were longer-form extensions of the half-hour and hour-long dramatic anthology series. Not surprisingly, Revue-Universal, which dominated half-hour filmed anthology series production in the 1950s, became the preeminent source of TV movies in the 1960s and 1970s.

One of the first was 1964's "The Killers," a remake of the 1946 film of the same name. This served as Ronald Reagan's last movie role, and he played a baddie in it.

TV movies allowed material that was too expansive for anthology series to be brought to the small screens. TV Movies had big budgets, which were later amortized by releasing them in theatres internationally. These movies brought viewers the big movie stars who did not normally work in TV. They also featured TV performers in roles outside the scope of their regular series.

Some of the most memorable were "Brian's Song" (James Caan, Billy Dee Williams), "That Certain Summer" (Hal Holbrook), "Duel" (Dennis Weaver chased by a menacing truck), "The Poppy Is Also a Flower" (Grace Kelly, Yul Brynner), "The

Affair" (Robert Wagner, Natalie Wood), "Izzy and Moe" (Jackie Gleason, Art Carney), "A Family Upside Down" (Helen Hayes, Fred Astaire) and "Stone Pillow" (Lucille Ball, in a dramatic role as a homeless lady).

Some TV movies, as were their half-hour anthology cousins, were pilots for regular TV series, including Columbo, Alias Smith and Jones, McMillan and Wife, Hawaii Five-O and McCloud. One of the best was the two-hour TV movie pilot to the series Rod Serling's Night Gallery, the first movie to be directed by Steven Spielberg.

With the popularity of made-for-TV movies, the next genre to emerge was the Mini-Series, consisting of two-part and sometimes multi-part sagas. Some of the best included "Sybil" with Sally Field, "Shogun" with Richard Chamberlain and "Backstairs at the White House." There were the all-star cast mini-series that enjoyed widespread attention and ratings, including "Centennial," "QB VII," "North and South," "Vanished," "Lonesome Dove," "Roots," "The Six Wives of Henry VIII," "The Thorn Birds" and "The Winds of War."

To date, TV movies remain the sources of the best writing, acting and production. They constitute TV anthologies (in the Four Star Playhouse tradition) and offer regular performing births for stars of past popular series (Melissa Gilbert, Jaclyn Smith, Tom Selleck, Donna Mills, et al).

Fortunately, cable television has continued the production and airing of made-for-TV movies. I particularly salute the Lifetime and Hallmark networks for their excellent and continuing series of TV movies.

The Nostalgia Boom

No matter how much planning one does (which I advocate and facilitate for business clients), many things just happen. Accidents that work are called strokes of genius.

Daily business is shaped by eccentricities, external influences and chance occurrences. By studying some of them, we gain insight into what modern business could be.

During a visit to the United States in the 1960's, Soviet Premier Nikita Khrushchev placed his hand on the tail fin of a Cadillac limousine. With seeming innocence, he asked, "What does this thing do?"

Eliot and Ruth Handler founded a toy company known as Mattel, Inc. They had a daughter named Barbie, who played with paper dolls, pretending that she was a mommy. Ruth watched her child play and got the idea for a doll with accessories, pretending to be an independent adult. Thus was born the largest selling doll in the history of the world...the Barbie Doll.

For those wondering the practical applications of outer space technology and research, look to items now normally found in the home, notably pocket calculators and microwave ovens.

So many odd-but-true happenings created the lifestyle that the populace embraced. Pop art, inventions, fashions, fads, and natural obsessions have contributed more to molding a society than textbook lessons. Historians continue to ponder the effects of pop culture.

As times change, the nature of nostalgia changes. While it is fun to remember the old days, we realize that pop art and culture set the rules by which we live as adults. Each generation relates to different phases of pop culture.

In 1965, a young woman in New York suggested to her boyfriend, a printer, that he make posters with Humphrey Bogart's picture. He acquired a negative for free, bought some cheap paper, and printed a batch of posters. Next, he ran a few ads to promote the pop-art posters.

Some kids came into a Greenwich Village bookstore, inquiring about the Bogart posters. The owner found the printer and bought his supply. The printer left town for a long weekend's vacation. When he returned, the phone was ringing. The bookstore had sold more than 1,000 Bogart posters, and could they have more. Realizing they were sitting on a goldmine, the printer and the bookstore owner formed Personality Posters. Thus, the celebrity poster boom began.

The atomic bomb is responsible for many societal reactions and phenomena...the most surprising being the bikini bathing suit. Rumors spread during post-World War II testings that the world would end soon.

Fashion designers scheduled the "ultimate" show with the most daring styles. One model shocked the world by wearing a skimpy two-piece suit. The costume—now accepted swimwear—was named for Bikini Atoll, location of bomb testings.

President John F. Kennedy was asked by a Life Magazine reporter for a list of his favorite books. Kennedy was a known intellectual who reportedly read one book every day. When the list included the Ian Fleming novel, From Russia With Love, the James Bond spy story craze hit America.

Hungarian design professor Erno Rubik devised a multi-colored puzzle in the mid-1970's. Each of six sides has nine squares, with each row able to rotate around its center. When solved, each side is one color. There are 43 quintillion possible positions. The least possible moves necessary to solve is 20. Rubik's Cube sold billions of units in its heyday. Knowledge of group theory and algorithms is useful.

Witness these fabulous firsts: The first product to carry the union seal was the cigar (1874). Franz Schubert wrote 1,000 musical works but left only one symphony unfinished. Ohio is the birth state of the most U.S. Presidents (seven). The last teenager to rule England was Queen Victoria.

People possess and vigorously demonstrate a passion for trivia. Stored nuggets of information may burst from the memory banks at any given time.

We can recite lyrics to golden oldies on the radio, yet the tenets of business etiquette are not so familiar. We remember movie dialog and old TV advertising jingles, yet policies and procedures are a little foreign.

It is the intention this book to merge the familiar with the meaningful. Media analogies help readers to connect with their own field of reference. Futurism and cutting edge philosophies have a basis in the familiar.

THURS. NIGHT, JUNE 2
7:30 - 8:30 P.M., CDT
CHANNEL **2** **13** **24**

"CLIMAX!"

JOHN HARRINGTON & THE NEWS

"THE UNIMPORTANT MAN"

A man with a conscience suddenly finds himself an unsure key witness to a major crime.

starring

MAC DONALD CAREY
RUTH HUSSEY

with

Bill Lundigan
as your host

Presented by

CHRYSLER CORPORATION
PLYMOUTH • DODGE
DE SOTO • CHRYSLER • IMPERIAL

13

Learning Business Lessons From the Entertainment Industry

This book was a source of enjoyment and completion to me. Back in 1969, I started going to Hollywood.

I visited the studios and the sets of current television shows...the same ones that are now being called "classics." Some of the shows that I visited were hits, and others were up-and-coming ones that the networks wanted to promote and find public attention for them.

35 years later, classic television is a hobby with me. It's fun, and you can share the shows, the memories and the messages contained therein with friends and family.

I wrote this book because pop culture affects all of our lives...always has, always will. By refocusing upon the industry that brought us our pop culture, we find new applicability to a changed and troubled world. Understanding how and why TV blossomed and came of age in the 1950s and 1960s helps us understand how organizations in general progress or stagnate in a changing world.

Thus, I took the bold move to take a nostalgic walk down memory lane and make the bold move to inject business book material into it. This book should empower audiences to reach within themselves for basic answers, to become their best and to realize that excellence is attainable thorough wider scope and focus.

My emphasis today is upon studying and advising organizations and businesses that really want to do the things necessary to grow steadily and be successful. I see too many businesses that think they can take shortcuts or believe that the recent corporate scandals do not apply to them. I've written other books about these business phenomena and the strategies necessary to turn the tide and create successful operations.

Working on this book, I see many analogies from classic television series to modern business strategies.

Reflecting upon the glory days of television and how the industry came of age, I see the following basic business thematic concepts that emerged in this book:

Entrepreneurism
Collaborations
Value-Added, Customer Service
Corporate Culture
Innovation, Strategic Priorities
Expanding to new marketplaces
Investing in the future
Technology
Creative processes
Leadership

Please allow me to elaborate further.....

Entrepreneurism

In the 1950s, the entrepreneurs of Hollywood sought to produce filmed programs for the infant medium of television. The New York network establishment was tied to having programming originate on the Eastern coast of the United States.

The innovative TV entrepreneurs proved to the networks that they could produce filmed programs on limited budgets. Many overshot their original budgets, betting on long-term residual benefits to accrue from reruns.

When the major studios saw the inroads that the entrepreneurs made into television programming, they wanted to join the action. They retooled their studios in order to meet economical production schedules and budgets. Like the entrepreneurs, the studios learned that quality popular programs could emerge, in spite of limited budgets and other factors previously seen as constraints.

Individuals and organizations amass values based upon a series of experiences. Often, values depend upon the context and reflect the facets of professional achievement:

- Core Industry...The Business You're In.
- Rendering the Service...Administering Your Work.
- Accountability...Qualities with Which You Work.
- Your Relationships-Contributions to Other People...Colleagues, Stakeholders.
- Professional-Leadership Development...Your Path to the Future.
- Your Contributions to the Organization's Overall Goals...Your Place in its Big Picture.
- Body of Work...Your Accomplishments to Date and Anticipated Future Output.

Collaborations

The best tends to attract the best. When entrepreneurs Lucille Ball and Desi Arnaz founded Desilu Productions, they attracted the best talent from the film community. The results were superior productions that have stood the best of time.

Many great talents joined forces with Desilu, sometimes working with them and other times working in collaborative productions. This set the tone for the multiple production company situations that are the rule in contemporary Hollywood, rather than the exception.

The biggest source of growth and increased opportunities in today's business climate lie in the way that individuals and companies work together.

It is becoming increasingly rare to find an individual or organization that has not yet been required to team with others. Lone rangers and sole-source providers simply cannot succeed in competitive environments and global economies. Those who benefit from collaborations, rather than become the victim of them, will log the biggest successes in business years ahead.

Here are my definitions of three terms of teamwork, intended to help by differentiating their intended objectives:

Collaborations — Parties willingly cooperating together. Working jointly with others, especially in an intellectual pursuit. Cooperation with an instrumentality with which one is not immediately connected.

Partnering — A formal relationship between two or more associates. Involves close cooperation among parties, with each having specified and joint rights and responsibilities.

Joint-Venturing — Partners come together for specific purposes or projects that may be beyond the scope of individual members. Each retains individual identity. The joint-venture itself has its own identity...reflecting favorably upon work to be done and upon the partners.

I have observed the greatest successes with collaborations, partnering and joint-ventures to occur when:

- Crisis or urgent need forced the client to hire a consortium.
- Time deadlines and nature of the project required a cohesive team approach.
- The work required multiple professional skills.
- Consortium members were tops in their fields.

- Consortium members truly understood teamwork and had prior successful experiences in joint-venturing.
- Consortium members wanted to learn from each other.
- Early successes spurred future collaborations.
- Joint-venturing was considered an ongoing process, not a "once in awhile" action.
- Each team member realized something of value.
- The client recommended the consortium to others.

My own disappointments with previous collaborations include:

- Failure of participants to understand — and thus utilize — each other's talents.
- One or more participants have had one or a few bad experiences and tend to over-generalize about the worth of consortiums.
- One partner puts another down on the basis of academic credentials or some professional designation that sets themselves apart from other team members.
- Participants exhibit the "Lone Ranger" syndrome...preferring the comfort of trusting the one person they have counted upon.
- Participants exhibit the "I can do that" syndrome...thinking that they do the same exact things that other consortium members do and, thus, see no value in working together, sharing projects and referring business.
- Junior associates of consortium members want to hoard the billing dollars in-house...to look good to their superiors, enhance their billable quotas or fulfill other objectives that they are not sophisticated enough to identify.
- Junior associates of consortium members refuse to recognize seniority and wisdom of senior associates...utilizing the power of the budget to control creative thoughts and strategic thinking of subcontractors.

Here are the reasons to give the concepts of collaborating, part-nering and joint-venturing a chance:

- Think of the "ones that got away," the opportunities that a team could have created.

- Think of contracts that were awarded to others who exhibited a team approach.

- Learn from industries where consortiums are the rule, rather than the exception (space, energy, construction, high-tech, etc.).

- The marketplace is continually changing.

- Subcontractor, supplier, support talent and vendor informa-tion can be shared.

- Consortiums are inevitable. If we don't do it early, others will beat us to it.

The benefits for participating principals and firms in collabora-tions, partnering and joint-venturing include:

- Ongoing association and professional exchange with the best in respective fields.

- Utilize professional synergy to create opportunities that indi-viduals could not.

- Serve as a beacon for professionalism.

- Provide access to experts otherwise not known to potential clients.

- Refer and cross-sell each others' services.

- Develop programs and materials to meet new and emerging marketplaces.

Value-Added, Customer Service

Television has its own Customer Service Index. The ratings sys-tem, though often criticized, is a fair way of measuring audiences. Public tastes are catered to, as well as measured. Usually, programming is designed to address public tastes. The most innovative programs predict public appetites and deliver hit shows that beat the competition into the marketplace.

In today's highly competitive business environment, every dynamic of a successful organization must be toward ultimate customers. Customer focused management goes beyond service and quality. There is no business that cannot improve its customer orientation. Every organization has customers, clients, stakeholders, financiers, volunteers, supporters or other categories of "affected constituencies."

Customer focused management is a concept that goes far beyond just smiling, answering queries and communicating with buyers. It transcends customer service training. In today's highly competitive business environment, every dynamic of a successful organization must be toward ultimate customers.

Companies must change their focus from products and processes toward the values which they share with customers. Customer focused management goes beyond just the dynamics of service and quality.

Everyone with whom you conduct business is a customer or referral source of someone else. The service that we get from some people, we pass along to others. Customer service is a continuum of human behaviors...shared with those whom we meet.

Customers are the lifeblood of every business. Employees depend upon customers for their paychecks. Yet, you wouldn't know the correlation when poor customer service is rendered. Employees of companies behave as though customers are a bother, do not heed their concerns and do not take suggestions for improvement.

There is no business that cannot undergo some improvement in its customer orientation. Every organization has customers, clients, stakeholders, financiers, volunteers, supporters or other categories of "affected constituency."

Corporate Culture

The television industry took upon a different corporate culture, once it reconciled the differences of its New York establishment and the influence that the Hollywood film community added.

Corporate cultures, if allowed to occur unchecked, will develop the negative qualities of those organizations from which its key players previously came. In forming a new corporate culture, which filmed television was in the 1950s, it is necessary to plan and build a hybrid of the best transferable qualities.

How organizations start out and what they become are different concepts. Mistakes, niche orientation and lack of planning lead businesses to failure. Processes, trends, fads, perceived stresses and "the system" force managers to make compromises in order to proceed. Often, a fresh look at previous knowledge gives renewed insight.

The purpose of re-examining and refining an organization's corporate culture is to:

- Think Big Picture.

- Conceptualize and communicate your company's own goals.

- Understand conflicting societal goals.

- Fit your dreams into the necessities and realities of the real world.

- Find your own niche...do your thing.

- Get satisfactions from doing something well and committing to long-term excellence.

- Seek truths in unusual and unexpected sources.

- Share your knowledge, and learn further by virtue of mentoring others.

In many industries and professions, business development has occurred primarily by accident or through market demand. Because of economic realities and the increased numbers of firms providing comparable services, the notion of business development is now a necessity, rather than a luxury. Competition for customers-clients is sharpening. The professions are no longer held on a pedestal...a condition which mandates them to portray or enhance their core values.

I would encourage business leaders to fill out a Core Values Worksheet These are the key criteria for basing your professional vision:

- Core Industry...The Business You're In.
- Rendering the Service...Administering Your Work.
- Accountability...Qualities with Which You Work.
- Your Relationships-Contributions to Other People...Colleagues, Stakeholders.
- Professional-Leadership Development...Your Path to the Future.
- Your Contributions to the Organization's Overall Goals...Your Place in its Big Picture.
- Body of Work...Your Accomplishments to Date and Anticipated Future Output.

Innovation, Strategic Priorities

Television is predicated upon the newest thing being supplanted by the next new thing. Innovations of one season become the water-marks for others.

Organizations must periodically assess and review their value systems as part of Strategic Planning and corporate Visioning processes. Every business leader should likewise develop and commit to nurturing their own personal value statement.

Here are some examples of Core Values which could be included:

- To be truthful, forceful and forthright in personal relation-ships.

- To treat others as I would like to be treated.
- To expect that I deserve and will receive the best out of life.
- To be the kind of person that others can count upon, like, love and admire.
- To be true to my word and consistent in my actions.
- To show loyalty and commitment to those causes and projects which I undertake.
- To show loyalty and commitment to family and those friends who are important to me.
- To never stop growing emotionally and continuing my journey.

Here are some examples of Strategic Priorities which could be included:

- To be the best that I can be.
- To be the best in my chosen field.
- To create new applications and set new standards for my chosen field.
- To successfully mentor others.
- To creatively approach projects in ways that others did not or could not do.
- To achieve results that are realistically attained and honestly reached.
- To continue building respect for myself and the self-assuredness to stay focused.
- To know that I am doing the right things and taking the best possible courses of action.
- To never stop growing professionally and continuing to evolve to the next tiers.

Expanding to New Marketplaces

In the late 1940s, there were only a few television stations. As their numbers grew in the early 1950s, network affiliates began dotting each major U.S. city. As more channels were added, independent stations experienced a demand for programming.

Since there was not yet a body of reruns in the early years of television, a radio syndication company headed by Frederick Ziv moved to television. They shot filmed shows that could be shown anytime and anywhere, with local sponsorship opportunities. The first shows were Cisco Kid and Boston Blackie, reviving the old movie serial format.

An early original Ziv series was "I Led Three Lives," the story of a government counter agent working as an undercover Communist Party member. In the city in which I grew up, the local furniture company sponsored the show. Its owner sat on a stool in the local TV studio, delivering the commercials and some occasional civic commentaries. Due in part to the fame created by his TV show sponsorship, Louis Shanks was subsequently elected to our city council. That was the power of early TV at the local level. Organizations put disproportionate attention behind image...if the sake of business is only to become rich and famous.

In analyzing the promotional hype that one hears, some companies claim that purchasing their product is the "be all, end all" panacea for life's dilemmas. If only you will buy their version of "The Answer," then you can surely fast-forward your way to instant riches, success and an easy life.

This is not written to take swipes at responsible branding, marketing and advertising. More than 80% of what one sees and hears is clever, informative, research-based, sensibly executed and intended to orient target audiences toward marketplaces. This is written to address the bigger issue that some companies believe the hype that they are issuing.

Some companies behave deceptively. Some either skillfully lie to get what they think they want...or may really believe themselves to be what they hype to publics who don't know any better.

Many consumers are gullible, "name" crazy and susceptible to grandiose claims. They take what is said at face value because they have not or don't care to develop abilities to discern what is hyped by others. They believe distortions faster than they believe facts, logic and reason.

This negatively impacts our society...which continually seeks button-pushing answers for life's complex problems without paying enough dues toward a truly successful life. Consumers naively believe mis-representations...to the exclusion of organizations which are more conservative, yet substantive, in their information-al offerings.

Here are some of the worst "red flag" expressions. When you hear them, beware of false claims:

• Our Mission.

• Family Tradition.

• Fastest Growing.

• In One Easy Lesson.

• Better.

• #1 in Sales.

• World Class.

• The Best.

• For All Your Needs.

Many of the hucksterisms represent "copywriting" by people who don't know anything about corporate vision. Their words over-state, get into the media and are accepted by audiences as fact. By default, companies have the appearance of credibility based upon mis-representations.

Companies put too much of their public persona in the hands of marketers and should examine more closely the distorted messages and partial images which they put into the cyberspace. Our culture hears and believes the hype, without looking beyond the obvious. People come to expect easy answers for questions they haven't yet taken the time to formulate.

Investing in the future

In television, trends come and go. One must expect that the current crest of success will not last forever. One must predict, plan and constantly re-examine what will work. Futurism means creatively planning for alternate eventualities.

In 1960, Warner Brothers was at the top of its television game, or so they thought. Its programs occupied 30% of ABC-TV's schedule. As stars left or sued the studio, they were interchangeably replaced by other actors. Scripts were retread from one series to another, often giving the writing credit to "W. Hermanos" (Warner Brothers in Spanish).

The studio's accountants and lawyers called many of the shots. They insisted that each episode make a profit, little realizing the investment in better productions toward longer-term residual rights.

The episodes began to all look alike. The quality dipped. There was too much sameness to the productions. Alas, the shows began getting cancelled. WB had not diversified its productions to other networks, syndication and changing public tastes. Soon, they were without any TV productions. The surviving studio became a home for independent production companies, rather than try to captain all the productions.

Futurism is one of the most misunderstood concepts in business and organizational life. It is not about gazing into crystal balls or reading tea leaves. It is not about vendor "solutions" that quickly apply band-aid surgery toward organizational symptoms. Futurism is not an academic exercise that borders on the esoteric or gets stuck in the realm of hypothesis.

Futurism is an all-encompassing concept that must look at all aspects of the organization...first at the Big Picture and then at the pieces as they relate to the whole.

Futurism is a connected series of strategies, methodologies and actions which will poise any organization to weather the forces of change. It is an ongoing process of evaluation, planning, tactical actions and benchmarking accomplishments. Futurism is a continuum of thinking and reasoning skills, judicious activities, shared leadership and an accent upon ethics and quality.

I offer nine of my own definitions for the process of capturing and building a shared Vision for organizations to chart their next 10+ years. Each one gets progressively more sophisticated:

- Futurism: what you will do and become...rather than what it is to be. What you can and are committed to accomplishing...rather than what mysteriously lies ahead.

- Futurism: leaders and organizations taking personal responsibility and accountability for what happens. Abdicating to someone or something else does not constitute Futurism and, in fact, sets the organization backward.

- Futurism: learns from and benefits from the past...a powerful teaching tool. Yesterdayism means giving new definitions to old ideas...giving new meanings to familiar premises. One must understand events, cycles, trends and subtle nuances because they will recur.

- Futurism: seeing clearly your perspectives and those of others. Capitalizing upon change, rather than becoming a by-product of it. Recognizing what change is and what it can do for your organization.

- Futurism: an ongoing quest toward wisdom. Commitments to learning, which creates knowledge, which inspire insights, which culminate in wisdom. It is more than just being taught or informed.

- Futurism: ideas that inspire, manage and benchmark change. The ingredients may include such sophisticated business concepts as change management, crisis management and preparedness, streamlining operations, empowerment of people, marketplace development, organizational evolution and vision.

- Futurism: developing thinking and reasoning skills, rather than dwelling just upon techniques and processes. The following concepts do not constitute Futurism by themselves: sales, technology, re-engineering, marketing, research, training, operations, administration. They are pieces of a much larger mosaic and should be seen as such. Futurism embodies thought processes that create and energize the mosaic.

- Futurism: watching other people changing and capitalizing upon it. Understanding from where we came, in order to posture where we are headed. Creating organizational vision, which sets the stage for all activities, processes, accomplishments and goals. Efforts must be realistic, and all must be held accountable.

- Futurism: the foresight to develop hindsight that creates insight into the future.

Technology

In 1951, Desi Arnaz got the call from CBS-TV. His "I Love Lucy" series had sold, and when were he and Lucy coming to New York to perform the show live?

Desi stated that he and Lucy would stay in California and film their show. He went out and recruited one of Hollywood's top cinematographers and devised a three-camera technique, so that Lucy could work her best in front of a live studio audience. Desi saw the added expense of filming the shows as creating a permanent record and an after-market, thereafter known as "TV reruns."

As a result, American TV shows could fly on film anywhere in the world. Filmed programs opened up new opportunities for local independent channels, foreign film sales and, alas, cable television.

Technology is important....but not the most important part of running an organization. We must learn how to use it, in order to put it into perspective.

Often, technology is a "bells and whistles" project that companies readily put money behind, rather than first addressing total-organizational issues, problems and opportunities. It does not solve all problems, nor should it be blamed for creating all problems.

People need more than technology to be productive. Yet, without adequate technology, they are handicapped. We must not give a disproportionate amount of attention to technology and leave people (any organization's best resource) the short end of the stick.

Each year, companies spend billions of dollars on the latest technology but do not reward their people for creative thinking. People are trained in the use of technology but are not trained adequately in other aspects of business operation...notably in the powers of reason, communications and the people skills necessary to work optimally with each other.

The bigger priority is to apply creative thinking to all aspects of company operation. Use technology as a tool. Utilize people as the masters of that tool. Encompass planning and bigger-picture thinking into all business operations. Therefore, those who use technology do so with a bigger understanding of its place in the Big Picture.

When technology is thought of as a component in the "macro," rather than a "micro" world unto itself, it will have mature utilization. Otherwise, it will be viewed as a bunch of high-priced toys which are played out of context to the main game.

Creative processes

The three-camera technique was adopted as the industry standard for TV situation comedies, both those produced live on tape and those produced on film.

Videotape was first introduced into the industry in 1954. By the late 1960s, it was dominantly used by the networks and by local TV stations. By the late 1970s, videotape was utilized for the home market. Many of us recorded programs off the air and began stockpiling libraries. For others, an innovative marketplace and creative marketing process brought us retails stores that rented videos for home exhibition.

Along with knowledge of the industry in which one works, there is a creative art to being effective at every aspect of running and sustaining each facet of a successful business. These are details per each of the seven categories on my trademarked Business TreeTM:

Branch 1: The business you're in. There are skills attached to rendering the service or manufacturing the products. People get into businesses because they have expertise in an area, such as widget making. It is for this that they have received education, training, professional development, mentoring and much more. Business founders and leaders are good at making widgets and are exceedingly comfortable with Branch 1.

The art comes in amassing professional abilities, specialties and skills in working with industry consultants, technical specialists, sub-contractors, vendors and core business suppliers.

Branch 2: Running the business. This involves administrative practices, procedures, operations, structure, the physical plant, technologies, equipment, supplies and distribution. Once people get onto Branch 2, the problems begin and start to multiply. Few widget experts are taught how to manufacture widgets and deliver them to market. Nor, are widget makers really taught the multi-dynamics of actually operating a business. Hence, all decisions are made from a Branch 1 perspective, mentality and orientation.

The art comes in working with lawyers, engineers, technology experts, non-core business suppliers, communications providers and repair-maintenance companies

Branch 3: Financial Components include cash flow forecasting, budgeting, equity and debt financing, accounting, record keeping, banking and investing.

No company stays in business without money...incoming and, to a hopefully lesser degree, outgoing. Making money is not the only reason for being in business. Usually, it's to make the best possible widgets and, then, to be very successful at it. Financial expertise helps Branch 1 founders stay focused upon fiduciary responsibilities.

Branch 4: People. Leadership tasks include recruiting, hiring and supervision. Companies are successful by possessing an attained art to human resources management, empowerment, team building, training, incentives and professional executive development.

This is the largest and most under-nourished branch on the tree. Organizations cannot operate with people. However, many organizations tend to misuse, ignore, ill-advise, misguide, neglect and mistreat the people working for and with them. Employees are most often hired for Branch 1 expertise and put to work. Like the company founders, most widget experts are not well versed in the other branches of the tree. Even in their Branch 4 interface with other employees, they function from a Branch 1 vantage.

There is an art to motivating people and optimizing their performance. Research studies show that money is rarely the primary motivation for people in careers and their professional lives. All people in the organization need lots of professional attention, mentoring, training and administrative support. Few ever get their needs satisfied, and thus, companies realize reduced work output and a less-than-zealous attitude.

Management cries, "Fix those people," without realizing that they are a large part of the problem. All of us can stand having our people skills refined. That's why widget makers, administrative staff, bean counters and all other leaves on the tree must embrace empowerment, team building, open communication and other concepts to relate better to human beings.

Branch 5: Business development. The components include corporate imaging, marketplace perceptions and realities, sales, marketing, public relations, advertising and research.

One cannot stay in business unless they market and sell something. Branch 1 creators think incorrectly that they are in the "widget" business. Actually, they are in the "widget manufacturing and marketing" business. Many companies are principally in the "widget marketing" business. Having a better widget is but a small part of that equation.

Branch 1 experts in management tend to fight marketing and sales, branding those two different professional specialties as necessary evils that someone else must deal with. The astute upper management will integrate all five branches and participates personally in Branch 5...taking their widget to market.

Using another analogy, a person who gives birth and does nothing more toward their child is not a good parent. That person is successful after shepherding the offspring through the various stages of growth and facets of life.

Categories 6 and 7 are the nurturing-strength (basis of business), which enable Branches 1, 2, 3, 4 and 5 to interrelate and function most successfully.

Category 6 (trunk): Body of Knowledge. The components include professional development, product-service development, external influences and information, collaborations, partnering, joint venturing, government, regulating factors, marketplace limitations, community standards and niche constituencies.

No company can stay in business without understanding the relationship of each branch (business function) to the other, each limb (department) to the other, each twig (niche consultant) to the other, each leaf (employee) to the other and each part of the Business Tree has its proper responsibility and should learn to interface with the others.

This sophisticated and vital category includes research and consultation with management on external forces affecting company growth...mostly outside their control but which can limit business opportunities. There is an art to fine-tuning the processes by which management gains new insight about the future of business, viabilities for change management, emerging issues and the next necessary steps. This category also includes crisis management and preparedness programs and the building of strategic business alliances.

Category 7 (roots): The Big Picture. The components include building a shared vision, corporate responsibility, creative business practices, strategic planning, innovations, outside-the-box thinking, the quality process, ethics, changing markets and walking the talk.

The successful company takes the time and appropriates the resources to develop a Big Picture. This costs one-sixth that of continually applying "band aid surgery" to problems as they arise. Business is approached as a Body of Work...a lifetime track record of accomplishments.

Leadership

The biggest problem with business stems from the fact that management and company leadership come from one small piece of the organizational pie. Filling all management slots with financial people, for example, serves to limit the organizational strategy and focus. They all hire like-minded people and frame every business decision from their micro perspective.

The ideal business or organizational executive has strong leadership skills first. He or she develops organizational vision and sets strategies. Leaders should reflect a diversity of niche focus, guaranteeing that an overall balance is achieved. Those with ideologies, strategies, process upholding and detail focus are all reflected. The best management team looks at the macro, rather than just the niche micro.

None of us was born with sophisticated, finely tuned senses and highly enlightened viewpoints for life. We muddle through, try our best and get hit in the gut several times. Thus, we learn, amass knowledge and turn most experiences into an enlightened life-like perspective that moves us "to the next tier." Such a perspective is what makes seasoned executives valuable in the business marketplace.

Many people, however, stay in the "muddling through" mode and don't acquire seasoning. They "get by" with limited scope and remain complacent in some kind of security. As their clueless increases, they sink through the following seven numbers, like they would fall into a well.

Life has a way of forcing the human condition to change. Due to circumstances, people start "cluing in." By that point, substantial career potential has been lost. Much damage cannot be recovered. Therefore, many people likely will stay on safe tracks...which will rarely ride the engine to glory.

The most effective leaders accept that change is 90% positive and find reasons and rationale to embrace change. They see how change relates to themselves, realizing that the process of mastering change and turning transactions into a series of win-win propositions constitutes the real meaning of life.

Leadership is learned and synthesized daily. Knowledge is usually amassed through unexpected sources. Any person's commitment toward leadership development and continuing education must include honest examination of his-her life skills. Training, reading and pro-activity are prescribed.

14

The Tube's Greatest Hits

Remembering the Golden Stars and Shows of Baby Boomer Youth.

The Appendix to this book is a reference body of work all its own. This section consists of essays, interviews and profiles written by Hank Moore during television's Golden Age.

These period piece reprinted articles that investigate TV's impact on the Baby Boom culture and interview recollections of major TV stars.

These articles by Hank Moore originally appeared in magazines and newspapers from 1969-1973. They review the overall themes and social significances of selected shows.

When we review classic TV in its contextual era, we realize even further the applicability of the shows and their teachings toward modern life.

Lucille Ball interview, by Hank Moore.
First published in October, 1970.

THE GREATEST LADY

by Hank Moore

HOLLYWOOD — The dictionary got two new words the day I was entertained in the home of Lucille Ball, who in my opinion has got to be the greatest of them all on television. To see her on TV (as EVERY-ONE has), one thinks she must be awfully nice and so charming. That's an understatement, so I've coined a new term to describe her: Fantabulous (which is a combination of being fantastic and fabulous at the same time).

Her home in Beverly Hills is smart looking,   painstakingly kept, and has a warmth of a family which comes across on "Here's Lucy," which features Miss Ball's children, Lucie Arnaz and Desi Arnaz Jr. I saw 3 dogs rollicking in the yard and affectionate to the guest (me); a big shaggy white one named Junior looked to be the most comical.

"Junior is used to this sweet little thing," smiled Lucy, pointing out a highly pedigreed white snowball of a dog. "It's funny to watch him when Lucie comes over to visit and brings her dog. A fiesty little animal.   I think she feeds it dynamite!" The mongrel takes after Junior all the time, "and afterwards, he is so out of breath."

As we sat in the living room sipping cocktails (scotch), Lucy talked fondly of her visit to Austin a few years back as honored guest of the Headliner's Club at its annual party honoring the famous. "I loved going into the Governor's mansion, and the Connallys were such nice people." She asked if he were out of politics and I said yes, officially, though he still had interests in certain candidates. "I had the feeling that he wasn't happy in politics and wanted out," she observed.

The biggest highlight to Lucy was being in the company of Cactus Pryor, the Channel 7 personality who is celebrated as an emcee and toastmaster in many circles. She termed Cactus "a very valuable man, the go-getter of that place." I told her he had appeared in a couple of movies, and she supposed he was quite good. I said he found the tedium of making films too slow-paced, and Lucy chided, "Not fast enough for him. He runs the circus himself!"

Fondly reviewing the Richard Burton-Liz Taylor appearance which kicked off

Lucy's current season on CBS-TV (Channels 5, 7, and 10), she felt "it paid off very well well having THEM and THAT diamond." I felt that Burton surpassed in the comedy role many of the costume parts he has done in recent years.

"I had to get him to throw the lines out front," said the master coach of comedy. "The English throw them away. I said to him, 'You have 9 or 10 laughs in here.' He said, 'Are you sure?' After some working on it, he would shout them, and I said, 'Not so loud!' That's the transformation of a subtle sense of humor."

Reflecting back to Texas, Lucy asked if Neiman-Marcus was still going strong, and wasn't it under corporate control now; I supposed management was still the same. "I have a friend in New York. His wife used to go to Neiman-Marcus regularly to do all her Christmas shopping. Wouldn't that be something, to make one trip and do it all!" I noted that other Neiman's stores were beginning to dot the state, and she laughed, "Yeah, that's the corporate management talking there."

A nut on novelty items, Lucy told of a newly-developed craving for going to auctions. "I don't get a chance to go many places for very long. Now it's auctions instead of the crap table at Vegas! I first got hooked on them a few years ago through Cara Williams; she would take me to auctions, and it all sounded like gibberish to me. I never thought to open my mouth for very long." Now she loves it and boasted her newest findings, some copper buckets. "I couldn't do it without an interpreter!"

Perhaps the earliest starting program, "Here's Lucy" commensed filming back in the spring and therefore was able to wrap up the year's shows at the end of September. "We kept saying, 'We'll be finished in September' and kept expecting something

to go wrong. Everything happened right, and we were finished, which I kind of feel guilty about because it's too late for a lot of the crew to get on other shows. It's a time of year everyone else is working. I felt terrible about it. They stuck it out; they didn't leave me."

One thing noticeable is the great love Lucy actually has for her crew, and they generally adore her. Most have been with her for many years to attest to their devotion. "Oh, they were sad at the end of the season. Men who hadn't been with me that long cried," which to her was too personally touching for words. "One man came to me and said he was retiring. 'I said I don't want

Lucille Ball in a dance routine and with Sammy Davis Jr.

Continued on Next Page

to retire' was his answer. I kept telling him, 'You're gonna play golf, fish, go on boats.' He told me, 'I don't like boats'."

Naturally, Lucille Ball, with her season completed, is in great demand for everyone else's shows. She is set for Carol Burnett, Merv Griffin, Jack Benny, Danny Thomas, Pearl Bailey, Bob Hope, Johnny Carson; i.e. all the big ones. "I like a steady routine," she explained in qualifying enthusiasm over all the guest shot invites. "I have plenty of work to carry me up to Christmastime. But it doesn't interest me; it's different."

She has a definite routine on "Here's Lucy" and sticks faithfully by it. Otherwise, "I can procrastinate a long time," she confided, sheepishly taking me to an adjoining room of the house. "Take a look at that living room. Those things have been sitting there for 3 years. The housekeeper says someone is under there. But everything is neat and in place to me; I know where it all is if nobody else does!"

Again lilting into another room, Lucy carried back a scale model of condominium apartment units. "I have to intersperse these guest shots with my trips to Colorado. I want to believe these letters coming in." Businesswoman Ball has a new investment, a resort 15 minutes from Aspen, Colorado. (the famous ski resort). "It's an entirely newly developed community some 9,000 feet high. We've sold Buddy Hackett a town house there, and here's ours, and all these are going to be rented." High prospective praises have been coming in from realtors and managers who are developing Snow Mass to take the overflow from Aspen.

Desi Jr. came sauntering into the den to ask mom to sign a check, just as he frequently does on the show. I supposed it must be a joy to have the kids on "Here's Lucy." Mom herself chided, "It's nepotism, plain and simple. I've got my husband, my sister (Cleo Smith, producer), and my kids all on the show!" I wondered if the music Desi had on upstairs was for practicing, and she said no, it was just for listening. "He has never practiced, only a half-hour before he goes on," even for the show they recently did with master drummer Buddy Rich as guest star. "That was a dream of Desi's, to play with Buddy Rich, since he was a little boy!"

A couple of dogs flitted through the room, and Lucy sighed over the job of house breaking them. "They get confused, especially with a green rug, of where to go. Have you got any dogs? I've got a lot of dog ashes around here!'

Lucille Ball is of course the idol of millions like myself who were literally raised on her comedy, which is of course a joy. "The biggest thrill is staying there. Shows fall by the wayside because you don't see them long enough. No grass was ever greener for me. Perpetuation of the whole setup was important for me. Our show was built very carefully so that you've got a lot going for you after a few years, let alone 18. Some shows don't have writers to spell it out to people what the show is about and who these people on it are and why they are doing what they are doing. America was raised on our style of comedy; it was spelled out for you: the situation, how it was accomplished, and the windup."

Mass adulation, philosophized Lucy, is only part personal. "It's the advent of television, the most intimate medium of our time. We started with TV. You recognize Tom Mix because he looks and acts the same." She pondered that statement and coined the second new word of our day together, "Sameability. I feel almost compelled to stay the same because so much is changing in this world."

And that's why those early-1950's comedies are rerun today just as often as new episodes, or more so. I supposed that the reruns are the most gratifying security as to Miss Ball's staying power. "It's funny, she sighed. "People are always talking about the residual checks. I've never seen one. I sell a product, my work, outright. I don't know why...I do. I need the money, to buy some little thing I want at the moment!"

The sameability factor makes the character Lucy (Ricardo, Carmichael, or Carter) everywoman. "She can go almost anywhere, do anything," her portrayer asserted. "I'd like to travel the show and take Lucy all over America. We did it a few times, and they break you; you spend the rest of the year recuperating, not physically but financially. We tried to do a show down your way at the Johnson Ranch but conflicted with something else. So we're still looking for unusual places to go."

And the talk with Lucille Ball went on and on, from imported fashions to the dogs to the family. Conversationally she is indeed everywoman. I finally had to boyishly admit that now I had met a life's idol. Suddenly the comedy stopped at Lucy's Place. "Thank you, dear," she replied, touched.

Fantabulous, that's what she is!

Candy Store feature, by Hank Moore.
First published in August, 1970.

INSIDE THE TUBE...

By Hank Moore

HOLLYWOOD - Saying you are going "to the Store" out here is not a grocery shopping errand. What you're saying is you are going to tinseltown's "in" spot, THE private club discotheque. I made the scene on various occasions, and it's something to behold, in the eyes if nothing else.

The Candy Store is the town's most posh house of GO-GO. No more memberships are available, though at last soliciting the joining fee was $1,000. In exclusive Beverly Hills on an unlikely-named Rodeo Street, you are met by a uniformed parking guy who kindly deposits your wheels at a nearby parking meter or loading zone (there is no lot). The building front is modest and sports (surprise!) a counter with candy jars filled with motley - colored canes.

I got met by a receptionist wearing a pair of dungarees reminiscent of my yard work and a yellow translucent blouse, sucking on a peppermint cane as she unlocks a door which appears to be signed by every patron who ever crossed the portal. First of the greeters was a spritely mod dressed Gene Shacore, a Beverly Hills hair stylist and boutique operator who also owns the Store. I'm told he makes three quarters of an annual million skins off this project alone.

Each time my party was the guest of an axciting young actor, Don Knight. He co-stars with Charlton Heston in "The Hawaiians" and with Chris George in ABC's new fall series "The Immortal." (An interview with our multi-faceted friend is upcoming in TV Digest in September.)

The building is rectangle with a bar on the right as you enter and booths on the left. In the middle of the room is a dance floor, where I noticed Dean Martin whooping up and a table full of girls at a facing booth. Toward the back are more booths and a stairway leading to the "game room" (pool, etc.). All the top rock hits are blasting away from a 2-turntable console operated by an especially limber chick who dances to her own music. I hear she's not as involved as her departed predecessor, who insisted on doing her thing topless.

Joey Bishop enters with a couple of friends who are hardly ever away from him the rest of the evening. One looks like Marty Allen with short hair and the other like a television engineer I used to know. Joey and Dean exchange several quips, but Joey sits on the stairs watching the action for the most part with sad eyes. A member of our party said Joey's so sad these days that he's getting a bald spot in his hair transplant!

I'm drinking my usual bloody mary, and it has an after taste of ammonia cleanser. The waitresses are dressed in various fashions from Shacore's boutique: one evening a floor length gown, another a white pantsuit creation with a 3-stage gold belt. The girls' tableside manner sounds like something out of the mind of a public relations agency

(Continued on Page 17)

copywriter, which is good in that they are diplomatic at taking orders, enthusiastic about the business atmosphere, and socially ingratiating.

The customers were a sight to behold. Across the way was Don Mitchell of "Ironside" and Bill Bixby of "The Courtship Of Eddie's Father" with their girls. I think Dino is having the best time of anyone in the place. Most of the guys and gals appear to be secretary-actor types and are dressed in a colorful array of fashions.

A guy wanders by in a crocheted shirt I could have easily mistaken for Grandmother Hill's tablecloth. There's a guy in dungarees buttoned up by 2 rows of snaps (sort of a double-breasted zipper). A chick at a neighboring booth is in a backless frock with a mane of blonde hair draped over one shoulder. Dino is in a black turtleneck, and our Don is wearing a shirt right out of "The Hawaiians." We've got to heave sighs of interest as a steady parade of chicks pass in review, wearing everything as sightly as a bedroom sheet loosely draped, see-through fashions of all kinds, and an air 5 feet off the ground

We're in the half of the crowd which is really having a good time. The other half seems to be on parade and looks at others having fun before they proceed to "join in." I asked various people why, and the typical Hollywood self-consumption syndrome seems to be a trait of the secretary-model types rather than of the actor types. There are some out on the dance floor who I'm sure do not realize they even have a partner.

Presently, the original good humor man, Frank Sinatra, steps in, and a hushed reaction by the crowd acknowledges his presence. Flanked by his bodyguard "Sarge," Frank is brandishing his left hand in a sling. I stepped over to find out that he just had a cancerous growth removed from the hand and is doing just fine, thank you. Frankie will discuss his recent endorsement of Ronald Reagan with any and all. I wondered if he wasn't instead simply opposing Jess Unruh, one of the clan who kept President Kennedy from visiting Sinatra at Palm Springs in 1960. "You got it, pal!" Sinatra looked like he remembered graphically the who and where of the incident(Continued on Page 32)

More of Inside the Tube.......

A chick drifts by in a stoned daze. One of our party asks, "Janet?" She floats awhile and turns to me: "You can call me anything you want!" I give a "That's quite alright" nod and decline in favor of another swig of cleaning fluid.

As the crowd gets thicker, the manager is quickly jamming in other tables and stools for more customers. Next thing I know, a couple of guys ask if they may join us. I nod and surreptitiously whisper to a companion if the guy who's ordering a refill on the table's drinks isn't football star-actor Jim Brown. Dogged if it isn't, and the big guy is congenial company.

I notice Joey and Dean are speaking, Dean and Frank are speaking. But Joey and Frank aren't. On comes Stevie Wonder's latest record, "Signed, Sealed, and Delivered," which moves Bishop to dance, right across from Sinatra's table. Next is Norman Greenbaum's "Spirit in the Sky," and Frankie has to dance too, 'cause his record company waxed disc.

The girl at the turntables is agonizingly good at programming the evening's music. I observed that she didn't miss a single record cue, and the "musical crests" that we refer to in radio were flowing right. (12 years in radio, and I'm not that good!) The music prompts Jim Brown to dance, and darned if he didn't end up with that stoned chick; he could have done lots better.

Another evening I'm on vodka collinses, and an aside that they taste like Gatorade cracks up the waitress. Dean Martin is trying hard to get upstairs, but the action keeps him bugalooing away. Bishop's men are try-

ing to meet new girls while Sinatra is brandishing his cast "goodbye" to all; he and Sarge have a good comedy act going, as they stop at each table to take pokes at each other.

I am told to notice all the out-of-work actors: Dennis Cole, who's no longer on "Bracken's World," and Don Marshall, whose "Land of the Giants" got cancelled by ABC and who's better known to my "Julia" cronies as Diahann Carroll's ex-boyfriend. Rejoice, for the next time I saw Don, he had news of just forming his own production company, and he was getting lots of work.

Good pal Dan Doran, an ABC publicist, shrugged at the early-morning hour, speculating how rough it would be to get going in the morning. "I can tell them I was looking after Joey Bishop and Don Marshall," he chided, adding that he at first didn't recognize Bishop when he first started coming to the Store. "And I worked on his show!"

The Candy Store, like Hollywood itself, is a state of mind more than a place. If you have got a motive for having a good time, then it's phonysville; and phonies contrive motives. Yeah, there are scads of people to be seen and to be seen by. The concept of the Store is pure fun with a little status involved; suddenly Jim Brown, Frank Sinatra, Dean Martin, et al, are not considered for their professional stature but instead are your friend and mine.

I can think of very few people asking what I did workwise. They figured I must be something to get in. Otherwise, they knew you because you were there to have a good time. The Store is a place to really dig!

Green Acres, interview with Eva Gabor and Eddie Albert, by Hank Moore.
First published in February, 1971, and February, 1970, respectively.

Matching Charm Each Week

By HANK MOORE

HOLLYWOOD — Vivacious Eva Gabor is a charmer in any circle. With a definite distinction of class about her, bejeweled and all, you just know that by day she labors along with the swine like the rest of us. Her swine is of course the world's best-known pig just short of Porky Pig: the incomparable Arold of "Green Acres."

Reflecting on the season just past was a pleasure as always for me, for Eva is one of our regular hostesses. "I don't know where to start," she sighed. "I've been going so fast and can't relax yet." First prescription for rest for her was a Christmas at Palm Springs populated by the entire Gabor clan.

Eva's Other Animal . . .
Duchess, the high–society heiress in the Walt Disney cartoon movie feature "The Aristocats," now playing all over the country. Eva supplies the feline's voice.

Secondly, Eva, a non-fan of football, evidently got lots of rest while her football-fan husband, producer Richard Brown, watched all the bowl games. "Well, not boring, but they're a little noisy for me. I went to one, and it took me a week to recouperate! Anyway, darling, I had one heck

of a busy season. You saw my shows with Dean Martin and Kraft."

And of course she also has a wig franchise company, which Miss Gabor unveiled in an earlier interview in TV Digest. Business is going fine, she is now happy to report. "We have 150 boutiques all around the country.

To A Hamlet And A Ham

Also in Macy's. And I went to Florida in January to open some more stores."

The glamour parlors are unique, Eva pointed out, in that they are housed in various types of locations, unlike other franchise operations which are virtually indistinguishable. "Some of them are in department stores, and then you can also open boutiques on their own. In Kansas City, we have 5 of our own boutiques. So, things are hectic and well!"

Christmas was indeed a joy for Eva, who gave some 70 gifts to the cast and crew of "Green Acres," as shooting on their sixth season wrapped up some 10 days before the big day. "The family had a big Christmas Eve. It was very cozy; we had a big tree. I must say, I missed the snow. Christmas is really only beautiful in snow; it's most peculiar to see Christmas trees in the desert. "
So, to get all the snow she could handle, Eva went up to Lucille Ball's condominium in Colorado to ski and bask in the winter atmosphere.

Miss Ball and Miss Gabor are off-screen very close friends. "She is one of my best girlfriends. I love her," remarked Eva. I noted that through the Colorado tract Lucy is also becoming very interested in real estate properties. "Whatever she does is brilliant, and she has a perfect mind for that sort of thing!"

This year, CBS decided to group its "rural" shows into one lump time block, termed under the name of demographics. "Green Acres" was sandwiched in between "The Beverly Hillbillies" and "Hee Haw." Eva is quick to point out that "Green Acres" is quite sophisticated in tone, but that the new time slot has not diminished their ratings. "We don't kick, but we don't enjoy being moved every 5 minutes."

Like most performers, she believes demographics are proven wrong by the success of shows in spite of points and percentages. "I know we're a big hit; we've been on the air for 6 years. So I don't care what they demograph about. As long as it's a hit, that's all that matters."

Glamorous Eva Gabor enter—taining Hank Moore at her home

The scripts to her have been funnier than ever this season, and any prospects for cast additions next season will be in animals. Arnold the Pig and the like have been tried and true building blocks for comedy routines for her. "We have an adorable Hungarian duck, darling little thing, followed me all over the stage!"

Among the off-season work for Eva is a movie in the planning stages with her sister Zsa Zsa. "That will be wild, I agree with you. That's the right remark. We've never worked together. This will be our debut and should be quite exciting."

Some family chit-chat about Zsa Zsa's success on Broadway in "40 Carats," some political pundits, and another session with Eva Gabor came off well. "Are you sure I've brought you up on all the news, darling?" I assured Eva she had indeed, and charmingly so.

"Chit Chat"

Editor HANK MOORE
Interviews EDDIE ALBERT

He plays Oliver Douglas
on CBS' "Green Acres" series
Saturday at 8 p.m. on Ch. 5 & 7.

Transcribed from a telephone conversatic

What reflections do you have on "Green Acres" now as you are finishing filming your fifth season?

"I think we're pretty fat for the next season. You never can tell those things, but we're looking forward to it. Our ratings have been up, and the stories have been up, and the stories have been good; so we keep our fingers crossed! I like our time slot a little earlier in the evening because I think it gets more kids that way and they like it. When we were on Wednesdays, we were on at 9:30, so a lot of kids missed it."

Eva must be fun to work with.

"Oh yeah, she's a kick. She knows her business and is responsible and works hard. She's always jolly; I wouldn't want anyone else."

What plans have you for the series' summer hiatus?

"I did a record of 'Prepare For the Seventies,' which should be out and around pretty soon; I did that on the Ed Sullivan show. I didn't concentrate very much on singing guest shots this past season on the variety shows, but I'll be doing a lot more coming up now.

"I've gotta go around the country making a lot of speeches on pollution. I've gotten dozens of invitations to the college campuses: Georgia, Florida, Michigan, Illinois, and so on. They ask about smog, water shortage, oxygen, salmon: things of that sort; I've been studying pretty hard on it, so I'm pretty well informed."

When did you first get interested in polluted waters?

"Years ago. It's a thing that I take a serious interest in, along with Arthur Godfrey; we're the two guys who are working on it. But a lot of people are becoming interested now; so we can be grateful for help coming in. The oil derkes off the Calif. coast do not help much, do they. And there's not much you can do about it because the bottom keeps breaking up now. Eventually, maybe they'll get those birds back, clean up, and things will be like they always were, I hope."

You were an adventurous youth. Your biography says at one time you hunted treasure.

"Yes, off Guadalupe Island; it was one of those adolescent things. I didn't care if I found any or not. I didn't find anything then or when I excavated the Mayan ruins. It was a little enjoyment to prowl around the jungle."

Visiting Dr. Albert Schweitzer at Lambarene must have been one of the high points in your life.

"You're quite right, that was. Very rewarding. I'm very happy I did that before the old gentleman passed off. His philosphy about reverence for life impressed me; that's part of the pollution thing for me.

(Continued on Page 30)

"We were there for meals for millions, a protein that we were making which was sent around Tom Dooley's hospital and the Schweitzer to feed all the patients. It was to keep the disease from spreading and was a good nourishment for the people. We were feeding maybe 110 countries at that time. Now the government has taken over most of it.

"The project originated here in Los Angeles. Clifford Clinton started it, and it developed into quite a thing finally, even in the film colony."

Is "Green Acres" kind of a change of a change of pace from what you've done before?

"A change of pace except that television is the name of the game today. Sooner or later, everybody's going to get into it; I got into it a little earlier than most. Oliver Douglas is a good juicy part, well-written, and very suitable for me. The people around me - Haney, Eb, and Kimbal - these are good characters, funny people."

Eva was saying her dogs get a little jealous of Arnold the Pig sometimes.

"Yeah, that's true. They want to be in films themselves."

Do you think television is lacking in the field of public affairs programming?

"Everything is lacking in that area. The government is doing very little about it, in spite of the publicity; actually, they don't even understand what the problems are. By default, very little aggressive action is being taken. The public is beginning to demand some action, fortunately, as a result of most of us talking on television and arousing them. But there's no great understanding of the amount of money involved."

If given the choice do you think the public would want more such programming?

"No. The general public, doesn't enjoy too much public affairs. They prefer the fictional things, unfortunately, because there are so many serious problems that require the public's knowledge and understanding. We just don't have enough of that on the air, that's all. They'll tune them out. Of course everybody tries hard to make a good show, but sometimes we have to turn it out a little too fast."

Do you think a person can successfully perform and direct themself?

"It's very difficult; there hasn't been too much success in that. Both of them are serious jobs. Orson Welles tried it and didn't do too well; he was a genius. Jerry Lewis has a special kind of thing; he plays himself all the time, and it's not a typical situation. But there's been no great record of directors who are actors. Oliver did it once quite well but there isn't an awful lot of it. Nobody wants to do two jobs at once unless he is a little nutty."

Would you say "Green Acres" has brought, more fans and recognition than all those years of doing character parts?

"No question about that. We perform for 25 million people every Saturday. I get asked for a lot of autographs; the people are very nice and courteous. I enjoy it. That and the fact that I really like acting keeps me busy."

What do you think is luring many of the longtime holdouts, like Doris Day, into television now?

"It's a very healthy business, and pictures for the time being are not very healthy. But I suppose they'll keep moving over. A lot of the new people who were not in pictures are very good too: I watched Michael Parks last night and think he's a splendid actor."

Would TV do well to develop schools for talent?

"No, they haven't got the time, nor do they know how. There was never very much of it in the big movie studios' heyday. They talked a lot about it, but they did not know how to select talent in the first place. Talent has to pop out itself through the heart; it's very hard to spot good talent early. You've got to see it come out of the fire because it's more than simply being able to act. It takes discipline and desire."

Editor HANK MOORE
Interviews EVA GABOR

She plays Lisa Douglas
on CBS' "Green Acres" series
Saturday at 8 p.m. on Ch. 5 & 7.

Transcribed from a telephone conversation

"How's everything in Austin?"

It's winter and not too cold

"I don't think it ever gets too cold these days. I have some friends there: the President and his sister. I saw his interview on television, and he is looking in great shape. I guess once the whole burden of the world gets off your shoulders, you look better!"

Have you known the Johnsons long?

"I met them in Austin, where you are, years ago; and then, when he was in the White House, we went over for the inaugural ceremony. Mrs. Bobbitt, the President's sister, and her husband are very good friends of ours. I used to go a lot to Texas before I started my 'Green Acres;' now I don't go anywhere.
"We're just finishing our fifth season. And I'm doing the new Pat Paulsen show, and then after that the Tennessee Ernie Ford special. And in between, I've got a wig company and a decorating business; otherwise, I have nothing else.

So you're a businesswoman now!

"I have a new wig franchise company which I am terribly excited about. Our headquarters are in Kansas City. Oh, you should see my office; it's just marvelous.

How is it decorated?

"Beautifully, in great, great taste. And the boutiques, which an artist and I sorta

designed together. When the franchises buy one, they get it already made and can set up business in one day. It is a ready-made business and is the biggest business in America, believe it or not. There isn't a woman who doesn't wear wigs or wiglets nowadays."

How big a wig collection should the well-dressed woman own?

"Quite a lot! You'd be surprised to hear that even men have acquired a lot of wiglets. It takes an awful lot of time for women, especially those of us in show business: I have very long hair and if they would have to curl the whole thing, I would have to get up instead of 6 o'clock at 5 o'clock to get ready. So, we just do the front and and put some pieces in the back; I have 5, or 6 changes during the day. It saves a great deal of time and also saves my own hair not to have to fiddle with it all the time.
"I'm sure you're thrilled. Isn't it boring,"

Only when the guys at the local pool hall talk about, then you know you're talking too much about it.

"Oh do you play pool? My husband does; we have a table in our house. I'm very bad about it; I'm not very good at it. It's a big fashion in Hollywood; everybody plays pool."

Your boutiques are decorated in pink. Is that your favorite color?

"You know, they made a survey of what makes things sell the most. I never

(Continued on Page 29)

knew until I got into this business that they could just about survey everything. Pink color makes people want to buy; don't ask me why. So, we have pink rugs.

"Our home is very **big** and we have all, sorts of color schemes in it. My bedroom is green and white, my drawing room in blue and white, and my office in yellow. The pool house is red, white, and blue; we're being very patriotic. We're decorating a lot of condominiums in different colors."

I guess you like having a number of homes to go to.

"Yes,..I like that. Palm Springs today is beautiful and sunny, and Hollywood is very gray and sort of winterish looking. When you think it's only two hours, and you can have sunshine, it's sort of lovely.

"I was laughing the other day about the Hollywood life of movie stars. We went over to have dinner with Lucille Ball. The help was off, and Lucy was cooking, and I am, doing the dishes, I'm not very handy in the kitchen, but Lucy is terrific. She was saying 'Do this, do that.' When I set the table she siad, 'Are you left-handed?' I said no. So, she said, 'Then set the forks properly!' She knows just about everything in this world."

You and Eddie were recently picked by a photographers' guild as television's most photogenic couple. How do you feel about that?

"Well I think it's just great. Anything to be awarded is terrific; I love to win awards."

Do your pictures flatter you?

"I had some pretty awful pictures of myself. Some pictures are better than others. But I try to do my best, learn how to dress, and try to do everything around it. Things somehow turn out alright. I don't look the same everyday; I'm a human being. Sometimes I look good, sometimes not so good."

I understand you are an antique collector.

"Oh yes, I adore them. That's how I got into the decorating business. I inherited it from my father, who used to collect antiques in our house in Hungary; the attics and the basements were so full we couldn't move. Beautiful furniture lasts so long and and gives you so much joy; I find that anti-

ques fit in any house. I have pieces that I've had since I was a kit; they've been in a house in Hollywood, our town house in New York, an apartment in New York; now they're back in Hollywood; they fit everywhere."

You are an animal lover!

"Oh you read my biography. I have two Yorkshire terriers sitting in my lap, one over there, and two cats. I have a very funny Persian cat, Sade Sade Married Lady, with a very funny pink nose and a black moustache, and she's a girl and cross-eyed. There's another Persian we got in London, called Super Boy."

Do you take your pets on the "Green Acres" set with you?

"I take the dogs with me. They are in my dressing room off the stage, my bungalo, they go with me everywhere. The Persian cat comes down to Palm Springs, but Sade doesn't like the car; she is sick and has to stay home."

Does Arnold the Pig get jealous of your pets?

"Arnold doesn't get along with other dogs because he is a movie star. He is really a star, with his dressing room and everything. I had a scene with him yesterday; he is really amazing, that Arnold! The kids love him."

How did you get involved in "Green Acres." It's a change of pace for you.

"Not after five years of living on it. It seemed like a very good idea and did turn out to be a very good. Our set is known in Hollywood to be the happiest. We have a great company and Eddie and I are great friends. So, it doesn't really ever have any problems, which is unheard of out here. We live together so closely, and we spend so much time together."

What's Zsa Zsa up to these days?

"She's in Las Vegas doing a show and has a big success. Zsa Zsa and I talk on the phone everyday; we get together as much as possible." (Continued on Page 22)

Week Of January 3—9

Listings for Austin, Waco
San Antonio, Temple

T.V. Digest's Gala "Mission: Impossible" Issue

This week the Impossible Missions Force begins probably its most grandiose adventure to date, "The Falcon," a 3-part episode beginning Sunday at 9 p.m. over Channels 5, 7, & 10. Pictured are the stars of "Mission: Impossible," Peter Graves (left), Leonard Nimoy, Lee Meriwether (guest starring), Greg Morris, and Peter Lupus. To spotlight this popular adventure series, T.V. Digest presents an issue devoted entirely to "Mission: Impossible," with exclusive interviews with ALL of the series stars!

READ REPEATEDLY IN THE HOME EVERYDAY BY ALL MEMBERS OF THE FAMILY

Gunsmoke, interviews with John Mantley and Milburn Stone,
by Hank Moore. First published in October, 1970

INSIDE THE TUBE... By Hank Moore

HOLLYWOOD—The closest thing to an anthology series on television today is one of the small screen's traditional westerns, "Gunsmoke." Phenomenally successful for 15 years, the production staff still looks at each new season as a challenge, rather than sit back and stagnate.

That's the impression I got while talking with John Mantley, executive producer of "Gunsmoke," in an effort to see what has made the show what it is. A 50-year-old native of Canada, Mantley has authored screenplays for everything from "Rawhide" to "The Untouchables" and has been with "Gunsmoke" in all creative capacities through the years. He and the show have been cited by western heritage societies.

Chemistry among the regulars was working in early episodes, although Mantley chuckled that Matt would make asides at Kitty for being a prostitute then. A dialogue sample: "I wish all the men in the world would disappear" (Kitty). "What would you do for a job?" (Matt). "Viewers didn't like Kitty giving her favors to other men," he added. "Of course the Longbranch is still little more than a social club, though we don't say so."

Although Matt Dillon was a prevocator of violence in personalities in the early years of the show, he has never shot a guy without warning. "The audience now knows what Matt will do in a given situation," said Mantley.

The series can be equated in message content to chapters from the Bible. "The honest, basic morality of the West in this period has a Biblical parallel. Several of our shows have demonstrated how a small transgression can lead to a major tragedy," he noted, although there's only half the violence in "Gunsmoke" today than in past seasons. "Violence is always indigenous to the plot."

Audiences seem to like shows most in which star James Arness is in them a lot. Mantley noted that it's not because he works less that Arness is light in many episodes. "Jim appears less and less because he is a marshal and wears a gun on his hip. In this brutal and callous period, he has to be functional on the screen."

Dillon is every man in the morality plays, clarified Mantley. "We try not to do detective stories because that's not Matt Dillon's bag. "His staff doesn't look in the Bible and then correlate stories." The plots seem to coincide by themselves.

Overall this past television season, "Gunsmoke" was rated number two nationally. "In recent years everything that opposed us has gone down the tube except for Rowan and Martin," he beamed. "Ratings are just like death and taxes. Indifferent ratings do lower a good western some. Even the most loyal fans do switch channels."

A fresh look in "Gunsmoke" this coming year is to get outdoors from the soundstage at Studio City more. A two-part blockbuster, "The Snow Train," filmed in the Dakotas over snow-capped mountaintops this spring, is a fall offering, as is another segment done in New Mexico.

Character development is the secret to what Mantley looks for nowadays in choosing scripts, for the show has to in the future lean more and more toward the anthology approach. "It's hard now to do the classic western where people shot first and asked questions later," he is firmly convinced that the future cannot bring anything but more successful years of "Gunsmoke" on the air.

Dick Clark interview by Hank Moore.
First published in February, 1971.

Pied Piper To Teens:

By HANK MOORE

HOLLYWOOD — To any young adult today, Dick Clark is an idol. As THE purveyor of the recorded sounds of the day, Dick must surely rank as the most celebrated disc jockey of all time. Because of the nature of oldtime rock 'n' roll music, which I was brought up on, and the longtime appeal of his personality, I have to rank Dick Clark as one of the all-time greats of television.

As host of "American Bandstand" on ABC-TV since 1957 (it now airs Saturdays at noon over Channels 7 and 12), Dick has remained perennially young. And his charm with teenagers is still undisputable.

Since I encountered Dick in the "be bop shoo bop" days of rock 'n' roll, I somehow imagined his office to have Fats Domino blaring from the loudspeakers. Quite wrong, for the decor is something out of an antique museum, with Western posters, a barber's chair for guests (flanked by a row of theatre seats), ancient telephones, and the rest. Music for him is provided via a 1930's juke box, and the records on them were likewise in vintage: Glenn, Tommy, Benny, Artie, and the rest.

"Bandstand," Dick was proud to point out (as Dr. Peppers were served, naturally), was a first on TV, with live dancers, guest stars, and lip syncing to the tunes. He knows of some 100 copies of it that went on after his show became a smash success. (It had been Philadelphia's Number One show, a local daily from WFIL-TV, for 4 years before ABC picked it up.)

As one might imagine, the corridors of Dick Clark Productions on Sunset Boulevard

are adorned with keys to the cities, plaques, press clippings, and other memoirs of a music industry which is so attuned to this man...and vice versa. Really a very humble guy, Dick glanced at the walls. "The keys and plaques were thoughtful gestures, but they're cold now," he exclaimed. "The people who meant a lot to us and the memories and interesting experiences are the thing. Ironically, we never got a key from Philadelphia. It was the biggest attraction of its day. People saw 'American Bandstand' right after Independence Hall and the Liberty Bell."

In 1964, after "Bandstand" had been cut to one show a week, and offers from movies and other shows had been piling up, Dick moved his operation to Hollywood. From these offices, he produced "Where the Action Is," the Paul Revere and the Raiders series, and other TV shows, including 2 other nighttime series for himself. Also from here, Dick books concert tours for the biggie acts: Dionne Warwick, Tom Jones, Engelbert Humperdinck, the Iron Butterfly.

The Diversified Dick Clark

Creedence Clearwater Revival does Dick Clark gigs. "They borrowed their style a great deal from Chuck Berry and Little Richard," he explained. "It's interesting to see a Creedence audience. They are conservative young people with modest dress and shorter hair. The audience goes in, applauds, enjoys the music, and leaves without incident and without drugs."

As for the group of the year to watch, Dick picks the Jackson 5, whose shows he also books. "Their audiences are similar to who used to go and see The Monkees and the Raiders. They are 85 per cent black, yet whites buy more of their records." Clark thinks the Jacksons signify a breed of really young performers, as the bubblegum set thinks of people in their 20's as old. "These boys are the first very young black act exposed to very young audiences. Before, all they were exposed to were old men and women. The Supremes in their day were old women!"

I wondered if he could pick the fad singers through any extra sensory perception. Dick doesn't think so, remembering he thought nothing of Elvis Presley at first hearing. "I was still playing middle of the road music," which is where Dick pegs himself as to basic tastes. "Middle of the road stations are amongst the most successful in the music business. If you get too young, you can't sell products!"

Some 200 of his old gang of regulars

**Dick with Creedence
Clearwater Revival**

from Philly still keep in touch with Clark, which thrills him. They have reunions frequently which sets them apart from Dick's dancing friends of the '60's and '70's. Since 3 or more "Bandstands" are taped at a time, people come in for taping sessions but rarely return.

When he was in the music publishing business, Dick used to get over 100 unsolicited tapes of songs or acts a day. Now, he still finds some 100 a year and forwards them to people who can help. Among his ownings is a country and western radio station. "Country music is one of my favorites but its main problem is that it is not successful in attracting young people in great numbers."

Reminiscing over moldy oldies like "Pink Shoelaces," the pitiful singing career of Tab Hunter, and the funky lyrics of the '50's, Dick confessed still listening to many of them from his multi-thousand record and tape library. "Today's recording techniques are far superior to the 1950's. Let's face it, those records are bad!"

Television, Dick feels, is a medium which has many powerful yet untapped resources it can explore. He feels the magazines and critics who charge the medium is dying are wrong and are biting the hand which feeds them. "There is no doubt in any thinking person's mind that there isn't going to be

**Dick Clark with Oliver
(singing star)**

(Continued on Page 17)

More Dick Clark Interview . . . . .

any great change in TV. The newspapers and movies have stuck around through it all."

Like TV itself, Dick fancies himself as a durable individual. He looks about the same as he did years ago; his hair is a little longer but not unstylishly so. "The better part of valor is to stay as familiar as possible!"

Being typecast as a teenager and as a model of wholesomeness doesn't bother Dick Clark at all. "I could live with it or throw it like a nightmare," he reasoned. "Thank goodness for it, so I live with it." On the pictures and TV guest shots he did, Dick played the guy least likely to do it: the psychopaths and killers in sheep's clothing. "You could have spun me off in 'Mod Squad' as the adult member, and that would have blended in." But otherwise, The Image would not have lent authenticity to pursuing a career as a fulltime dramatic actor.

How coincidental it was that I brought up Dick's acting, which is more in his past than his present. Dick recalled subbing for Peter Falk in a pilot for a series on a youth counselor done 8 years ago; the producer called him up the other day and talked of reviving it. Clark wouldn't mind if his Kincaid character hit the screens but instead yearns to do a talk show in the nighttime. (His ABC contract forbids him appearing before 6 p.m., which is the time bracket where he has been swamped with offers from everyone.)

Believing in his products was his bag, and many people associated Dick with many items which bought time on his show without his endorsement. To Dr. Pepper he became for 11 years what Ed McMahon has become for Budweiser, its spokesman. "Ed should be as lucky as I have been," he talked of the liaison which ended early this year because they had to change their ad campaigns. But Dick will still entertain at bottlers' conventions for Dr. Pepper. "I know every bottler on a first name basis by now!"

His company is involved in counseling with other companies on product image and youth appeal. The client list numbers the likes of Sears, Borden's, United Airlines, and the Thomas Organ Company.

As it's about time, there is a "Best of American Bandstand" of sorts on the way, in the package of a new movie which Dick Clark is producing. "The Years of Rock" is a documentary "tracing the impact of music on people and people on music," he explained. The Warner Brothers release will draw most of its film clips from all of Dick's shows and other sources. It begins in the bobby sox era of the middle '50's. "I still think girls' legs look about as good as ever in bobby sox and loafers," he quipped about the styles of that period.

Suffice to say, Dick Clark is quite an active man. "I would hate to do 'American Bandstand' on a daily basis now. We did it as long as 3 hours and 15 minutes a day. If I had anything else I could do, it would be a talk show like the other 4 guys who do it now." Dick is an active producer and not just an aging disc jockey. "That's probably our fault that people don't know what else I do because we haven't told them enough. Television is a very small part of people's lives."

What has Dick Clark learned from his very successful career in music, I asked. "That young people are very well versed on the music business. That's the way to reach them," he believes. And probably no other man has done more to communicate with youth than Dick Clark, a man to whom the music industry must be indebted.

To Hank
THANKS FOR THE
MOST KIND
WORDS -
Dick

Jack Lord interview, by Hank Moore.
First published in November, 1969.

"Chit Chat"

Editor HANK MOORE
Interviews JACK LORD

He is known as Steve McGarrett on CBS' "Hawaii Five-O" series

Transcribed from a telephone conversation

"I talked to a man yesterday in St. Paul Minnesota, and he said he got the first snow of the season. Gee, that's strange. We're sitting here in this tropical paradise, and you're getting snow on the mainland. You don't get it, but have got a hot football team!"

Do you do a lot of your own stunts?

"Oh, yeah. I do it all. I've had a background in athletics, had a football scholarship at NYU. I was a quarterbakc, but was the only football player in the history of NYU that ever graduated with a degree in art."

Did you get ribbed about that a lot?

"Oh, yeah. Constantly! But it never troubled me. I knew where I was going. I wanted to be a painter all my life. I did up until the time I was sent to Washington during the Korean War to illustrate a book for the Maritime Service, & that's when I got involved with acting for the first time. I had never even thought of being an actor, never had any desire. I didn't like actors! But, it's interesting the way things evolve, & when you don't force them, they have a way of working out.

You spent time as a seaman in your youth.

"Yes. I went to the academy in New London. I was attached to a visual aids unit after I had gone to sea. Because I knew how to launch lifeboats & splice wife, I ended up doing a series of training films. And that was my introduction to acting. I tried to become an actor after the Korean War and found out it was not an easy job. So I decided to go to school and be a professional actor at night, and I sold Cadillacs during the day."

Pick up a lot of commissions?

"I was a very good salesman, as a matter of fact, because I knew the product very well, and I believed in it. It was nothing more than a transfer of convictions to a buyer, which is what all good selling is, I think. When I quit Cadillac, I was making $18,000 a year as a salesman; I went to $1,100 my first year as an actor."

Do you still get much time for painting?

"Our schedule here, Hank, is very tough. I work about 80 hours a week generally. We work 6 days a week, and our basic workday is 12 hours, which is the 'glamorous life of a television star.' People think you get up leisurely in the morning, & you have a long breakfast, & then you get made up, & that's a lot of bologna! We work from 6 in the morning until we lose the light.
"But, fortunately it's working. We have a hit now. We dominate the time slot. And then you're assured of another season, and that's what we want. I want to do 100 films and then quit and do what I always wanted to do: to paint and to direct one picture a year."

You really must be sold on Hawaii!

"I'm writing a book on Hawaii, kind of a travel book. It's going to be illustrated with about 90 of my photographs, and I'll have

(Continued on Page 31)

about 50 pages of text. It will be out by February and will be distributed by one of the largest pocketbook distributors in the U.S. We got an initial order for 100,000, & we're having it printed in Japan. Beautiful color separations!"

How do you and your family live?

"We bought a condominium on the beach at Kahala, a suburb of Honolulu. I'm going to walk out on our lanai right now. From where I'm standing now, we're on about 60 of water, and I'm 3 stories high. So I can look out at the most glorious sunrise. It is only about 6:00 here. The sun is just coming up over Kokohead, a famous landmark here. We're in a sheltered cove between Kokohead and Diamondhead. And the sun now is just peaking over Kokohead.

"The whole sky is shot with pinks and purples. Here they have fantastic sunrises & sunsets, because the atmosphere is so pure. They have these tradewinds which blow away all the smog and all the industrial waste that accumulate on the mainland. They do not have that problem here."

"Every ship that goes into Honolulu harbor goes by the door here. All the Naval vessels going into Pearl, and now I see coming

out of the horbor little lights on fishing sand pads, commercial fishermen going out to catch ocpu, which is a kind of tuna. And that's what my life is like. I go off and play McGarrett and run home and paint and live the good life."

It's quite different from the rat race of the cities.

"I can never go back to that again. It's so fary away now. There's a kind of naivite here, a kind of sweetness in the poeple that is so refreshing having lived in big cities all my life. And that's what I'm trying to convey in my book. They call them the Golden People, not because of the color of their skin; they really are! The children on the beach are very beautiful, little mixtures of all nationalities.

"Well, I've given you my talk for the morning, Hank."

It was beautiful just listening.

"There's a beautiful Hawaiian word , Mahalo, and it means 'Thank You.' So I say mahalo!"

HOLLYWOOD - I finally got a chance to see the fabled Brown Derby Restaurant

"Chit Chat"

Editor HANK MOORE
Interviews BILL BIXBY

Bill is Tom Corbett, sophisticated father on "The Courtship Of Eddie's Father," hit weekly ABC-TV series.

Live from Hollywood.

added.
The show this season has developed

Henry Fonda and Janet Blair interviews, by Hank Moore.
First published in March, 1971.

Fonda's Family Fare Forbids Fads

By HANK MOORE

HOLLYWOOD — "Nice is a funny word in these times, but he is that!" Janet Blair always thought Henry Fonda was a nice man, and fresh from an international tour as "Mame," she finally got the chance to work with him. Janet plays Betty Smith in ABC's new hit family series "The Smith Family." And she is kinda nice too!

A former band singer and Broadway musical-comedy star of considerable renown, Janet's only other television series was "The Summer Chevy Show," which she hosted as Dinah Shore's summer replacement in the summers of 1959, 1960, and 1961.

But the musicals were just an extension of her own flamboyant character, and "Mame" encompassed all of the roles. "I'm a nut myself," she gleamed as we chatted one drizzly California morning. "I hate imitations, and I think a lot of the people who did 'Mame' did imitate Angela Lansbury. But I completely saw 'Mame' from within myself because I do kind of any nutty character like that. You can't look and say, 'Who did it before?' You must bring all the things you have through the funnel, so to speak, of your creativity. And then it can come out in your own interesting way."

The fun of acting to Miss Blair is the discovery of the fact that she has been playing so many of the roles all these years, including Auntie Mame and Betty Smith. "I didn't know I had so much 'Mame' in me anyhow. The fun of acting is the sheer discovery of, 'My God, that's me. That's what I have felt.' Each one I dearly loved and found very corny and funny."

Her other stage hits includes "South Pacific," "Annie Get Your Gun," "Peter Pan," "Anything Goes," "The Sound Of Music," and "Bells Are Ringing."

She thinks the best part of "The Smith Family" is that the network is under a long-term contract, and longevity will insure growth and improvement within a show. The show was already picked up for next season before it debuted this month. "It's that magic word: Henry Fonda. Sure, it's good," she chirped.

Janet believes the show will start a trend back to family television, not so much in the stumble-bum situation comedies but in the vignette type of program. "With so much

Janet Blair

violence on television, and mod and crazy, and with the psychedelic things, the strange shots, and the nudes: that craziness has just about blown everybody's mind. I know I'm sick of it. There is always this desperate need for people to laugh and for people to laugh and for people to just be entertained. I think that's why these great comedians and comediennes have survived over the years, don't you!"

Gotta be the reason.

A show that's escapism but not quite, comedy but not quite, drama but not quite; that's her recipe for a family show. "Several times during the shooting, Henry or I felt perfectly comfortable saying, 'No, this just isn't real.' Let's hope that as the show goes on, it will become even more real."

A concerned professional, Janet Blair also uses volunteer charity work as an outlet for her civic and humanitarian ideals, particularly with the Crippled Children's Society of Los Angeles.

"As a parent, I'm terribly concerned about raising my children," she observed, as we talked about the stresses of travelling by virtue of the nature of show business and how it often keeps performers away from their families. "So many times, you come home and overcompensate. You know you are overcompensating, or they will take advantage of the situation. If you just don't sit down and say no, and mean no, they'll do it. By the same token, I've seen where with too much discipline, the child grows up and reflects this same kind of rigidity. And they grow up in their little way very crippled too. So I came to the conclusion that I would say no as little as possible; I would give them choices."

A mature outlook yet a colorful character. That evidently sums up Janet Blair. But to convey all that into a TV series without turning to saccharine is the trick. And judging from "The Smith Family" thus far, she seems to be turning the trick quite handily.

***

Henry Fonda, starring as Detective Chad Smith in "The Smith Family," is described by Janet Blair, who plays his wife in the series, as an "impeccable actor."

Henry Fonda

The same word aptly describes Fonda's preparation for playing a plainclothes detective, and the father of three, in the new half-hour series about the home life of a policeman.

"I had no hesitation about playing a policeman," Fonda confided recently. "I think the image is a bad rap. I'm for law and order, and cops take a bad rap from kids today. I don't think policemen should be put down because of a few bad officers any more than all college kids should be put down because of what happens on the campuses."

Fonda began his research for the role last spring when he accompanied executive producer Don Fedderson and producer-creator Edmund Hartmann to the Los Angeles Police Department headquarters in Parker Center.

"We had lunch with the chief and many of the police commissioners," recalled Fonda. "Then made arrangements to return the next day for a full tour of the center.

"We began at 8:00 a.m. I saw everything from the Bertillon system of fingerprinting to the commissary." On another day, Fonda visited the Police Academy, watching recruits in various training activities. The actor sat in on classes and inspected the facilities, which include an obstacle course and firing range.

One entire day was spent at a Hollywood Precinct house where Fonda met detective sergeants, like the one Chad Smith is modeled after. "I joined 2 of them in a routine day... and it showed me just how undramatic police work can sometimes be," said the actor. During the course of that day he sat in on interviews with suspects and helped police to research criminal cases.

A lunch with 3 off-duty policeman filled Fonda in on some station house gossip and the "shop talk" of men in the front line of America's never-ending war against crime.

Henry Fonda did one other TV series before, "The Deputy" on NBC in 1959-60. Ths show to him is a big step up. "It's been one of the better experiences I've had in any medium," he noted. "To work with good people is what it's all about!"

Lee J. Cobb interview, by Hank Moore.
First published in September, 1970.

"Chit Chat"

HANK MOORE
Interviews
LEE J. COBB

Cobb stars on "The Young Lawyers,"
new ABC-TV series starting next week

Live From Hollywood

HOLLYWOOD - Lee J. Cobb is in my opinion the world's finest actor. An intense man in his craft, his key is believability, be it Judge Henry Garth in "The Virginian" (whom he played from 1961-65) or bigoted lawyer Ohman Hedgepath (his character in the new movie "The Liberation of L.B. Jones"). Pesonally, he is a man to admire and/or idolize because he has warmth, convictions, and believability on a personal basis.

A must in coming out to California was to meet "The Man" himself. He gives out few interviews, for they conflict with his ever-intense concentration on the roles he is undertaking. Not that he has nothing to say publically, but involvement in his roles is everything to Lee J. Cobb, who was anxious to talk with me. And vice versa!

This fall he assumes the head post in the Neighborhood Law Office on ABC-TV's "The Young Lawyers." As a mindblower, I said upon introduction that wouldn't it be strange if Ohman Hedgepath was head of the NLO. (Hedgepath was defending Jones in the controversial new picture, the screen's ultimate in depicting Southern racism, where Hedgepath ends up letting Jones' killer, a policeman, go free.)

"This may surprise you," said Cobb, "but I think he would head such an office. Hedgepath was a man who knew better. He was a product of his culture, incapable of doing the right thing, although he knew right from wrong." Maybe Hedgepath would have rallied to the fore when confronted by a new environment: an office full of compassionate individuals.

"I was very much taken with the project and wanted very much to do it," he added. The picture was delineated from the book in that the racial tones were added which he thinks made the film so much more impacting.

It was a coup for the television industry to get such an accomplished actor back for a weekly series, but Cobb is taken with the "Lawyers" project too. I speculated that this summer's reruns of his best "Virginian" segments was just the thing to get audiences primed for his fall return, as high ratings will surely justify. "I'm glad," he replied. "That show was physically demanding. I wasn't free to do other things." (He hasn't watched the repeats.)

I asked by what gage Cobb planned acting projects to accept in pursuing his career. "I keep several sets of books," he said, "loft, sentimental, impeccable. Now I'd like the time to pursue impractical impulses." An obviously mellowed man, he looked completely absorbed in thought. "If I were in a position to make plans, the world would be in a much better shape. I don't have the courage to make predictions anymore."

It's impossible for Cobb to do his kind of acting on TV, in movies, or in the theatre anyway. "The ideal is real only in a social structure in which the idea can flourish, in an endowed theatre. The arts are very delicate. You have to need them and realize you need them. Older countries have a rich heritage of needing the arts."

But then it's a matter of what we think we need. "It's going to take time for exertion to be made without some Congressman saying it's a boondog," Cobb believes. "Is the Post Office surviving? We need it and pay its losses. These dreams I propose instead of commercial arts."

(continued on next page)

Theatre and films are in the hands of indifferent people, he proclaimed, and we both agreed. Apologizing that it may be "self indulgent for me to despair the conditions," he is still concerned about quality of entertainment and restrictions made to stifle that quality. "I have a conflict because I'm far from being a prude. I don't want to be denied from seeing anything spicy."

Differentiating again that he is "not biting the hand that feeds me," he termed television a professional compromise but one at this point in his career to be "the best bargain. Television is a concentration of these problems that have invaded the other ideal media. Why should the fate of a work depend on whether the sponsor likes it? It's not a question of television but instead of advertising." And the audiences have not complained either. "The people it is going to don't know any better. We cannot blame them because what do they have to compare with?"

I asked if he thought TV had progressed any since he did "The Virginian." Cobb

wrinkled his chin and sighed, "Not a whit! I don't know if it has retrogressed. And that includes radio. Of course air pollution is more palpable poisoning than some TV."

Was he slamming the likes of "Hee Haw," I mused. Cobb gestured exactingly: "Leave it on. Just don't deny me what I want to see." Commerciality gripes him, as on music stations. "They say, 'We're going to play Beethoven's Fifth, but first,' You could take a nap before then."

I asked Cobb to rank order the types of media in which he preferred to perform. It was: theatre, live television, taped television, radio, motion pictures, and filmed TV. That order obviously showed a preference for immediacy, "to use the previous moment as a springboard for the next. For an actor, the gratification is in the doing."

And films are chopped up and pieced together.

He did lots of radio drama. "The loss of a language is something that's immeasurable," morosed Cobb "Radio was an avenue for mutual involvements of millions of people." and it was the heighth in immediacy.

Re-evaluating his colorful career, which included everything from "Golden Boy" to "On the Waterfront," Cobb couldn't exactly pinpoint a favorite part he created. "You're speaking with a man who is in love with so many of my parts. You love all your children. Do you ask Jasha Heifetz what he likes to play?" But if singling out was required, the more-or-less favorites had to be King Lear (in the 1968-69 season Lincoln Center production) and Willy Loman (in Arthur Miller's "Death of a Salesman").

Creating roles to Cobb, despite any acknowledgement of his own talents, is a collaborative effort. 'I didn't take Willy Loman and build him. I took the genius of other people." The script is "The Thing" to Cobb. "I raise my sights very high. So there cannot be very many good writers or actors. Talent should always be very rare."

He is quick to defend the weekly format of television quality-wise by proclaiming that there's no such thing as a good series. "I don't care what Pulitzer Prize winner you've got. He can write only one or two good scripts." He doesn't like to see rough drafts of his scripts because he automatically begins developing characters. When the script is changed up, there's still something of the former self in the current project.

The 59-year-old actor rared back his head in laughter on his relationship to the Young Lawyers in the show. "I think they thought it would add something if the character (David Barrett, the fatherly figure he portrays) was on his last leg!"

Things are going well to him, even for a television series. "We're now in a period of birth pains, trying to get the logistics down." The cast is not fixed yet; Cobb feels additional members of the NLO will appear later in the season. "Maybe some religions will be offered!"

The highlight of "The Young Lawyers" to Lee J. Cobb, a concerned citizen, is that it sticks to convictions. "The chips can fall into a wider radius, even in commercial TV. Our time is coming." The important thing is not to give up one's beliefs. "Dream on what you believe in, but don't kill off

(Continued on P. 38)

Lee J. Cobb

the rest," he advised. Sage philosophy!

A longtime character actor, Lee J. Cobb is now billed as the lead of a show like "The Young Lawyers." Still people call him "the guy who played so and so." Cobb grinned that it pleased him as an attestment to his believability in certain roles. I asked him if he would rather go down in the all-time books, however, as Lee J. Cobb or as "the man who played so and so."

Cobb perked up, bowed his head, then perked up again.

Week Of March 20—26

Listings For Austin, San Antonio,
Temple, Waco

The most established "family" in television is the cast of "Gunsmoke", the durable Western series which is preparing for its 17th season. Pictured from left to right are Glenn Strange, James Arness, Buck Taylor (seated), Amanda Blake, Milburn Stone, and Ken Curtis, as Sam, Matt, Newly, Kitty, Doc, and Festus on the show. "Gunsmoke" producer John Mantley is interviewed on Page 3. Ken Curtis is featured on Pages 4-5. "Gunsmoke" airs Mondays at 6:30 p.m. over Channels 5, 7, and 10 (CBS-TV).

Lawrence Welk interview, by Hank Moore.
First published in June, 1970.

"Chit Chat"

HANK MOORE
Interviews LAWRENCE WELK

Welk and his Champagne Music Makers
entertain on ABC-TV's "Lawrence
Welk Show" Saturday evenings on
Channels 10 and 12.

Your show is one of the few that runs new episodes during the summer.

"I think it helps because they have too many reruns; there's not the interest there that you should have. It seems to agree with us; we've been busy for many years, and our kids seem to like it. It's a good format."

Do you think most variety shows have to narrow a variety of music?

"Of course we point our show towards the American family: mother, father, and the children. And in order to please all of those people, we have to have a variety; so we put on a few songs which the little children can enjoy. By the way, children like the bubbles best of all. We lose out a little bit on the teenagers."

Do you think teens understand you?

"They don't really dig that kind of thing. But on the other hand, I doubt if any kind of music could interfere with their life because when you get up to that age you're thinking pretty much so about your partner and the love business."

Do you think guest stars are an asset to your show?

"We've managed to get on quite a few. But actually it's very difficult for us to put on guest stars because we have 45 people in our own group, and whenever we put guest stars on, we have to miss someone in the orchestra. And it doesn't make a hit with the people that you hire by the year and then not use them. So we're not too crazy about putting guest stars on."

I'll bet you're always scouting around for new talents.

"We like to keep our eyes and ears open. We think it's important in a show that wants to keep on year after year after year, that

you don't grow old with it. And also like I'm doing with you here, I also have many friends around the country and put a bug in their ear to ask them to look out for. So you never know if sometimes you can do somebody a favor.

"The little girl and boy that we have, Ralna English and Guy Hovis, a married couple, are being accepted very well. She is from Lubbock, and he's from Mississippi. They were playing here in town at a little club, and one of our boys in the office came in one morning and said how good they were. So we tried them on one show; today they're getting more mail than anyone else in the band. They can do any kind of song; a sweet song or a swinger."

Did you ever fool around much with jazz or try to do any improvising?

"One of my first loves in life was dixieland music. I think I bought every record, and wore out many of them, that Red Nichols used to make with his wonderful dixieland band.

"Last time I played New Orleans, Pete Fountain, who used to be with me, came out with his limousine and picked me up at the airport. And everytime I have a chance to find dixieland bands, I'm always in front of the band listening to it."

Do they invite you to join in?

"I'm not that good! I somewhat enjoy it. Are you somewhat of a cat too?"

A pitiful clarinetist.

"I think Pete Fountain is the best clarinet player that we have in America. He understands the feel for music and his tonal quality. He plays very good; we don't have too many of the real good clarinet players anymore who play that type. He doesn't know this, but when he left my band, he broke my heart because I thought so highly of him."

One of the coming musical trends is to link jazz or classical sounds with rock to produce unique pop sounds.

"I like it; I noticed it in the recordings. Many of those groups (Chicago; Blood, Sweat, & Tears) have a bigger band. They quite often do those recordings in Los Angeles or New York City, and they take those older musicians that used to play in name bands and put them into orchestras in the background.   They really get good sounds."

Do you think classical and pop music can suitably compliment each other?

"To a certain degree, yes. There are some people who don't like both kinds, but I kinda like it. Of course I love any kind of music, so I might not be a regular run-of-the-person.

"I think a great many people who haven't had musical training only know what their natural talent allows them. If they're a little bit like I am: I actually don't understand some of the music that's being played nowadays. And I think the public is a little bit the same way. I wouldn't want to say that the newer music today is good or bad because I don't understand much of it. But when it gets too far out......

"For instance, I don't understand jazz too well. I understand dixieland jazz but not the modern jazz. Never did understand it!"

What touring will your band do this summer?

"We'll do altogether 3 weeks at Lake Tahoe and then another 2 or 3 weeks the rest of the nation. Our schedule is very heavy: we can't possibly take all the things that come to us. If we were to take all the offers, we couldn't sleep. America is a wonderful place; it takes a long time to make it when you're in demand."

Is it the cost of one-nighters that pro-hibits the big bands from coming back?

"It's not the cost that's involved so much. If we had the time where we could go out and do one-nighters, we could actually be kept busy for a long time. But there are many towns where we've had offers for the past 6, 7, or 8 years and still haven't had a chance to give them a date. The medium of television is so powerful that if a band makes good on television, you can really keep yourself busy from coast to coast."

Of course there are your recordings.

"We had a certain amount of young people accept some of our records. Another thing is we have a very good stable business. Our memory album or something like that doesn't sell millions, but it does sell 100,000 or 3 or 400,000, which are very good sales; and you come out very good."

Do impersonators flatter or bother you when they mock you?

"I think at first when we got out in business, while our skin was quite thin, it bothered us. But after awhile you get used to it and have an understanding that it's actually a very healthy condition. I did a show recently on the Lucy Ball show, and the whole show was around 'Wonderful, wonderful' and that 'one and a two' business. And it's a fun idea."

Do you pay much attention to critics of your music?

"We do, yes. We get about 5,000 letters a week, and about 98 per cent of them are favorable letters. So we actually watch the 2 per cent a little bit more than we watch the 98 per cent.

Walter Brennan interviews, by Hank Moore.
First published in December, 1970.

PLAYING AN OLD MAN SINCE HE WAS 30
. . . . Because His Teeth Were Kicked Out

by Hank Moore

HOLLYWOOD - "I'm from the silent picture days too. All those guys are kicking off. I've got to read the obituary column each morning to see if I'm here. And if my name's not there, I shave," chuckled one of the film world's most lovable characters. At 76, Walter Brennan is a veteran of 50 years in pictures and television. Everybody knows that squeaky old man; he's been in that role since he was a young man too.

"I was interested because they are good clean pictures," he remarked about going into CBS' "To Rome With Love" series, his fourth venture on TV. As we talked on the "Rome" set, I could see the affection for Grandpa Brennan from technicians to the two cuddly little girls who star with him and John Forsythe on the show. "I would rather be associated with something for the family than all these other lousy things!"

A veteran of more than 100 movies, Brennan starred on "The Real McCoys" for 6 years, "The Tycoon" for one, and "The Sons of Will Sonnett" for 2. By far, Amos McCoy was his favorite character. "I had trouble shaking that walk he had. It wasn't in the first 3 pictures. I have an arthritic condition in my back, and I got up walking that way one morning. They thought it was funny, and it was in the other 221."

One thing he has consistently been is lovable, having played villains in only 3 films. "I never had any aspirations of being a star; always had feature billing." But playing grandpas just stuck. "The only reason I first did it was from force. I got in a fight and got my teeth kicked out. I've been doing old guys since I was 30. I always figured I was very fortunate to have a job. And I think I'm very fortunate to be wanted at my age!"

Pantomime to Brennan is the finest art. "I work from here up," he annotated, pointing at his chin. "Very few lines, that's how I like to work. Pantomime to me is a much higher art than acting. I can watch Red Skelton forever; I think he's the greatest pantomimist in the world today. Marcel Marceau can't touch him."

Walter Brennan is the kind of guy who takes his lunch to work in a pail marked Amos McCoy ("just a sandwich, a couple of cookies, and my vitamins"), who loves the easy home life on his 10-acre spread in Thousand Oaks, California ("once I get home, I stay there"), and who downed the idea of a big shindig for his and wife Ruth's recent 50th wedding anniversary. "We never figured the kids had to be home. It's like one of my kids who went to war. He said, 'So long, Ma,' and my wife didn't even ring a tear. She's not the type; if that kid came back and she wasn't there, that would be his last memory of her. I thank my blessings 'cause I sure have them."

He's also the kind of guy to proudly admit watching all his old pictures when time permits. "It's like 'The McCoys.' They're pretty good shows. When I first saw them, I saw holes and bad things. You blot that out if you haven't seen them in a long time."

In addition to not aspiring to be a leading man, Brennan likewise saw no gleams of directorial talent in his lengthy career. "Not anybody can direct," he reasoned. "If you're successful at one thing, why be a jack of all trades. I've worked with some awfully fine directors, fine because they had an understanding of other people."

Walter Brennan (left) with Susan Neher (center) and Melanie Fullerton on CBS' "To Rome With Love"

A confirmed Republican, Brennan stands for "the Constitution as written. I'm for America first, last, and always. I don't care if a guy's a Jew, a gentile, a Negro...as long as he's for us. I am a Catholic and don't like what's going on in the church today either. Guys who think that because you don't think like they do, why that's a lot of bologna. It'd be great if we all thought the same; we'd have a totalitarian form of government." But he doesn't make controversy about having his beliefs; actually, he'd rather observe and respect those of a different nature. "Those political guys are always getting me to speak out and make a controversy of it."

Pretense is what gripes him about Hollywood, or any other business for that matter. "Everybody's gotta start somewhere. That's the thing that gripes me: they're always trying to give you the impression that it's always been like that. It certainly hasn't been with me. I used to fall off a horse for a buck. Sure this guy's a millionaire, or he hasn't got a dime; if I don't like him, nuts to him!"

The same common sense approach dips over into Walter Brennan's acting. "The dough doesn't mean a thing if I'm gonna be miserable. Your mental attitude toward a thing is very important. Even in your business: you get hold of some guy who gives you the business; that's no good. I like to have everybody happy. Because the main thing is the contented mind, which you cannot buy with money."

Working conditions to Brennan must be easy-paced to keep the cast and crew happy and alert. "When we were making those 'Sonnetts,' they said they'd do them in 3 days. I said, 'Not with me you won't! You'd better get Forrest Tucker. 3 days and 3 nights, no sir.' So they made them in 4 days and found it didn't cost them any more because they didn't get into overtime, which gets up to triple time. And you don't get the same performance if you work all night either. The next day you come in and you're half dead."

Retirement to Walter Brennan is definitely out. He plans to keep plugging away until the end. And with the set life for him is a steady stream of good-natured chiding and conversation. "Old flapjaw," as Brennan terms himself, is having a whale of a good time while doing things strictly professionally.

And he's everybody's favorite 76-year-old youngster because of it!

George Maharis and Yvette Mimieux interviews, by Hank Moore.
First published in November, 1970

HOLLYWOOD — Hot on the trail of mystery and adventure this season are two of the movie world's most glamorous people. George Maharis and Yvette Mimeux are the folks, and television is their arena for a change, as stars (along with Ralph Bellamy) of ABC-TV's "Most Deadly Game" series. (Saturdays at 8:30 p.m. over Channel 12).

Maharis is a broken field runner of sorts, I found as we lunched the other day. Rarely one to play life by the numbers, George has taken some falls as well as some glories. His biggest fall, that of his career, can be directly attributed to the week he spent in Austin, Texas, in February of 1962, where he was filming an episode of his phenomenally popular, "Route 66" series. It was in Austin that he contacted infectious hepatitis, an inflammation of the liver that had accumulated from overwork on the show; he had to taper off, then be replaced. For 2 years, George ailed, then he climbed back to the top in movies.

An astrology bug, he chuckled, "I'm a Virgo. We've gotta be involved in everything." Since the crew on "Most Deadly Game" has compatible zodiac signs, he feels there is a good working relationship on the set. "It's interesting to see how things come out by the astrological signs. But you cannot rule your life by it!"

There have been some uncanny correlations between "Route 66" and "Most Deadly Game," and Maharis has to look to the stars for an answer. Both titles were changed before they went on the air ("The Searchers" and "Zig Zag," respectively). There were deaths on both shows (a crew member on "Route" and costar Inger Stevens on "Game").

Miss Stevens was replaced by Miss Mimieux. "Yvette for my standpoint was on the top of the list," asserted George, who hopes he won't get sick again.

Television to him is a lot of trial and error, but that's the only way to work out the kinks into a good show. "TV is more expensive now and consequently more difficult to do the things you want to do," Maharis believes. "I think we really haven't made our pace yet. Like a swimmer or athlete, once you get in your stride, you hit it. It's terribly difficult to take a series and have an instantaneous success. It's like a successful marriage; you have to have time to adjust."

GEORGE MAHARIS
.....'Route 66" brought him to Austin

A believer in the free spirit, George cannot plan or speculate on a career. "I cannot be the chef and the gourmet. When we were born, they wound up the clock, and you might as well use the time well." A man of perpetual motion, Maharis loathes hobbies. "The word hobby implies   someone is bored and needs to find something to do." He does want to learn to paint, to "do exactly what you want and don't care what others think about it."

Another thorn in his side is censorship, which George feels shouldn't exist. "If you don't like something, turn it off," he charged at the people who would keep certain kinds of entertainment, no matter how

This Time They're Detectives!

By HANK MOORE

wild, from being available to the appropriate aficianados. "If they want to tell me what to read, let them pay my taxes!"

Reflecting back to "Route 66," Maharis feels it would have been even more popular today. The show was an extension of himself, the story of an adventurer who worked at such unlikely places as A&P, Sears, a garage, and a dance studio. "I found out how to use my hands quite young," he winked with a cheshire cat grin. If "Most Deadly Game" could do its investigating on location, he feels viewers would be much more pleased. "The feeling is much more different: the air, the sun."

An athletic guy, George works out at the gymnasium regularly and participates in many sports. A confirmed bachelor, he did participate in marriage. "I did that once. I don't do that twice!"

* * *

HOLLYWOOD — "I wasn't interested in doing a series until this season," explained lovely Yvette Mimieux, one of the movies' most comely creatures. Also a free spirit, the costar of "Most Deadly Game" is hardly what one might call a dumb blonde. "I have involvements!"

And most diversified too is Miss Mimieux, as we found out about her on another luncheon date. She wants to do deep sea diving and excavation digging. Her thirst for such adventure was treated last summer at Fiji and Tahiti, "the second largest barrier reef in the world," Yvette exclaimed with bubbling blue eyes and a slightly tilted head, projecting a lilting quality of personality.

She got into archeology on a vacation off the coast of the Yucatan Peninsula. "That reef ends just east of Honduras. And British Honduras is so unexplored. I'd just love to live on an unexplored Pacific island." That's just the way she modeled her canyon home in Beverly Hills, I found. "It's my own ranch, a little island," Yvette envisioned her life's surroundings.

For extra fun, the bouncy actress manages a rock group, Andromeda, a term she borrowed from Greek history, a reading love of hers. A born promoter, Miss Mimieux last spring turned filmmaker and produced celluloid on the musical combo for worldwide distribution as a short subject to movie theatres.

With a self-confessed yen to be a theatrical set designer, Yvette got into acting as a cofounder of Theatre Events, a Los Angeles group she organized while still at Hollywood High School. Director Vincente Minnelli saw her in one of their plays and introduced her to MGM, where there evolved a long-

(Continued on Page 29)

YVETTE MIMIEUX
.....one of the screen's most glamorous

YVETTE MIMIEUX........

term movie contract. "But I'm still going to sew and paint before I'm through," she gleamed.

Miss Mimieux, who also speaks 4 languages fluently and is a professional pho-

tographer, stressed the importance of characters on television who are likewise far from being dumb broads. "Vanessa Smith (whom she portrays to George Maharis' Jonathon Croft) relates to people as she deals with them. It's not just a job. A college-trained criminologist, she is feminine at all times; how often do you find that in the professional world!"

Both Maharis and Miss Mimieux could be mistaken for hellions in their own right. Adventurous and free-wheeling, yes. But they embody a breed of Hollywoodians who are free spirited, yet responsible citizens. Their thirst for life and adventure always concerns other people; they are not islands in their own interests.

"Chit Chat"

Editor HANK MOORE
Interviews DANA ANDREWS

Andrews, longtime stage & film star, stars on NBC's "Bright Promise"

Thanks Hank, Dana Andrews

I know you're a native Texan. Were you involved in acting around here?

came over to buy the stock of the company I worked for. Mr. Steck himself offered me

Andy Griffith interview, by Hank Moore.
First published in January, 1971.

COUNTRY CORN FROM
A SENSITIVE PERSONALITY

by Hank Moore

HOLLYWOOD — Andy Griffith can talk about anything on earth and make it sound like a comedy narrative. Spinning yarns with the master is always fun, I found out in an early-morning session aboard his own pride-and-joy vehicle, a motor home van, where the coffee's always brewing, with some casual chit-chat right behind.

Which is why his "Headmaster" series didn't work this fall. It wasn't the real Andy Griffith, and the viewers chanted for a format change to the style they knew and loved from all his other years on CBS-TV. "I'm glad we recognized that it was failing before we were told," he admitted. "And we went on and made our own change, me Aaron Ruben, the producer."

"The New Andy Griffith Show" is like the old one "in flavor. We use the front porch a lot," explained Andy. "After the very first 'Headmaster' went on the air, I went over to see Aaron and said, 'I'm homesick as I can be, and I miss playing scenes on the porch. And I wanna go home, I just have to'." In the old show and its descendant, "Mayberry RFD," the town was the star. "And here it's a family because I have a wife, 2 children, and my wife's sister lives with us."

To insure a big start for the show (Jan. 8), Andy had Goober, Emmett, and Don Knotts from the old show come to visit. Show number 2 (Jan. 15) has Glen Campbell, "playing himself. He did a fine job for us!"

But "Mayberry" did get along without Andy, as he knew it would. "I realized that was happening in our first year. We started out with 4 characters and kept adding them. And all of those characters made up a whole town and gave it a flavor. I think it will work right on."

I asked Andy how the 2 leading men on "Mayberry," he and Ken Berry, both low-key, differed. "We're both low-key, but I hit a little harder than Ken does, a little bit. You know, it's great when you find guys who really get along with one another. I have this big Winnebago bus and belong to a hunting club. Last Sunday, we'd take that bus. And these are really high mountains. And then we'd go up and shoot for awhile; me and Jack Dodson (who plays Howard Sprague over there) and Ken Berry and Lee Greenway (who's the makeup man for both shows and a world champion with a shotgun) and my little son went with us this time. There were 5 of us."

It was beginning to pleasantly sound like a famous Griffith monologue. "We had 3 90's strapped on the outside and a 90 and a 70 on the inside. Then we'd pull over out of sight of the club or anything and park the bus. I had a generator running and a television on where they could watch the ballgames. And we'd get on our bikes and must've ridden 30 miles up in those mountains. Aw, it's really run. It took us 2 weeks from before to heal!"

Suffice to say, it's a family-like atmosphere around Andy. "You take on one another's attitudes after awhile. We hired a little girl to play our daughter, 8 years old, named Laurie Rutherford. In the show that Glen Campbell was on, I asked her mother if she could sing. There was an old songwriter called the singing brakeman, Jimmy

Rodgers, who died in 1933. Well, I got one of his songs, called 'My Little Lady' and taught it to this little girl. And she winds up singing with my phrasing. She sang that with Glen Campbell, and it's really nice. Really nice!"

Griffith, who has guested on former co-star Don Knotts' variety series on NBC, feels situation comedy is more Knotts' bag. "It's difficult because it's all sketches. I think he needs some music in there somewhere," was the comedian's belief. "Of course he'd like it to run for awhile, I guess, but I don't think he really cares because he can do a situation comedy next year if he wants to."

Andy thinks he and Don find it hard to adapt to different characters besides themselves. "Oh, my Lord have mercy, I've got to tell you. I was over there with 'em, and it just took forever; it's really hard work. Don and I both basically play one character; he may take on different colors, though."

Helping other talents launch careers, like Knotts and Jim Nabors, makes Griff feel his oats. "Do you know a man named Glenn Ash," he quizzed. I replied affirmative. "Well, he's in our new show. He's a client of my manager. Don was influential in this whole thing, said he'd been down to Texas and met a really funny guy. There's a place out here called The Horn, and he asked me could I get him into The Horn so some people could see him. My manager got to going over there looking at him and signed him. We've used him in 3 shows so far, and in 2 of them he came off strong. He doesn't have any technique and doesn't know how to act; so we're trying to teach him."

Making solid careers for others, Andy feels, is good for both of them. "You get a guy who hasn't been seen all that much, and it helps the show if he's good, such as when Jim Nabors came along. And George Lindsey and Jack Dodson. Don and I had been old friends before he ever got on Steve Allen." One such person on the new show, I suggested might be former Miss America Lee Meriwether, with whom viewers may now identify on a weekly basis. "She's wonderful, very cooperative, and looks like a wife," Andy chortled.

I wondered what made Andy go into comedy. "There's something really strange that would make a person go into this. I used to be scared to death to walk out on a stage. Now I'm doing it all the time, but I'm scared to death everytime. You hear stories about people being scared to death, and you just wonder then if that's the truth, what would possess a person to go into that line of work."

continued on page 37

Andy Griffith and Mayberry pal Don Knotts

Andy Griffith Continued

Andy Griffith is still questioning his own fright and how he is trying to overcome it. "I have walked around that way all my life, feeling like an inferior citizen. And yet I have the presumption to walk out on a stage and demand that everybody in that audience look at me and listen to what I'm saying," he said in earnest, followed by a faint chuckle. "Now why those 2 go together, I don't know. But you'll find that's true in almost every case."

But fighting supposedly insurmountable odds kept Andy in the ring. "The last time I played up at Lake Tahoe, last spring, I found I was on the stage and wasn't scared. It fascinated me; I didn't know what was going on. The wohle time I found that I wasn't really scared to death; I was just so excited about it. When the man told me I couldn't sing: I'd spent all my life training to be a singer, and the man said I didn't have a good voice. He said, 'Your voice is overbrilliant, almost unpleasant.' I believed him and thought, 'What can I do?' And I don't know whatever possessed me to go home and ask a friend of mine if I could be in a play."

The play required a monologue, which he miraculously wrote. "I guess the inspiration came from where 'What It Was Was Football' came from. When I was in college, I played a sousaphone in the band, and guys used to pour drinks down the bell of the horn. A guy told me a dirty joke about a football game once, and those 2 things rattled around in my brain. One time I needed an extra monologue and made it up in the car on the way to the job. I never wrote it down; it was taken down from the record later on. Things will stay in your head, and finally they'll come out, I guess."

Analyzing his talent brings out the shyness in Andy Griffith, but he humbly knows he has got it. "But I tell you the truth, I'm so thrilled that I am in comedy, do understand it, can write a little bit, can perform comedy, and can recognize a good comedy performance that I just don't know what to do. It's just great. And I'm glad I recognized that 'Headmaster' was a bomb and walked away from it in time to hopefully change and salvage something."

"Chit Chat"

Editor HANK MOORE
Interviews DIAHANN CARROLL

She plays Julia Baker on NBC-TV's "Julia" (Tue., 7:30 p.m., Ch. 4,6,42)

Live From Hollywood

HOLLYWOOD - Escorted onto the lot at 20th Century-Fox studios in Hollywood, we were taken to the office-dressing room suite of Diahann Carroll, glamorous star of music and comedy. The interior was plush.

you get to the hotel, you take it off of the earphones, into your room, turn it on and rehearse all the show by yourself. You can have such FUN!"

Efrem Zimbalist Jr. interview, by Hank Moore.
First published in February, 1970.

"Chit Chat"

Editor HANK MOORE
Interviews EFREM
ZIMBALIST JR.

He stars as Inspector Lewis Erskine
On ABC's "The FBI" series

HOLLYWOOD - "I'm happy to be able to rest," sighed handsome Efrem Zimbalist Jr. at the prospect of finishing his fifth season on "The FBI." The actor stars as FBI Inspector Lewis Erskine and graciously welcomed us to his Warner Brothers set the other day.

"I'm a good script scanner but don't have much memory for anything else," he noted, questioning what other actors had as a secret to remembering things.

Strolling through the soundstage, he inspected a living room set. "If you used that phony stuff in a house, would you ever know it wasn't stone," he asked a technician who replied no. Zimbalist took mental note, as he is a great handyman around the house. "All the major work at our place, the construction, is now done. I like to touch it up a bit now and then." His hands, full of calluses, look more like a pair belonging to a carpenter rather than to an actor.

I asked about his regular visits to FBI director J. Edgar Hoover, and Zimbalist said his next was scheduled for May. "This man is apt to talk about any topic in the world that hits him. He is an extraordinary conversationalist who talks at great speed. A very agile mind!

Conversations with Hoover and technical advisers have taught Zimbalist much about the workings of the law enforcement agencies. "A lot of people think the FBI should protect others; they are not allowed to protect. It is primarily an investigative organization in interstate cases. One of the benefits, if you can call it that, to be derived from our show is to be shown what the FBI jurisdiction is exactly, what deliniation there

is; before, that was clouded in my mind".

He of course reads up on departmental changes within the bureau. "It used to be in kidnapping cases there was a week's delay in the FBI being able to cross state lines. Fortunately, that time has now been reduced to 24 hours, which is still a little slow. One of the things the Nixon administration is trying to bring about is teams formed to pool resources of the various governmental agencies, which is good sense."

"I'm not a director, but Philip Abbot, (co-starring in the show as Arthur Ward) is showing great promise," Zimbalist noted. The two did a special for a future air date based on the drama "Kansas City, I Love You." Abbott was directing the episode we were watching being filmed.

We had to ask Zimbalist about our idol, Audrey Hepburn, with whom he co-starred a couple of years back in "Wait Until Dark" "Audrey is an absolute perfectionist. I would break my back to work with her anytime as was almost the case in 'Dark'. We had about three weeks to go in our 'FBI' season when shooting on the picture started. Since both projects were at Warner Brothers, I jockeyed back and forth. After the season wrapped up, it was less hectic, but I was gasping for breath".

Zimbalist was born into European music royalty. His father, Efrem Sr., is a famed concert violinist. His mother, the late Alma Gluck, was a renowned opera star. Young Efrem studied piano and deep down must have yearned for a musical career.

(Continued on Page 30)

More Efrem Zimbalist Jr. Interview . . . . .

Between takes, he eyed a piano in a living room set where Erskine and lieutenants were to question a witness. He sat down at the instrument and began immersing himself in an original contata. The crew was treated. "I just fiddle around with that now," he noted somberly.

His first acting career had ended with the death of his first wife, Emily McNair. Zimbalist retired to the Curtis Institute of Music in Philadelphia, which his father headed for four years to,compose.

He returned to his second acting career via a soap opera, "Concerning Miss Marlowe" "That was great training. I had to wear these gray hairpieces, which were a terrible bore to put on."

Oh yes, he received fan mail. "The letter was always directly to the character, not to me. They'd say, 'You should treat her better,' and would take it very personal. They were either happy I'd done something nice or unhappy I hadn't, so who can you please!"

Like many soap opera exes, Zimbalist is occasionally recognized only as that character by steadfast "Marlowe" fans. "It's always a shock when they do," he asserted, because of the phenomenal successes of both of his TV series since then, "77 Sunset Strip" and "The FBI."

For years he would enter amateur art competitions with his charcoal and painting works. "I painted long enough to know what my limitations are," Zimbalist assuredly noted, a trick which he feels has also kept his acting in stride.

As far as other hobbies, he is an excellent tennis player, skier, and horseman. He will on weekends be seen tinkering with his ancient Packard at his Encino, California estate. Until "The FBI" begins shooting for next season in May, Efrem Zimbalist Jr. will be catching up on a lot of sleep. to boot.

The series is seen Sundays at 7 p.m. over channel 12, Mondays at 10:30 p.m. over Channel 10, and Tuesdays at 9 p.m. over channel 7.)

30

December 6-12
Listings for Austin, Waco San Antonio, Temple

Open daily from 7 a.m. to 11 p.m.

Accomplished actor Efrem Zimbalist Jr. shows his credentials as Inspector Lewis Erskine on ABC-TV's "The FBI," based on actual criminal cases from the Bureau's files. Sundays at 7 p.m. on Channel 12, Mondays at 10:30 p.m. on Channel 10, and Tuesdays at 9 p.m. on Channel 7.

Ed McMahon interview, by Hank Moore.
First published in May, 1971.

Ed McMahon and Johnny Carson on "The Tonight Show"

NEW YORK — Ed McMahon is one guy who both knows where he's been and knows where he's headed. A proverbial dynamo of energy, the towering force of the late night TV audience is every bit as cordial and conversational as is on TV. His on-camera assignment is of course as Johnny Carson's sidekick on NBC-TV's "The Tonight Show," and he has developed that feat into an art these past 9 years.

Visiting with Ed at NBC the other day, I chanced upon a jar of specially prepared Hellman's "Mahonnaise" on his desk. That originated as a gag on the show, with Ed claiming European ancestors as the namesake of the popular sandwich spread. (His 5th great grandfather was President of France.) "John and I will take opposite polls because it gives us things to fool around with. Would you believe I got 75 letters siding with me on the issue, one of them in French. We do the same thing with the pig and the horse. He says one is smarter; I say the other."

More than just a second banana, Ed is regarded by television viewers as a pacemaker, for his voice and presence adds solidarity to the products he sells on "The Tonight Show." One of the first to uncover W.C. Fields, Ed noted to me, "I won't say I'm responsible for his insurrection, but I'm a contributor. He was the first balloon buster; he fought pomposity."

As a child, McMahon adored the Fields brand of comedy. "I was a fan of his from the start. I must've seen 'My Little Chicadee' 200 times and can do it line by line." Such cornball humor used to bother him. "By liking slapstick, people thought I was in low taste. I've never liked opera. But I discovered that many other millions don't either and dig Fields too. So who's to say you're in low taste?"

The honors and titles have knocked on Ed McMahon's door many times since his popularity through "The Tonight Show" was firmly established. The Bedside Network named him Man of the Year. A chairman of Easter Seals and a devoted worker for Catholic University, his productional abilities are always being sought. In 1968, he was honored guest at the Austin Aqua Festival, an event which he remembers as one of his best experiences. "They named it Lake McMahon only for the day," he recalled of the visit where we had originally met. "The touching thing was the kids pouring their hearts out to finish. And after they got there, they fell into the water!"

He glanced at the calendar on the wall and began reciting projects ahead which would take him over the country: a beauty contest; a California trip; a visit to Florida for a housing community which he is helping to promote. (We looked over brochures and designs for the City in the Round, surrounded by water in the canal, with each home's backyard containing either a golf course or waterfront. McMahon wants to have the area's first McDonald's Hamburgers franchise.)

"It's scary. Your whole life is laid out for you," Ed commented. "I get to the point where I don't want a luncheon date, and I want the freedom to call people up." But he is still interested in building a reservoir of products to be spokesman for. There's already Budweiser Beer and Uncle Ben's Rice; now he is lining up an insurance company. "If you have a few years under your belt, people believe you," he reasoned as a father figure.

We talked about our mutual friend Frank Sinatra and his recent retirement. Ed thought that was a good thing to do. "Why not leave as the top entertainer in the whole world. Who else could teach phrasing to young singers better than Frank Sinatra." All of which will leave Frank free to do more of the humanitarian projects for which he received his Academy Award. "The poor guy is so maligned," Ed added. "He does more benefits and free things than people know about. For all the bad things you hear, there are 50 great things."

McMahon himself considers his work with Catholic University "not a token position. If I get involved in something, I really want to do it well."

The impact which he has made upon the public as an overall nice guy has been substantial. "The farther away from New York you go, the more important you are. Parking guys say, 'Hi, Mr. Budweiser' when they see me, like they knew me 20 years, and it's a great feeling. It's television that did it, bringing us people into the home as friends." He also thinks his personal magnetism may be attributable to his role as Carson's Number 2 Man. "There are more second bananas in the world than chiefs. More people see themselves as climbing second bananas!"

The public who identifies with Ed McMahon has shown it in little gifts and trinkets. He showed several of them to me: a sign saying "Ed's in town," a statue of W.C. Fields, the Lake McMahon street sign, the McMahon family crest, and a myriad of ornaments made from Budweiser cans and bottles (a lamp, pin cushion, and the most ingenious of all: pencil holders made by cutting bottles in half and simply regluing them the other way around, with the bottle neck against the bottom, serving as the stand).

Add to that the fact that "The Tonight Show" is a firmly established viewing habit, and that spells the cause of both Ed's success

A Skilled Conversationist

by Hank Moore

and his humility. He traced the day's schedule in preparing for the show, rehearsing, warming up the audience, and going on the air, the main ascent to showtime starting at 4:50 p.m. "The funniest thing is to be out town or on vacation, sitting in a club at 10 of 5. There's a little thing in my brain that tells me to jump up; I'm so married to that instinct."

Acting is in his scope too. Another idol of Ed's youth was actor Paul Douglas, a man who could be rough yet kittenishly gentle and warm, a very humanistic sort of character actor. "I saw myself as a kind of Paul Douglas, a part which is not being done by anyone now. I see myself as not totally married to the movies (should he leave TV after Carson's run is through). I'll still have my Products."

The demise of either he or Carson from the medium are improbable in the near future. Ed in fact wants to keep "The Tonight Show" as a long-running series and the

Continued on page 21

Ed McMahon *Continued*

show's "family" intact. "It's a habit, but I'm pleased. Jack Benny was so smart to develop a family. Everything we do stems from a family concept. Nobody worked with Milton Berle, but they knew Rochester and Dennis Day. Those family relationships were so true in their own day. That's built on love, and that's where you get junior high schools named after you."

Ed McMahon was leaned back in his office chair, looking at the momentos on his office desk, the pictures on his office wall: him with John Wayne, him with Johnny Carson, and him standing in front of the Jack Benny Junior High School in Waukeegan, Illinois. That to him is knowing what he did was worthwhile, some kind of public thanks. His daily gratification in the meantime is coming from homemade nick-nacks.

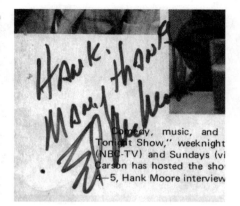

...dy, music, and ...Tonight Show," weeknight (NBC-TV) and Sundays (vi ...Carson has hosted the sho ...4—5, Hank Moore interview

"Chit Chat"

HANK MOORE
Interviews MACDONALD CAREY

One of Hollywood's all-time film stars, Macdonald stars on NBC's "Days Of Our Lives" daytime serial.

Transcribed from a telephone conversation.

How many days' scripts do you prefer to learn, several ahead or just one?

"Oh, only one at a time; because sometimes, as you know, a scene will be repeated from an exposition point of view with the

Gems stars of Canada (for the Expo) and Mexico. That was work too, really!"

You probably approach new audiences of fans that you may have never have appeared before in pictures.

Buddy Ebsen interview, by Hank Moore.
First published in May, 1970.

"Chit Chat"

Editor HANK MOORE
Interviews BUDDY EBSEN

_Buddy stars as Jed Clampett on
CBS' "The Beverly Hillbillies"
comedy series (Wed., Ch. 5, 7, 10)

Live From Hollywood.

HOLLYWOOD - Have you ever eaten a sweet tasting sauerkraut? It sounds impossible but delectable. Throw in a generous helping of Polish sausage and turnips, and you have a pretty tasty luncheon menu. The chef was none other than Buddy Ebsen veteran actor, television star, millionaire, and one of Los Angeles' leading citizens.

We had a rare treat: lunch with and fixed by the star of "The Beverly Hillbillies" himself, not to mention a private recipe of martini that bears no resemblance to the helping of corn mash Buddy serves as Jed Clampett on the show.

After a visit to the "Hillbillies" set, where the season's final episode was being filmed (with Phil Silvers as guest star), we journeyed with the star to his bungalow for two more hours of solid conversation. Though Ebsen was dressed in Jed Clampett garb, and very much looked the part, he didn't talk mountain talk, and the subject of the series was hardly brought up. After all these years, what can be said about "The Beverly Hillbillies" that already hasn't been said?

Ebsen is a guy with a zest for living. "When I go, they'll have to cut me up in pieces like a snake," he grinned as he served cocktails.

I called to his attention a mutual acquaintance, Fess Parker, who worked his way through the University of Texas as my father's janitor, and with whom Buddy co-starred in the "Davy Crockett" movie and TV series. I showed him a copy of the Parker interview in the Nov. 15th TV Digest, and Ebsen smiled. Slow and easy of movement, he observed, like Jed Clampett would "The boy looks well fed! Did he say any-

thing about me? That's nice to know."

He recalled accompanying Parker on a Texas homecoming to address the state legislature when "Crokett" hit. "It's nice, to be associated with a local fella who made his pile (of debris) there," Ebsen smacked.

Filming on the "Crockett" pictures Ebsen noted, was always behind schedule due shots. "Disney was flying in to check on us, and Norman Foster, the director, was rehearsing a scene that was two weeks late, pretending his doom was behind him. Disney arrived, walked up, noted that on the rushes a bear's zipper was showing, got back on the plane, and said nothing else."

Buddy Ebsen originally studied to be a doctor. Then he turned to dancing (his father owned a dancing school), performing for years on Broadway with his sister Vilma. Hollywood beckoned in the 1930's, but Vilma got more of the spotlight. Ebsen turned actor after W   /ar II service in the Coast Guard. "Crockett" established him as a character player and "Hillbillies" as a major star. He is an expert fisherman and sailor, having entered various yachting contests with his 38 and 35 foot sloops.

He is mainly a very involved man, feeling that because of his recognition to the public he can contribute an active role in civic affairs. He also wants to influence others to involve themselves with the issues of the day.

To wit: he serves on the board of directors of a Negro newspaper in Watts. "It's gotta be done in an incentive way," Buddy remarked in explanation of his encouragement of black power through black business ownership. "It is people doing their best

More Buddy Ebsen Interview.....

with what they've got. We (the board) turned a few corners for them."

Also chairman of the Cancer Fund, Ebsen serves on Mayor Sam Yorty's Citizens Narcotics Committee, organized in January, 1969. The group has been charged to study and implement ways of reducing problems created by marijuana, dangerous drugs, and narcotics by "law enforcement and by education. Those of us who are known can speak, enlighten, and educate the public on the facts and falacies."

Ebsen explained the committee's structure as not contributing to escalation of any drug problem because it does not make policy. It is not responsible to the legislature and is therefore not a figurehead for politics.

"Human nature, being what it is, will thwart or negate education as a major deterrant as long as an easy supply of dangerous drugs is cheaply available," the actor feels. "If we are to reduce the drug traffic, we must hit the sources of supply and distribution, however organized or makeshift they may be."

He suggested narcotics courts should be stepped up. "Too many delays could shut our work down."

The group has appealed to the Federal Communications Commission to discourage narcotic jokes on the airways. "A laugh makes it instantly acceptable. We may be the catalytic agent in that area," he noted.

Buddy is a personal and political friend of California Governor Ronald Reagan but is also a political realist. "If it weren't for the hatchet job Yorty did on Governor Brown, Reagan wouldn't have gotten elected," he mused, yet turned his head to a Reagan-autographed picture on the rear wall.

It turned out that both Buddy and myself share the Civil War period as our favorite period in American history. "So many great stories about the Civil War have gone for years without being told," he said, admitting that the Civil War has been his most consuming occupation for the last 18 years.

That consumption has included scouring pages of little known diaries of such as General McClellan. A couple of years ago, Ebsen was moved to write a play on McClellan, "The Champagne General," making the militarist the villain and Abraham Lincoln (whom Buddy termed a "political dark horse from nowhere") the hero. "I saw a play right in the pages of history and wondered why nobody wrote it before."

Wherever he and his family go, terming themselves as "tin can tourists," Buddy makes a point to dig into local history and whatever a town's implication with the Civil War might have been. "History is not trouble," he grinned. "It's a pleasure!"

An undisputed top star in Hollywood, Buddy Ebsen is lovable as the uncut character Jed Clampett, even to viewers that pan the rest of the show. A durable star, he seeks total community involvement and even suggested a project for us (one of his latest) as we were leaving: working with the Boy Scouts to encourage households to keep old refrigerators out of children's reach.

Actors as Directors feature interview, by Hank Moore.
First published in January, 1971.

ACTORS AS DIRECTORS
by Hank Moore

HOLLYWOOD — The natural inclination of top notch actors is to direct, to create films and plays of their own craft. Stars like Mike Nichols and Gene Kelly have dispersed their efforts entirely in the directorial vein while others are sampling the other end of the camera - and enjoying it.

Fess Parker

Fess Parker of NBC's "Daniel Boone" series is one such actor we talked with on the subject. He is directing because he feels more at ease behind the camera. "I'll probably hang in there with directing and maybe phase out of the acting field someday," the 6'6" pioneer figure reported.

Parker has directed his own show, as have other stars, who vow never again. "I think it would be very difficult for me to do a 'Mission: Possible'," stated its star, Peter Graves. "I'd have to have two shows in a row in which I was very light as an actor because you need a good solid 10 days of preparation to direct a show.

"And then, I don't like the idea of directing myself," he continued in explanation. "I don't know how Jerry Lewis works. Maybe he has somebody who watches him from off-camera while he is performing and suggests things to him."

Andy Griffith, who admittedly plays one character all the time, with modifications, doesn't want to spoil his performance by even wanting to know technically how he does it. "I get a certain sound in my ear about a line reading on a script or how a scene should be played. I have fairly good instincts, and I'll stay with it til I pretty well get what I want."

That concept will stick, subject to change by an objective director. "Unless somebody has a better idea, and quite frequently they do, it sticks," Andy reasoned. "So far as direction and camera placement, I don't have that knack."

But spearheading productions is for him, as witnessed by Griffith's executive producer role on his own weekly CBS series and on "Mayberry RFD" script conferences. "The only part about producing that I do not like is casting; I hate that. You have to turn down so many; only one person can get the part."

Eddie Albert
*....resident ecologist
on CBS' "Green Acres"*

Mike Connors

Eddie Albert of "Green Acres" asserted that an actor-director loses his objectivity by juggling both balls. "Both of them are serious jobs. Jerry Lewis has a special kind of thing: he plays himself all the time, and it's not a typical situation."

Albert mentioned "no great record of directors who are successful actors. Laurence Olivier did it once quite well, but there is not an awful lot of it. Nobody wants to do two jobs at once unless he is a little nutty."

Mike Connors of CBS' "Mannix" mystery series countered the no-direct rule with the nature of a star's work in a series. "On 'Bonanza,' Mike Landon can direct himself because he has a supporting cast and can afford to be light. I think I can write, however, and then act in something without losing anything."

Professional productions are financially rewarding, but amateur theatre lures actors for kicks. "Sometimes you get some very interesting talent," Connors observed. "And the enthusiasm you find there, you don't find in the professional ranks. Wow!"

"At night they come to give three or four hours," beamed Joseph Campanella, a lawyer on NBC's "Bold Ones" trilogy. "I say, 'Let me know when it's 11 o'clock,'" and they never do because they're interested, enthusiastic, and want to go on; whereas in the professional theatre there's always a couple who say, 'Can't we get out of here?' When you meet people who want to work for the sake of the work, not for the money or glamor, it's a pleasure!"

These are the guys who are not performing hams. Some like Bob Crane of "Hogan's Heroes" admit it. "I'm too much of a showoff to sit behind a desk or camera," he quipped. "That's really unfortunate for the other actors I might work with."

Peter Graves

Bob Crane

Hal Holbrook interview, by Hank Moore.
First published in October, 1970.

"Chit Chat"

HANK MOORE
Interviews
HAL HOLBROOK

Hal plays Senator Hays Stowe on the
new "Senator" segment of NBC-TV's
"The Bold Ones" Sunday night series
(9 p.m. over Channels 4, 6, and 42)

HOLLYWOOD—NBC's "The Bold Ones" has gone several steps bolder this season by delving into pertinent social issues from both sides. Each viewpoint is seen by "The Senator," and that segment is generating great enthusiasm in the pens of critics in what viewers are saying, and in the soul of the folks who are putting it together. Hal Holbrook IS The Senator, and he thinks he's onto a winner. And alas, he is out from the cover of Mark Twain to proclaim success with his own face; and it feels just fine.

"It's been a really nice experience, better than I thought it could be," he gleamed as we talked on their set at Universal Studios. "When I saw the scripts, I began to realize we were going to do very good things. And as we have done the shows, and I've watched the dailies everyday, I've seen the performance level and the director's work. I think that it's all been of a very high calibre, certainly for series television."

This week's show was a favorite of Holbrook and tells the story of an aging Senator (guest star Will Geer) who has perhaps outlived his effectiveness. "After seeing that sort of thing and when I know of the others, I think we'll come off pretty good."

I wondered why a show about a Senator hadn't been done before, and Hal supposed it wasn't marketable. "The network was not that anxious. We originally had that in mind when we did the pilot (aired as a made-for-TV movie) and there was considerable discussion after the series was picked up as to whether I would go on being a Senator or not. I felt we could get into areas that were most relevant and controversial and which would be able to bear down on people. I have a feeling that what makes stories interesting is not so much the methods but that you feel you are actually seeing real, live people."

I wondered why "The Senator" was included in "The Bold Ones." Holbrook expressed wonderment and added, "At first, when we were picked up, for a day or so I thought that we were going to be one of

that 'Four In One.' Next day I heard we were going to go on 'The Bold Ones,' which excited me because it meant doing 8 shows instead of 6. I like the concept of not having to do a full season of shows because I think it's more probable to get 8 good scripts of a pretty even quality, where when you try to get 24 scripts of a high quality it's much more difficult for one series to do."

Besides that, Hal wants to act a variety of roles. The creator of "Mark Twain Tonight" on Broadway, he will co some Twain concert dates after "The Senator" finishes filming.

The Holbrook-Twain linking goes back several years. "I first got involved in his work as an actor," Hal commented. "It goes back to my last year of college. I don't think I ever had a class where we had to read any of his stories." Now he can look critically at Twain's skill as an author. "Sometimes it got a little shoddy toward the end; he got bored of writing. And in those days you had to make books very long because they were sold on subscription with pictures in them, with fancy bindings. And people really bought the book for its cover and for the pictures inside as much as they did the contents. Books really had to be longer so people would think they were getting their money's worth. And Twain would have to extend a story out and out longer than he really wanted to. 'Huckleberry Finn' is a good example of that. So is 'Life On the Mississippi;' at the end of it he just filled it with stuff from travel folders and just rewrote it to fatten it up. Those parts are often not as good as the fore part of the book. If you just stopped reading when you weren't entertained anymore, that's it!"

Having done Twain in a concert of readings and anecdotes on Broadway television, and in personal appearances, Hal has found a number of routines most popular with fans, although he doesn't base concerts on requests per se. "I usually have a pretty

(Continued on Next Page)

More Hal Holbrook Interview . . . . .

good idea of what I want to do. If I don't, when I get out there, I just do what comes to my mind. I think people like the Old Ram story a great deal. A lot of people have seen the Italian guide thing and like it very much. People love the ghost story and want to hear that; it's the only thing I repeat a great deal."

It was the TV interpretation of Twain that brought Holbrook an Emmy Award nomination and the linking in the public's minds with old Mark. "That's what television will do for you," he remarked. "That's one reason I wanted to do this series, so that I could try to get people to be familiar with me as I am and not as Mark Twain. It would

Hal Holbrook as Sen. Stowe talks with Bernie Hamilton (r)

be kind of creepy if all these years have the character you play completely obliterate you, and after a few years it kind of gets to you. It's nice to do different roles; I got hung up on that one."

Hal Holbrook's biggest longing is to do a western. "I've been out here for the past year riding horseback every weekend to get all in shape for that," he confided with boyish amazement. He doesn't care whether he is a hero or villain, "just as long as I can shoot and get on a horse, that's all." I admonished that they didn't allow such violence on TV anymore, and Hal said he would settle for shooting jack rabbits!

All sorts of historical characters enchant Holbrook. He did Abraham Lincoln on stage. One of his earliest assignments was a storybook of various characters: Disraeli, Prince Albert, poet Robert Browning, and a lot of Shakespeare. "You would be amazed how much material there is on historical characters if you really want to go and hunt it out," he observed. "For instance, if you are doing Richard II, there is a book called 'The Last Plantagenot,' which is quite entertaining and historically accurate about the

cruelty of the period. I was working on John Adams at one point and thought I was going to be in a play, started doing research on him, and had no idea he was such a fascinating character. When you're doing Shakespeare's plays, even the plays themselves can be approached on a rather scholarly point of view finding out the different interpretations, words, phrases, and scenes. It gives you a lot of food for thought."

Holbrook has 2 movies in current release. One is "The People Next Door" and is "involved with the drug situation in a suburban area, fathers and mothers like most of us who just don't understand what the devil is all about." And then a role in "The Great White Hope," with James Earl Jones. Hal feels the film script of "Hope" is better than the stage version because a lot of fat (a la Mark Twain) has been cut out.

Hal and his wife (actress Carol Rossen) are a rare example of a married couple watching and enjoying television sports together. "My wife is a nut on football," he sighed. "I wouldn't be watching if it wasn't for her. She watches 2 or 3 games on the weekend. On New Year's Day she watches 3 bloody games of football. I can't stand it that much, but she is in there!"

Reasoning is Hal's bag is "The Senator", and it would be great if both sides of the political issues were put into the hat, we both agreed. "It seemed odd to stop in the middle of a suspense story (the Senator's premiere on NBC Sept. 14). Then for 7 minutes 2 guys (Senator, policeman) sit at the end of a table and talk about that. While there was no resolution of that, you got 2 points of view. What we wanted to do on the show is have people with opposite points of view talk to each other. Because it seems lately in the country everybody is afraid to talk to each other; they apparently believe one thing or the other and don't want to talk about it, to try to arrive at some understanding."

Openmindedness to my belief is the key. And Hal thinks that might be the viewpoint of "The Bold Ones." For political ideologies are certainly not spouted. "I don't know if we have any sort of crusade in our series. Without pushing it too hard we would just like people to understand things," he asserted. "I don't think it's up to us to say one or the other is right. It's up to the audience to try to decide. The main thing is to let people think about it."

The Odd Couple, Tony Randall and Jack Klugman interview,
by Hank Moore. First published in October, 1970.

DOPY NICE GUY & STRANGE BIRD

by Hank Moore

TONY RANDALL
Tony is Felix on ABC's "The Odd Couple,"
Thursdays, 8:30 p.m., Channel 12.

JACK KLUGMAN
He plays Oscar on ABC's "The Odd Couple,"
Thursdays, 8:30 p.m., Channel 12.

HOLLYWOOD - Jack Klugman is a dopy nice guy on ABC's "The Odd Couple." In actuality, he is a nice guy who is far from being dopy. At the drop of a hat, he can portray a lovable character or then turn into a sinister villain. That's how versatile he can be, though he feels "Odd Couple" is more in his element.

"When I heard they had Tony Randall, I was interested," he reflected on how the series was put together. As we talked on the set at Paramount Studios, Jack noted that "Odd Couple" was the most expensive half-hour comedy on the air this season. "They were going top-notch all the way!"

Trained on the stage, Jack swears by television as gospel and as "the only way to get rich. As good as it is, you do 'The Odd Couple' or any series to make money." Financially speaking, he talked highly of Universal Studios, where he has worked most often in Hollywood doing most of their shows as a guest star ("Name Of the Game," et al). "They've always been good to me, always paid top dollar!"

The Neil Simon comedy, "The Odd Couple," was nothing new to Klugman, as he had replaced Walter Matthau on Broadway in the role of Oscar (likewise his role on TV). "I replaced Walter in New York in this play and made the mistake of going to see him," Jack sighed. "He was too great!" (Eddie Bracken later appeared opposite him in the part of Felix.)

He too chants the genius of Neil Simon. "The comedy's not that sophisticated," Klugman reasoned. "It is opena nd slapstick in a way. If it does fail, we've given it all we have. If it's a hit, I'll be in the production business looking for my own stuff. I should have done it 10 years ago and gotten it out of the way."

There's a lot of ad libbing done on the show, as directors like Jerry Paris (the Dick Van Dyke show), who was doing the show while we were visiting Jack and Tony, are constantly keeping the set uproarious.

But the scripts got careful scrutiny in the show's beginning, said Jack. "Tony and I agreed independently of each other on our criticisms of the script. We said that they were cartoon characters, and we cannot do that kind of show. They rewrote it, and everything came out well."

I marveled that Jack was particularly good in "Goodbye Columbus," a film which he agreed was one of the greatest things he ever worked in. He feels it could have been updated (the contraception methods used were out of date), though "the picture worked because there was a lot of love in it." He personally was most touched by his own scene with his daughter (Ali Mc-Graw) at the brother's wedding, in which pop tearfully told daughter she was a very good girl, and that he would never be ashamed of her; he did become ashamed of her at the picture's end.

As far as the next most exciting time in his career, Jack lauded working with Ethel Merman on Broadway. "She is my love" he gleamed. "I had heard such stories that she was a pain. Now I'd cut off my arm for her!"

As director Paris and costar Randall cut up during a scene rehearsal, Klugman breaks into a typical Oscar grin, inimitable even by Matthau. "You've gotta break it up once in awhile." Levity is one thing for sure that the "Odd Couple" set has got!

A veteran of live television and one forgettable series ("Harris Against the World" on NBC's "90 Bristol Court"), Jack Klugman acting and comedic talents are developed just fine, thank you, as "The Odd Couple" graphically attests each week!

HOLLYWOOD - Tony Randall is one of the world's most talkative sorts. A strange bird, he has an uncanny memory and an oh-so-wry sense of humor. A natural to bring Neil Simon's "The Odd Couple" to television is Randall, with whom I chatted madcap style over on their set at Paramount Studios. The series airs over ABC-TV Thursdays

"I think you'll find it easy to believe I haven't been offered anything as good as 'The Odd Couple'," Tony proudly pro-

claimed as his return to series television. (He did "Mister Peepers" with Wally Cox in 1953-55). "I feel the role of Felix was written for me. The thing is everyone who has ever played it was very good." Jack Lemmon, et al!

The show to him is "too good to be true this far. And it's not because of star talents either. The only star is the writer," he said in praising adaptors of the Simon storyline. "There's only one Doc Simon. But we've had a few scenes he need not be ashamed of." Randall played Felix on the stage in Las Vegas and Chicago, so he knows the script thoroughly, a photographic memory no less.

The uncanny Randall memory covers the gamut of radio trivia. "I know these things," he said with trademarked Tony Randall assurance. "I can still recall days and specific details about them. I just cannot explain it." And those Johnny Carson shows where he reeled off facts and figures were spontaneous.

To test, I asked the name of Stella Dallas' daughter on the old radio serial. He not only identified her as "Lolly, played by Vivian Molly, who now plays old ladies on commercials" but asserted that Ann Elsner, who played Stella, "now runs an antique shop."

To that, Tony topped the performance by reciting some 1930's vintage Sherlock Holmes movie dialog and sighed, "It astonished even me!"

Radio to him, as a performer, was a farce. "What kind of work was that? You would go in there, read through a part, and put it on air. And most of the time they would hire someone to read for them!" That's how Randall got his start, as a "reader" for Henry Aldrich.

Tony Randall has done Broadway and films, and poor or untimed writing bothers him. Scenes inserted for padding are annoying and should be cut out. He noted that this is how the Pigeon sisters were introduced into "The Odd Couple," as a shortening factor for the stage play. "They had to bring down the curtain somehow before things dragged along much longer. After the Pigeon sisters, the audience laughed so hard that it didn't occur to them to disbelieve the show after 2½ hours."

His secret ambition is to be a writer, to turn out masterful dialog worthy of Neil Simon. That's Tony Randall's very quiet dream. He is only very verbal on things when he is overly assured of them, which in itself is a Tony Randall trademark.

Barbara Walters interview, by Hank Moore.
First published in April, 1971.

Personable Hostess Finds Keeping Company An Art

By HANK MOORE

NEW YORK — The inquisitive girl re-porter on NBC-TV's "Today Show" is quite a busy-bee, combining family and work into a demanding schedule. Once in a blue moon, Barbara Walters will take some time off. Otherwise, she keeps America informed and entertained each morning on "Today", which seems to be a habit for too many mil-lions of people to count at one whack.

Just back from a week's vacation, her first without work thrown in, Barbara told me of the commencement address she de-livered at Ohio State University. "They awarded me an honorary doctorate degree, and if it had come from a small Eastern all-girl college like the one I attended, I would have been pleased. But no one there was as surprised or thrilled as I was at it coming from a University like Ohio State." The University's president, a fan of "Today," wanted a female speaker, and it gave her the opportunity to talk on women's rights.

"If I have one complaint against women's liberation," she said, "it has given the women who want to stay at home a national inferiority complex. Do not be intimidated. I know a lot of very dull, unrewarding jobs — and a lot of dull, unrewarded women who work." She feels the furor over women's lib has made the worthy cause of improving laws and working conditions simply "the number one butt of the come-dian's joke."

Barbara was the first of the television news personalities to be granted an exclusive interview with President Richard Nixon, with their chat on the March 15 edition of "Today" launching a series of fireside ses-sions which have since included the other TV networks. "The problem with the Presidential press conferences is that you're not able to follow anything up, and when you do the interviews individually, you are. I'm sure CBS and ABC were not pleased that he picked NBC and 'The Today Show'

Barbara Walters
....panelist on "The Today Show"

and me for the first," she reasoned for the President's new approach to the press.

Nixon asked Miss Walters during the course of the discussion her views on his TV image. "He did the show because he does realize the importance of 'Today' in Wash-ington. It's very high-rated because we do so many political features. And also, he and I have had a good working relationship in the past. I have interviewed him before, and a year ago he actually arranged for me to talk with Prince Phillip of England."

She worries about interviews afterwards. "Everytime you ask a question, particu-larly when you are working against the clock, you think, 'Is this the best question I could have asked?' I was talking about this with Walter Cronkite the other evening, and he said he has never done one against the clock," Barbara confided. "I'm a terrible second-guesser, asking was I too forward in talking about the President's image and saying there were those who thought him too stuffy!"

It takes practice to develop a technique, and Barbara believes in doing her own leg work in researching and obtaining the exclusive interviews. With subjects like Mamie Eisenhower and Ethel Kennedy choosing her and "Today" over others, the secret to her is simple: "I try to find the reasons that will incite these people to come on the program. You can't really teach somebody to interview. You can only give them some pointers."

Barbara Walters likes to be liked by both her subjects in the interviews and the audience watching. "I think the beligerent interviewer may make flashy television for a short time. Especially the hard-to-get per-

Barbara with President Nixon
....his "Today" interview
launched a series on the networks

son, who doesn't really need the publicity... it's important that they feel that you like them. If they feel comfortable with you, they will talk more. They also have to realize in these long interviews that you're not out to embarrass them, that you're not out to kill them. And this doesn't mean that you cannot be frank."

Dick Nixon a stuffy man! Barbara felt the context of their meeting was right and threw out prepared questions in lieu of a heart-to-heart talk, thinking he felt comfortable discussing his image with her. "When I thought of it later: to call the President of the United States stuffy? But you have to react to a certain extent to the climate you are in, and there's a certain line you don't cross into rudeness or being too personal."

Traveling "The Today Show" seems to score with audiences (with Rumania the next scheduled tour), and Barbara looks forward to a new wealth of subject material from new locales. "We try to travel individually, those of us on the show, to give it a different flavor other than New York. I was in Texas very recently myself!"

The fact that "Today" is doing great guns in television, when other shows around it are in economic and creative straits, reaffirms to Miss Walters the nation's thirst for substantial information. "It's very straight, the way we do it, and is quite heavy programming for any hour of the morning. I'm happy to say that the FCC cutback or loss of cigarette advertising has little effect on our day-to-day life."

Last fall, Barbara had a book published. "How To Talk With Practically Anybody About Practically Anything" is getting good sales and negotiable attention from men. "I just received a big fan letter yesterday from Barry Goldwater about the book," she bubbled. I commented that he stands in recent history as one of America's most misunderstood men, having "mellowed" in the public's eye since the 1964 campaign. "I think he is becoming more understood," she replied. "Maybe attitudes are!"

If information contributes to changing attitudes, "The Today Show" has to be a front runner in the trend. And Barbara Walters is proud of the opportunity to be a part of the working team behind it.

Burt Reynolds interview, by Hank Moore.
First published in March, 1970.

Sense of Humor, Rugged Actor Makes for Personable Image

By HANK MOORE

HOLLYWOOD — If one can be rough-and-tough yet gentle at the same time, Burt Reynolds surely fits that category. As the star of ABC—TV's "Dan August" series, Burt is a pursuant police detective. His off-screen remarks are off-the-cuff if not off-beat. The big guy is quite friendly and gently perceptive.

The cutdown of violence on television has even extended to the "American Sportsman" series, which we commented on seeing the day before, as we chatted in his dressing room at the Sam Goldwyn Studios, where "Dan August" is filmed. The program's content was reduced to fishing; no game was shot. "You're not going to learn something about fishing that you didn't already know," observed Burt of the sequence featuring "Gunsmoke's" Milburn Stone and Ken Curtis on an aquatic expedition. "You learned that these guys really love each other. It was a very entertaining little show."

Strangely enough, Reynolds thinks big game hunters do the most for conservation, though they kill a lot of beasts. "And we're

not talking about guys who go out and get a leopard skin for some broad's back!"

In college, Burt Reynolds was a star athlete. A high school footballer in Palm Beach Florida, he got bids from as far away as Baylor University and Tyler Junior College. Burt recalled really wanting to go to TJC most of all because he had a girlfriend there. He finally took a halfback position at Florida State College but did make it to Texas to play ball one time; it was a Sub Bowl clash against Texas Western College (now known as the University of Texas at El Paso).

An avid viewer of television sports, Burt digs the styles of Howard Cosell and Don Meredith. "Any guy who says Howard Cosell is a good commentator and who says Don Meredith is bad because he has an accent is wrong. I hope he doesn't like me." He thinks Meredith's objective analyzing is enhanced by the down-home approach. "Cosell was made a star because he had a black hat on!" He and Meredith are teaming up for a comedy-western made-for-TV movie, produced by Aaron Spelling. "It's the Bob Culp-Bill Cosby kind of adventure thing, and I'm coaching Don, who is a very good friend, on his acting techniques. We'll see what comes out of it!"

There's a very definite southern accent in Burt Reynolds' talk, as well as Cherokee blood. Earlier in his career, he did numerous specialty roles as Indians, like the blacksmith he played for a couple of seasons on "Gunsmoke" shows. "If somebody called me a dirty halfbreed one more time, I thought I was going to throw up!"

Such was the feeling he translated into one of his best achievements, this season's "Run, Simon, Run," a made-for-TV movie which he did with Inger Stevens. "They got

more mail for that show than any they had ever done. It was like they discovered me after 12 years," he proudly reported. "People who didn't know me started looking for something else I was in and started watching 'Dan August'." He snickered at the review that equated his performance very stiffly to

TV DIGEST
ANNIVERSARY ISSUES:
JULY 3rd & JULY 10th

Burt Reynolds

a piece of wood. "I got letters from chicks saying, 'If you're a piece of wood, I'd like to be a carpenter'."

Reviewing "Dan August's" contribution to the television medium this season, Burt felt it was in the area of quality dramatic production ($250,000 budget per show, of which his salary is $20,000). "No matter how you sliced it, Dan August was still a cop. When you're on film 90 per cent of the time, it's hard to be interesting. It's difficult for Lawrence Olivier to be interesting as a police lieutenant."

Some scripts had more than one murder in them, which made cross investigations and a more intriguing show possible. Burt feels August's strength was in not taking sides on the issues and making the stories a whodunit to the end. "We played moment to moment, just as he investigated."

The series met stiff competition this season, in part from "Adam—12," which is in the same genre as "Dan August." Burt joked about his other opposition: "If the CBS movie is lousy - and they must be getting down to mine by now - then we're in good shape ratings-wise. The only new thing about Dean Martin is the color of his hair!"

With the series completed, Burt is up for a picture opposite Candice Bergen. His own production company is developing a story for hopeful filming. He noted that it would have to be pretty off-beat to sell at the box office. "If I could make up the most interesting biography for the now generation would be the ex-killer as opposed to the war hero. You never see Audie Murphy on the talk shows. Every night you turn on the television and see some guy who just got out of prison who now makes flowers in Pasadena. And those will just be the actors we'll have in our story. I'm still working on the storyline!"

When not shooting in Hollywood, Burt is off to his native Florida, where he owns the ranch once occupied by gangster Al Capone. "I'm threatening if things get bad to go back and bulldoze the house and look underneath. There must be something there!"

Sense of humor is the order of Burt's day . . . everyday. His strength is his ability to laugh at life's little tragedies. One example was the cast that he was wearing on his right hand. Having done his own stunts for many years, Burt recalled never having broken anything major. It was during a dramatic scene in "Dan August" that he slammed his hand down on a desk that his first casualty came.

Burt Reynolds joked about his ex-wife Judy Carne, having seen her recently on the "Super Comedy Bowl," getting shoved through the window by a football player. "Gee, I cheered. I wanted to do that several times while I was married to her!"

Exchanging quips with Reynolds is a good time. That's why he is so in-demand for the talk shows. His humor is wry; his attitude is cheerful; and his conversation holds no bars.

Johnny Cash interview, by Hank Moore.
First published in May, 1970.

"Chit Chat"

Editor HANK MOORE
Interviews JOHNNY CASH

The troubador of country music
stars in his own weekly ABC-TV
variety-music series.

Live From the Grand Ole Opry House
in Nashville.

NASHVILLE - A visit to Music City is always enhanced by the presence of the Main Man. Johnny Cash is country and western music's Man of the Hour, and all eyes across the country - and in his own backyard - are on the husky 6'2" singer with his own gutsy, while oh-so-sincere approach to the songs of his land.

We made the scene at Nashville's historic Grand Ole Opry House, where Johnny's oh-so-popular ABC-TV weekly variety series is rehearsed on Wednesdays and Thursdays. We were at the Thursday afternoon session in preparation to an evening taping before an adequately packed house.

Johnny Cash was dressed in casual black slacks and a black shirt. He was coughing heavily and admitted feeling ill the last couple of weeks, though his show must go on. He pointed out a transistorized, battery-operated microphone, which he had attached to his shirt and therefore could be heard sound man willing - wherever he walked.

"It just calms me down," Cash noted as he lighted up a cigarette; he kicked the smoking habit last year but resumed again recently. He is called over to introduce an act (Tom Hall and the Glazer Brothers) while camera shots are set up; he hides the cig behind his back surreptitiously. The introduction is to talk about the boys coming from the back country. This time, Cash pulls a stagehand into camera angle and in jest redoes the introduction to him - and to a howling crew - "As I said before, the wind blew them off their little irrigating field and and into Nashville, where they got filthy rich. How about that!"

As the Glazers again run through their number, we join Johnny on a darkened living room set for a sat. He looks admiringly at the stagehands dressed in similar black outfits (with "Johnny Cash" scrawled on their backs.) "Those guys know how to work that junk. They put out their most for this show."

I observed that Nashville is becoming a booming TV production center, for financial and artistic reasons. "I'm in awe of how they do this and keep organization. I guess I'm their most cooperative worker!"

He starts getting edgy. "I can't sit still. So if you like to walk around alot, you're in good company," he chided. We were walking around, Cash with his arms crossed, when he suddenly looked up at the gallery, where a rehearsal audience had assembled. The look on his face was that of consternation; then he sheepishly turned his back to the audience, picked his nose, and sheepishly turned back around. "I couldn't let them see that," he chortled.

That little act appears to be the key to, Johnny Cash, the man and performer. He knows all eyes are on him and is uneasy. He appreciates the adulation of fans but feels they are overdoing it. "I worship astronauts and statesmen," he confided.

The Glazers finish, and Cash leads the crew in a round of applause. Then on come Tex Ritter and Roy Acuff, doing a portion of a show-long salute to the Country Music Hall of Fame, which will not be seen until May 13. I feel in the presence of giants, he said as the two greats were on camera; he sits admiring them, as Ritter interjects, "You haven't done so badly yourself, Johnny Cash."

More Johnny Cash Interview

We talked to Ritter, and he made lots of political patter; he is running for the Republican Tennessee Senatorial nomination to oppose Albert Gore in November. His credentials include a degree in political science from the University of Texas at Austin. Roy Acuff stood by playing with his yo-yo and carefully chiding the candidate.

While Cash is pacing, a lady comes over from her balcony seat to where Cash is standing on the stage 10 feet below. She tries seemingly in vain to get his attention and muses how to get her autograph book down to him. When the singer finally turns around and sees her there, he grabs for a stepladder and steps up to obligingly sign her into his permanent fanclub of devotees, so to speak. We observed her beam with pride as she returned to her seat. "I'm shaking," she remarks. "I almost gave up there!"

Afterwards, Johnny settles down in his dressing room in a building adjoining the Opry fro a serious chat. He sips coffee from a paper cup, and mocks a comedian's face: "This paper cup tastes better then the coffee does."

"We're in what used to be a honky-tonk called Possom Holler," he explained. "Roy Acuff bought it, and we're leasing it from him for dressing rooms and sound control rooms. I just feel comfortable in the whole Opry Hall complex; I really do. I was a regular on the Opry for only a year, but I've been a guest on it many, many times, and it's one of the best audiences I've ever played to."

I asserted that the prison crowds must be the most gratified bunch he has entertained. On that note, a tear came to Johnny's eye: "People say I've had hard times. Well, those guys know it; they've been down many crooked roads and need the compassion shown them."

His spritely wife, songstress June Carter, sauntered in. They had done a cute rendition of "Darling Companion" for the evening's show. She looked tired but smiled at being back to work on the show.

She talks about the family: 4 girls by Johnny's first marriage, 2 by her's and their newly born baby boy, John Carter Cash. "My girls live with us and are the greatest little helpers with baby John," "Johnny's girls come in the summer to visit. Sometimes we get them on holidays. I'd say we've seen them on the average once every 6 weeks. Johnny calls them quite often, at least once a week; we really try to keep in contact'"

For hobbies, Mr. and Mrs. Cash like to fish. They have frequently dinner parties, estimating 98 per cent of their friends are in the music business.

"I had a voice like a bell, a high soprano, to the time I was 18 years old," Johnny recalled as discussion turned to his musical virtuosity. "I remember once when I was 5, walking miles to hear a travelling singer named Bob Steele. Afterwards, all of us lined up for his autograph. Even at that age, I know I wanted to be a singer. I looked at Steele and thought, 'You don't know me now. But you will.' It took me 20 years."

We brushed over his well-known hard times. "They are gone for good, and we all know it," Johnny Cash humbly admitted. "I'm happy to be alive, lucky to be alive. I know damn well I'm a good man."

Hugh Downs interview, by Hank Moore.
First published in June, 1970.

"Chit Chat"

HANK MOORE
Interviews HUGH DOWNS

Hugh hosts NBC-TV's "Today Show"
and various other specials of news
and social interest and education.

From New York.

It's about noon your time. Are you ready for some sleep after a hectic morning's "Today Show" schedule?

"I wish I could! Sometimes I fall on my head right after the show and take a nap, and sometimes I'm up until way late. But there's no real pattern. Maybe there ought to be."

How do you spend mornings after the show?

"Usually by digging myself out from under a mound of stuff on the desk: other projects, some personal, some show. Meetings with the writers sometimes go until noon. I get everything wrapped up, and I disappear. Sometimes I'm here to 3 or 6:00. That's not a complaint because it's a free country, and I can always quit; it's not bondage, but it does get heavy."

I guess you do much reading.

"Yes, there is a great deal of reading connected with the show. I don't read every word of every book that comes out by any means. But it's possible, by getting reviews of the book, written by a staffer who read it, that you can get an adequate idea of the book to discuss it with the author, the guest. So I probably read about 15-20 per cent of them."

Have you contemplated taking speed reading?

"You know, I never formally studied that, and I don't read terribly slowly. But speed reading shows some records that are fantastic. I read at different speeds anyway; on some things I sail along. But there are things that must be near the periphery of my ability to comprehend, and I have to read them very slowly. I've been reading Toynbee lately and am fascinated with him; and every paragraph is worth stopping and thinking about after you've read it. He really is a superb historian."

Do you take any technical journals?

"A little bit. I've been interested in genetics and read some of that. I get the bulletin of the Atomic Scientist. But I really don't have that much of a grasp of quanto mechanics to follow them on the highly technical aspects of it. I do better where there's a good scientist writer who can digest this stuff and then put it out toward the interested layman; and there's still some mathematics in it."

Is it even workable to write the complicated for the lay reader?

"One of the problems, as C.P. Snow points out, is that the bridge of communication between some of these extremely specialized and advanced disciplines is such that the ordinary John Q. in the street is caved in. I got an idea of that from reading Ettington in the stuff he published from 1921-31, that you might have things literally forced into a translation of the English language from a mathematical language and becomes ludicrous.

"And it's the inadequacy of the language that is ludicrous, not the concept. The big danger is that atomic physics cannot be gotten across to a layman. And the fact that it has fiery, direct application to his life makes it all the scarier. The scientist is no longer a guy in an ivory tower who doesn't really matter to the community, because he has shown that he really does. There's kind of a distrust of scientists among the lay public because they represent awesome forces of nature that can be unleashed."

Continued on Page 29

More Hugh Downs Interview.....

Your major social concern seems to be ecology.

"The subject which I've dedicated everything I do outside of 'Today,' and a lot of it on the show, is the idea of saving this planet, the environment catastrophe that must be staved off."

Do you think Earth Day had a good impact?

"I think from a public education standpoint it can't help but be good. People must come to know in time that the earth is limited and overcome the frontier psychology of thinking that if you louse up one place you just move on to a new wilderness."

Will interest be translated into action?

"I think that's going to be forced even before the very young grow up. It'll have to be or we'll choke on the air and gag on the water. Some harm has already been done that may be quite severe and will take the earth awhile to recover from. It had to happen: I think the New York Daily News said it was a Communist plot to undermine our way of life! If that's our way of life, let's get it altered a little."

Why hasn't the legislation gone through already?

"There's an awful lot of lethargy on the part of companies with responsibilities to stock holders. The far-seeing companies

Hugh Downs is always investigating unusual news, social, or nature subjects for special reports on "The Today Show," which he hosts weekday mornings from 7-9 over Channels 4, 6, and 42. (NBC-TV). Inside, an interview with Hugh Downs.

More Hugh Downs Interview . . . . . .

know it's expedient now to get on the ecological bandwagon. They have no morals about it; they simply know they won't be in the business if they go on. So I think the companies will soon be packaging a lot of plastic things, and they're going to get over this terrible tendency to pollute. Companies like Coors Beer give you money back to return the beer cans. I think that's a statesman-like thing to do.

"They're going to be putting smoke suppressors on their factories. The smart ones will; some of them will just have to be forced into line, and it may be through citizens taking it to court. It's going to happen because we're simply not going to allow the atmosphere to go down the drain!"

You still turn up occasionally back on the "Tonight Show" as guest host.

"It's kind of fun to get back into that although the gap widens as 'Today' and they too fall into better directions. It used to be doing 'Today' and 'Tonight' was a more similar job. I now feel a little bit uneasy doing 'Tonight,' but it's nostalgic."

The fact that you're still doing "Tonight" is probably by virtue of being a former announcer with Jack Paar rather than being at the helm of "Today."

"Life tends to typecast people, and it's unfortunate because it happens in the United States more than it does in some other countries. I met a lady in England who was a Lady literally, the wife of a Lord. She also had her own television program and was a medical doctor and a practicing magistrate. Now that's a hell of a versatile thing; I say you wouldn't be allowed to do that over here.

"I used to go to a dentist who was very good at cosmetic dentistry; I had to have a couple of caps put on. The reason he was good was because he was in the Korean War and picked up the mouths of a lot of guys that got shot up. So he's good, but very young. I found out after I'd been going to him for awhile that he also was a rock n' roll singer. He wrote and recorded music and made more money doing that than he did in dentistry.

"Suppose I didn't know him, and I went to an A&R record party where they introduced me to this rock n' roll singer. And then when I went out, someone said, 'Incidentally, he's a good dentist. You might like to go to him.' I'd have never gone near him. So it's really a strange thing when you don't accept people at face value."

Therefore you detest labels.

"I don't want to be anything. I want to do things. And as soon as you be something, you're pegged there, and I think it's bad. I am nothing but a human being. And I think I've worked to avoid labels."

To Hank Moore, thanks & best wishes Hugh Downs

Captain Kangaroo, Bob Keeshan interview, by Hank Moore.
First published in October, 1969.

"Chit Chat"

HANK MOORE Interviews
BOB KEESHAN

Bob is known to millions as the amiable
"Captain Kangaroo," master of the
Treasure House. Weekday mornings,
8 a.m., CBS-TV (Ch. 5, 7, and 10).

From New York.

During "Captain Kangaroo's" run you have presented subject matter quite educational for the youngsters. Perhaps all those years haven't gotten as much credit as "Sesame Street," one of the year's hottest shows.

"I don't feel there's any competition. I'm just delighted with 'Sesame Street.' The amount of television children watch, there's certainly enough room for both. I think there could be 10 of us, and we certainly wouldn't be anywhere near filling the need.

wouldn't be anywhere near filling the need. Almost all of their people were trained by us and were with us originally. So it's no coincidence if so much of what was developed in 'Kangaroo' is there now."

At what point during the course of the show did you decide to go in for the meatier subject matter, that an hour of the Dancing Bear wasn't quite what the kids needed?

"We've really been doing this from the beginning. In terms of emphasis, there's been more of that in the last 5 or 6 years. We did our first Alphabet Day back in 1955, and we certainly worked with numbers back in those days. We perhaps didn't do it as formally as today. Certainly there was an emphasis on safety and good living habits way back when.

"We're tackling more difficult subjects today further away from the alphabet."

How many honors and awards have been bestowed upon the series?

"I guess there must be well over 150 of various natures, Hank. Going way back, you have the Peabody, the Television Executives 'Outstanding Program for Children,' newspaper awards. Freedom's Foundation citations, almost everything.

"The most gratifying part of it is what we do with the audience. Of course there are times when people within the industry or adults who are concerned with it don't clearly recognize what we are doing. We're not doing something to have somebody write an article in a newspaper or to have a television executive tell us we are doing well. If we feel we've accomplished something with our audience, then we've done our job."

Do you get much audience response?

"Not really because almost all of our total audience is under 7 years of age; so they don't write. It's only when we have the opportunity to see somebody once in awhile that you get the opportunity to communicate. Most of our letters come from adult women; so what we hear is second hand. We make most of our judgment on what mother in the home is able to relate to us. We do get a lot of good pictures however, crayon drawings and so on."

Do children tell you in person that they learned something from the show?

"If they did, we wouldn't be doing our job. What we are doing is entertaining basically. We hope that they never feel what we are trying to do is teach them something. If while being entertained they have grasped a concept, I'd rather it comes to them without knowing it.

"And the relationship is different than with the average show. Most relationships in television are sort of impersonal. This is a very personal one-to-one relationship. Most children treat us just like a good warm friend or a close relative because we're part of their homelife. It doesn't become a special event where they have to tell Andy Williams everything they saw on his show last week." (Continued on Page 15)

True, local TV cannot do things on as grand a scale as you do. But isn't there vast room for improvement in their children's shows?

"It depends upon direction given the local people. A lot of local programs are put on just to fill an economic need. And you go into the film library for what you can find and put one of the local announcers in a clown suit or policeman's suit. You haven't got a quality children's program, just something to fill an economic need. But if you have somebody with a philosophy that we've got a responsibility, there are all kinds of things you can do, things we are really doing on the network level: that very special one-to-one relationship. It all begins with a philosophy, and given that philosophy, they can do a lot."

I wonder if the comedians' monologues on the town drunk getting on and entertaining the kiddies aren't quite accurate on the local stations.

"Right. For a long time this audience has been looked upon as something half-witted and unimportant. Now people are beginning to think what effect we've had on them in 20 years. This is the media generation, and what effect did it have on the way they've grown up.

"Most people who do it on a local level are doing it just as a parttime thing, an extra dollar here and there, or a stepping stone to something else. They're not really thinking of making a career of entertaining on children's television."

You were the original Clarabell the Clown on "Howdy Doody." Did that have any effect on your creation of Captain Kangaroo?

"Not really because by the time I reached Kangaroo from 'Howdy Doody' I was really far removed from 'Howdy Doody.' I was a 19-year-old when I started with 'Howdy Doody,' and by the time I left them 5 years later, I had finished my schooling and had an entirely different attitude. It's a different world from a 6 and 19-year-old. When you become an adult, you start looking at things from a parental point of view; my attitudes in that 5 years turned 180 degrees.

"When I arrived at Kangaroo, I had done 2 years of local programming in New York that was very much in the Kangaroo format."

What did you study in college?

"I was going to become a lawyer and never quite made it!"

But I guess you've gone in for independent child psychology studies to get a grasp of what you are doing.

"We have conversations with experts on almost everything we do and what they would like us to do and then try to translate them into our particular language. Because we don't think of ourselves as educators; we are communicators."

Do you think parents can borrow any leaves from Captain Kangaroo in better communicating with their own children?

"Most parents don't spend enough time with their children. And I think that any parent who spends enough time will have opened up channels of communication and is going to be able to relate to the child and serve the child well. But most parents today are too darn busy, running the gamut of the affluent housewife who is busy with outside activities to the so-called middle class housewife who is busy keeping the house clean while using TV as a babysitter all the way to the ghetto mother who doesn't spend any time with the child. All of them in a way are raising motherless children. I don't think you have to worry about how you talk to your children; what you have to do is spend time with them, and the other will come quite naturally."

Does the fact that most kiddie show hosts are males suggest a departure from the female dominance of the mother?

"There's certainly a need for strong male image at the preschool level. What time the child spends with the parent is usually with the mother anyway. So, I think strengthening of the male image is important although that's not an overriding philosophy. We have a lot of strong women occasionally in the Treasure House, and the Romper Room things are all women and no male. 'Sesame,' whose special audience is the ghetto child, very much went for the strong male black image with that very much in mind. We're not so much dedicated to building of the male, although we think it's important."

It's difficult to deal with outstanding social problems with such a young audience. Could you even read the day's news?

"Reading the day's news is something that should be done and is a programming idea that we've been mulling for a couple of years now. Not for the preschool audience but for one just a little older.

"What we do is deal more with these problems in terms of how they relate to a

4-year-old. This great business about environment that we're talking about today: a 4-year-old doesn't relate to writing to his Congressman to do something about the environment. But he does to an ice cream wrapper thrown on the ground. You start with that in terms of direct action, and you start at this age level with a certain reverence for life. Because if you have an understanding of your position in this world, you will not be a polluter of the future."

Marcus Welby, M.D., Robert Young interview, by Hank Moore.
First published in July, 1970.

"Chit Chat"

HANK MOORE
Interviews
ROBERT YOUNG

Bob is the kindly family physician "Marcus
Welby, M.D." on the hit ABC-TV dramatic
series. (Channels 10, 12. and 42).

Live From Hollywood.

Hollywood - Dr. Marcus Welby has successfully been sued for malpractice, and he
is delighted about it. That's the subject matter of the show being shot this week for fall
broadcast, as a patient with back trouble,
diagnosed as routine, takes a sudden turn
for the worse.

We met Robert Young, old Doc Welby
himself, on the set during shooting. He
stands tall in stature but humbles himself in
every way possible. Bob is of course one of
the world's greatest stars, but it's all a job to
him; and being asked about the facets of
that job is still a wonderous joy for him.
Accompanying me watching Bob work was
David Victor, the show's executive producer
who is still on Cloud 9 from winning a
"Best Dramatic Series" Emmy Award.

Coming out of each take, Robert Young
greeted me with a grin that has worn well in
his 40 years as a movie and television star,
from being the screen lover of Greta Garbo
to the role of Jim Anderson, the world's
best-known father, on "Father Knows Best."

The malpractice suit makes for adult
subject matter, something controversial and
vital to the medical profession. "But what a
hornet's nest," declared Young, who lamen-
ted the public stigma against doctors who
get sued, whether or not they are found guilty. "It's not by the peers either. A panel of
doctors could probably be a stacked jury,
but by the public who remembers the case
could come an almost permanent condem-
nation."

He feels sorry for doctors in the highly
specialized fields, "whose insurance rates
are literally out of sight! A $100,000 mal-
practice suit means no Jamaica, around the
world, a new car. And suddenly it's more
dear!" To the ones who are guilty, Bob

understands the heavy punishment by such
persons by insurance companies; but it's
tough on the cases of doctors like Welby
who have been unfairly charged (and convic-
ted by an emotional jury). "Some people
in this town who have had fires cannot even
get insurance afterwards!"

Bob feels an American Medical Association investigation would be the answer to
malpractice suits unfairly filed and arbitrat-
ed. A future Welby episode would do well
to follow up on the suit, asserted Victor.

Looking over his film career, Robert
Young noted (diplomatically) that he really
had no favorite leading lady or part to play.
In terms of longevity, he obviously became
more attached to the longer running projects
like "Father Knows Best."

The Welby show brought him out of a
semi-retirement "because the script was a
departure from the easy-going 'FKB' image.
It showed I could get a little rough." He
felt had he waited awhile after the end of
"FKB," and had he modified the character
somewhat, his second series ("Window On
Main Street," 1961-62) might have similarly
succeeded.

Bob spends his lunch hour and production lags by napping. His wife Betty (they
were married in 1933) still occasionally
packs him a brown bag lunch. "I usually
snack at 11, at mid-afternoon, and around
6," he related. "I found by the sixth season
of 'Father Knows Best' that it works best
that way."

I asked Young which commissary served
the worst food, since his film career brought
him in contact with all of them.

"They're all about the same, pretty
testy," he chuckled. "At 20th Century-Fox

Continued on Page 36)

years ago, by order of Darryl Zanuck. they lowered the food quality and wrote the loss, which was about $25,000, off to production costs, which is about right. Years ago agents and whoever had business on the lot would time their business to eat there. It had the reputation as the best restaurant in town, not just the best commissary."

The episodes are shot on 6-day production schedules each week, but Bob works 4, venturing on weekends down to his ranch near San Diego. "That 3-day weekend is my salvation," he noted. The ranch is within baby-sitting distance of his 5 grandchildren. "I play golf very rarely but still read a lot. I guess a hobby is a way to escape from everyday boredom. And I don't get bored."

Yes, Robert Young is overjoyed at winning his Best Dramatic Actor Emmy. An even bigger thrill is that medical conventions (even the AMA) have conferred with him on principles of doctor-patient practice.

I left Dr. Welby knowing he would be independently boning up on malpractice in particular during the coming weeks.

"Chit Chat"

Editor HANK MOORE
Interviews JIM NABORS

He stars on "The Jim Nabors Show" and is still known to many as 'Gomer Pyle'

Transcribed from a telephone conversation

Hi, Jim, are rehearsals for your show going on today?

"Yeah, we're doing our Christmas show this week, and so it seems kinda silly sitting here singing 'Jingle Bells.' It's beautiful fall weather, but that's what we're doing. We're doing this one far ahead because of commitments of the guests: Kay Starr and Minnie Pearl. That's the reason that I had them on this particular show is that Kay was the first person that ever hired me. And we fell madly in love years (8) ago; and she has become part of my family ever since, and I hers. And Minnie is a dear friend of both mine and Kattie's."

When did she first hire you?

Do you keep in contact with the folks back home in Sylacauga, Alabama?

"Oh, sure — everyday. They'll all be here for Christmas: my mother and my 2 sisters, their husbands, and their children. I usually go home for Christmas, but this year I'll be working so it's very hard to get away."

Do you still play the clarinet much?

"Lord no! I haven't played it since high school. I've never had a singing lesson. The only way I can ever read those notes is because I took clarinet."

Merv Griffin, M.D., Robert Young interview, by Hank Moore.
First published in October, 1969.

"Chit Chat"

Editor HANK MOORE
interviews MERV GRIFFIN

Conversation transcribed from a
telephone call from the popular
CBS-TV star.

"The Merv Griffin Show" airs each
weeknight at 10:30 p.m. on Ch. 5 & 7

Hi Merv. Good to have you call!

"Have there been any barbecues on the
Pedernales lately?"

No, I think Lyndon's busy writing his
memoirs. I understand you are credited with
making one of television's earliest commercial goofs.

"I almost put the Hazel Bishop Lipstick
Co. out of business one night. Thier commercial was that a girl leaned over & kissed me on
the cheek very subtly while I was talking to
her, & I took my handkerchief & wiped my
cheek & said, 'See, doesn't kiss off, doesn't
smear off, doesn't anything.' We were right
in the middle of a live show, & she kissed me,
& I wiped it. But I looked at the handkerchief as I went to hold it up to the audience,
& I forgot about my makeup. All this brown
makeup was on it. I held it up with a shocked
look on my face, & the audience screemed for
2 minutes."

How do you feel about Arthur Treacher
& his outspokeness?

"He can always say the things I can't say.
Because of his age, nobody ever fights with
him. We all say he's 75 years old, going on
23. He loves to be kidded about his age.
He's a little cranky now because he can't
have another drink for another year. He
looked forward every night to having his 3 or
4 martinis before the show. Sometimes I
was talking to 2 whirling eyeballs. Lately he
hasn't had a drink, & it's making him crank-
ier than hell."

How did you meet your announcer (Arthur)?

"On the Jack Paar Show one night. We
were both booked on as guests. I just thought
it would be a wonderful combination of personalities. He's certainly not a 'yes man.'
He certainly doesn't laugh at my jokes if he
doesn't think they are funny. And he's funny about being cranky. It's a nice chemistry!"

"We hear, Hank, that there's money in
Texas!"

I don't know where it is. Have you ever
played here?

"I played Glen McCarthy's Shamrock Hotel one month after it opened. I played the
Emerald Room, & then I played Dallas. And
I played Beaumont for a private party. Oh, I
loved it down there."

This must have been in your days as a vo-
calist with Freddy Martin's band. How did
you get with him?

"I had a radio show in San Francisco & he
was playing there with his band, & he heard
me on the radio one day. He came out offering me a job singing with him."

I guess you know, you called during our
soap opera. How would you philosophize
your CBS variety series?

"When you really consider it, our shows
are kinda soap operas. Your audience gets to
know your cast of chars, myself & Arthur.
They see this constant traffic of celebrated
people or newcomers coming through our
door, & they're all real, live stories, they're a
very truthful format. In a sense, the audience
takes to them in the way they do to soap op-

(Continued on P.19)

eras. We have no rehearsal, no nothing. I don't get over there until 30 seconds before the show, and I walk on the stage. When those guests come around the corner, I'm seeing them for the first time. So it's really improvised soap opera."

Are many of your friends in show business? I know you reside on a farm in New Jersey.

"No, they are out at the farm because we are out there so much. First we used to go to all the show business cocktail parties that they have, but we found that it hurt the show. So many people I was seeing at cocktail parties were my guests on the show. It's very hard to interview someone if you know them well & know everything that's happening to them. It's almost better to stay away from that side of the business & lead a different kind of life, & then I think you're far more curious when they come on the show. We built a guest house out at our farm for Arthur & his wife; and they spend time out there. He loves the country."

What sort of personal appearances have you been doing?

"I got my first taste this year of country fairs. I love 'em. What I liked was you went for 2 days; you didn't have to stay for 2 weeks and do the same act twice a night.

Just as you're getting tired of your own show you close; you're perfect! Opening night I played the Pennsylvania State Fair in Allentown. You'd go out opening night, and they'd all rush to the front of the stage. They don't even stay in their seats. I thought they were making decisions, like Billy Graham.

How much did you have to do with renovating the historic Cort Theatre for your show's use?

"We were in on every meeting for it. We designed how we wanted it to look for the show. You have to do it because these are such delicate formats. Your audience is very coveted: we depend upon their reaction whether it's love or hate. Their sight line has to be perfect, the audio has to be perfect; they have to be able to see so that no camera is in front of them. We shoot over their heads and from the side.

(Continued on P.24)

More on Merv Griffin

"It's just like coming out into a live theatre every night. A Broadway theatre owned by the Shuberts, CBS put $2½ million into fixing it for television. The theatre is back to 1905, I think. It has a few bodies lying around there."

What other activities have you planned for the future?

"I just recorded an album of piano with 40-piece orchestra. It will be out the end of October, with songs like "Romeo & Juliet," some Rod McKuen numbers, and two original compositions. I want to do what I know the other 2 can't. I'm sure Johnny & Joey both can stand up & sing a song."

"We are working on specials. Our company produces 'Jeopardy' on NBC, a very popular show; been on the air 5 years now. We will do the Jackie Gleason Show and then take ours to Miami, and he will be on with us. Eventually we may tour the country. I just think it would be wrong to sit here in New York when there's so much stuff happening outside of New York."

Mannix, Mike Connors interview, by Hank Moore.
First published in April, 1970.

"Chit Chat"

Editor HANK MOORE
Interviews MIKE CONNORS

Mike is private eye Joe Mannix on
CBS' "Mannix" mystery series

Live From Hollywood.

HOLLYWOOD - If you think Mike Connors is a big, handsome guy on the screen as
he plays private eye Joe Mannix on CBS-TV
you'll be even more impressed with him in
person. We encountered the rugged actor at,
of all places, "The Red Skelton Show."

We entered the Skelton studio at Television City in Hollywood where the bulk
of a Skelton show had been taped the night
before. This morning, all that was to be done
was the dancers' and singers' opening production number (a big band styling of a
1965 rock hit "One, Two, Three") and
introductions of the stars.

Mike is a warm, friendly guy, the kind
who would invite you to step out for a cold
one and a round of laughs. Only, he was
dressed in a tuxedo and waiting for the
dancers to perfect a visual track (the audio
track was prerecorded) before he could take
his bows to a canned audience.

"This is a nice change from the tumbles
I usually take in my work," Mike nodded.
"This is especially fun to do when you're
...Look at the pretty legs on those dancers!
I can go back to the series feeling like
Vincent Virile."

"Mannix" has done very well in its
second season, after a so-so first year on the
air. "It's rough to do on Saturday nights
because you have a smaller audience."
he observed.

I asked if he did many of his stunts, and
Mike replied "90 per cent, but I may start
cutting down because I'm not getting any
younger." I speculated that he might have
been a college athlete, and he recalled years
of playing basketball for UCLA. He still
arises at 5:30 a.m. for a daily workout.

Another young lovely strolled by. Mike
poked me on the shoulder and chided, "I

see what we're looking at. I may not make
it before noon!"

I observed that Skelton was a gas to work
with. "Red is a wild man who completely
goes away from the scripts, and adds what
he likes, and generally raises hell for the
screaming audiences," he said. "I'm trying to
get Red to go straight dramatic for one of
our shows next season, and he wants to do
it." I speculated that it sounded like Emmy
Award material.

"I'd like to write and direct," Mike wist-
fully supposed as his ultimate career goal.
"I think an actor suffers greatly, however,
in directing himself. It's difficult to be objective; Olivier was not at his best when he
did it. On 'Bonanza,' Mike Landon can
direct himself because he has a supporting
cast and can afford to be light in that episode. I think I can write and then act in
something without losing anything."

I asked if he had in fact done any writing for a film he appeared in, and a 1960
script called "A Swinging Affair" was recalled. During the summer hiatus for "Mannix," the actor will "go to Hawaii to look at
a story property and mainly play a lot of
golf and tennis."

Connors calls himself "one of those
three months a year players. My only handicap is that I can't play golf!" It's really an
18.

He has done numerous guest shots on
variety shows in the past year besides
Skelton (the Pat Paulsen and Leslie Uggams series). "It's like stealing money, like
fun and games. I can fake comedy and
because I'm an amateur comedy performer,
just the excitement of getting on a stage in
front of people is still a thrill to a green
funny man like me."

More Mike Connors Interview. . .

Joan Crawford was highly praised by Mike. "She taught me a great deal. It's kind of interesting that I has my first professional job with her. It was in 1953, in my first picture: I played a lawyer. It's strange to think that after all these years I'm up for my first award, a Golden Globs, and she's the presenter."

I asked Mike if he thought television should get into the "message" business like so many films these days.

"I don't believe entertainment should have too many messages in it," he felt. "The word is entertainment: a little fantasy, a little excitement. I would much rather go to a college and speak on what I feel than put it on the screen under the guise of entertainment."

I asked if he would like to add any occasional comedy to "Mannix," a very heavy mystery show. Mike grinned at the possibilities but said the producers had turned thumbs down. "We tried it once, and it didn't go over well because people were expecting a serious action drama."

I asked what recreational forms he enjoyed, and Mike beamed pride at coaching his son's basketball team. He and his family also love riding horses and water skiing.

"Directing amateur theatre has been a thrill for me the times I've done it," Mike grinned (as he had by this point done numerous times for the Skelton camera until the dance sequence had been retaken perfectly). "Sometimes you get some very interesting talent. And the enthusiasm you find there you don't find in the professional ranks. Wow!"

A second wow was exclaimed for another passing dancer in an appealing costume. "I keep my back to it so I can concentrate on what we're saying," Mike exclaimed in his widest grin of the morning.

I Dream of Jeannie, Barbara Eden interview, by Hank Moore.
First published in November, 1969.

"Chit Chat"

Editor HANK MOORE
Interviews BARBARA EDEN

She stars on NBC's "I Dream of Jeannie".
Jeannie and Tony will be married on
this week's show.
Barbara also appears Tuesday as guest
star on Engelbert Humperdinck's
special.

Transcribed from a telephone conversation.

I understand they are planning big festivities for you and the "I Dream of Jeannie" show down in Florida.

"A wedding reception, really; that's what it is. It'll take about 4 days. We'll go to Cape Kennedy and the space center there. I was there just a few months ago. They had a Barbara Eden Day. I set off a weather rocket; it was really kind of fun!"

Don't you really enjoy public appearances of this sort?

"I do, when it has anything to do with NASA. It's like a fairy tale to me. I can't believe it's real. I've been very interested in it, you know, reading Life Magazine and all the brochures when I was in Houston. I did the Bob Hope Special in Houston with the astronauts, and of course they give me a lot of literature, which I read avidly, about their training techniques."

The astronauts don't seem much the hero type, do they.

"You know, they do. They're so bright, and visual, and great, that I was really overwhelmed when I met them. They're real people!"

This week seems to be your big week on television what with getting married on the series and a guest appearance on Engelbert Humperdinck's show.

"Engelbert's a hard worker and a lovely, lovely man. Very cultured; he's a gentleman. I think the audiences will like him; he has a very easy, warm personality, with a sense of humor, which is kind of hard for the guys who are screamed at.

"We did a couple of interesting things. I sing "Matchmaker," and Engelbert does little comedy vignettes in between each one. It's really funny, different for him. And then I do "Son Of A Preacherman" with the chorus. I'm kind of proud of it."

What other song and dance appearances have you slated?

"I'll do Dean Martin's and Andy William's shows. I'm probably going to Japan for the Expo '70 and then on the way back go to Australia. I'll take my nightclub act that way and it'll take a couple of months."

How do you feel now that Jeannie and Tony are getting married?

"Oh, wonderful. They made me an honest woman. Only thing is now I'm a bigamist; I've been married 11 years in real life, and suddenly I'm married on television."

Was it fun filming that particular episode?

"It really was. It's a cute show. The problems we get into because Jeannie can't be photographed. And of course NASA wants to photograph the wedding. Consequently, she is the only girl who has ever watched herself walk down the aisle. And the things that happen when she forgets, of course, and has to pop in at the last minute to say I Do. It was fun!"

Are the camera tricks on the show as intriguing to you as to the viewers?

"I should say so! It's amazing; all the

(Continued on Page 30)

wires, the smoke, and lights. Each one takes a unique and different kind of contraption to make it go."

Have you had any accidents on the set by the gadgets?

"No, knock on wood! I was almost squashed once. Remember, when I was in the safe? We had a great big interior of the safe built. And I was in there with all the big lipstick, and purse, and comb when I made myself known. We had money and vitamin pills, things like that. They had the third wall of the set that they were rolling in, and the darn thing started to slowly fall over on me. I didn't know it until I heard a lot of people screaming; this wall was coming toward me. If 8 big fellows hadn't jumped on the other side of that wall to counterbalance it, I would have been seriously injured. But, thank God they were all thinking so fast."

Would you want to do a variety series?

"Yes, I would. I think I would really enjoy it. Of course I love acting, but the bug has bitten me with the variety series. I like the fact that you can talk to people and be yourself; it's fun for your ego. The variety artists have guests, and they chat; it's like being at home."

That's probably why you enjoy appearing in the clubs so much.

"It really is, you're right. Immediately you get the response from the audience. That's very gratifying."

Have you calculated how much you travel performing each year?

"Oh my, I've been all over the world. It's been in short trips too, in and out of the suitcase, which is a little wearing."

Tell me something about your husband, Michael Ansara. I think he's one of the finest actors, and have been a fan of his for years.

"Thank you. I agree with you. We met on a publicity date. The studio thought I should go out with him and take some pictures. It kind of boomeranged on the studio when 2½ months later we got married; they didn't intend for it to go that far."

"Michael is better known for drama, but he enjoys doing comedy very much. Last week he was on 'The Governor and J.J.' This week he's doing 'The Survivors.' Next week he will be on 'Then Came Bronson,' filming all these. Now, he was supposed to be doing a running part on 'The Survivors,' to be Lana Turner's love interest. Lana's out, and I guess that the casting will be different; but they have committed him to several shows."

Are many of your friends in show business or out of it?

"I'll tell you, I've been so busy for the past 2 years, I'm lucky I have any friends left at all. Naturally the ones in show business we see more lately because of work. We like to play bridge, but golly, I don't think we've played in 2 years!"

Will Jeannie and Tony have any children?

"I really don't know. I guess it depends on what the Ansara family does. It's not in the plans right now!"

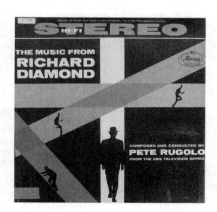

Excerpt from Star Interviews interview, by Hank Moore.
First published in July, 1971.

**This Is A Fictional Story, Reprising Interviews with All of TV's Top Stars.
Quotes & Situations Are True, Having Appeared the Past 2 Years in TV Digest**

Our Past Blasts

By HANK MOORE

HOLLYWOOD - Waylayed by some interesting people, I finally arrived at the gala second anniversary party held in behalf of TV Digest. Gosh, it was nice of the top stars in the industry to turn out in our honor.

The event was held at Beverly Hills' Century Plaza Hotel, which is a little expensive for me to stay at when I go out, but the TV networks love it, and after all, their budget was putting the shindig on. I caught Bob Hope puttering about the ballroom the afternoon before, readying his performance as our master of ceremonies.

Hope has a staff of 9 writers on-call to provide pleasantries for any occasion. I suggested that formula jokes might play a part, like the gag: "La Dolce Vita, or what to do until the spaghetti gets warm." Hope recalled adapting that line to fit numerous occasions. "I think people know those formulas, like you do. If they wanted totally original pundits, forget it. That must be my bag, if you can call it that, to see and adapt in a form easily recognizable to any Joe on the street."

The renowned comedian was in rare form as he emceed the evening's musical-comedy revue. Time Magazine had recently published vast reports on Hope's wealth. "I think they're computer drinks," he quipped, wondering where his earnings went. "Dolores (his wife) is home cutting up all the mattresses looking for my money. She says the kitchen needs painting. Time and Fortune got it all wrong: I'm a TV comedian, not a TV repairman!"

First on deck to sing was America's favorite bubblegummer, Bobby Sherman, who sang his latest hit, "The Drum," and commented to the older-than-teenage crowd: "Bubblegum is young, yet the oldtimers like me can dig it. I'm not facetious; 24 is old to

teens, who don't really understand hard rock yet. For us, though, it's good toe-tapping music and kinda a change of pace after a steady diet of rock." Off the bandstand, Bobby commented that he was looking forward to getting back to series TV, as indeed he will this fall on ABC in his own half-hour situation comedy show. He remembered the 2 years on "Here Comes the Brides" and added, "I got to where I wanted to devote more time on my singing, while acting was indeed a gas. I really found myself loving to sing all over again!" That's why his new show will be heavily dotted with bubblegum ditties, and the kids oughtta love that.

Glen Campbell was gruff as a bear because he was feeling under the weather. "Got a damn cold," he declared. "I'll just sound a little nasally, that's all. What I need is about 6 months' hibernation." After his special renditions of songs were performed, Glen confessed a great hankering to get to the golf course more this summer. "I've got a 7 handicap," he told of his game. "I play with Frankie Avalon a lot, Andy Williams, and Dick Martin is about the funniest one to play with. I'm gonna start doing more exhibition matches in the spring."

Lovely Diana Ross next performed her new hit, "Reach Out, I'll Be There," and in a discussion afterwards shunned herself as a message singer. In her days as leader of The Supremes, Diana recalled, " 'Someday We'll Be Together' was about the closest we tried to give any messages. I'm not one for preaching, really. I'm a singer and like to sing love songs. The closest I would get to giving some kind of message is something that could be taken either way. I'm really not a pushy type of person, where I would try to push my feelings on the public. I have that chance

Continued on page 32

More TV Digest Anniversary Spread. . . .

because I am in the public's eye. I don't think that it is my duty; I can do what I have to do in other ways."

Tony Randall of ABC's "The Odd Couple" favored the crowd by reciting some 1930's vintage Sherlock Holmes movie dialog and sighed, "It astonishes even me!" He reeled off some radio trivia for the skeptics. "I know these things," he said with trademarked Tony Randall assurance. "I can recall days and specific dates about them. I just cannot explain it." To wit, I asked him the name of Stella Dallas' daughter on the old radio serial. Tony not only identified her as "Lolly, played by Vivian Molly, who now plays old ladies on commercials" but asserted that Ann Elsner, who played Stella, "now runs an antique shop!"

Next on deck was Hal Holbrook of NBC's "The Bold Ones," doing some of his critically-renowned impersonations and readings of 19th Century author and lecturer Mark Twain. He traced the link with Twain back to his college years. "I don't think I ever had a class where we had to read any of his stories." That's why he can as an actor look critically at Twain's works. "Sometimes it got a little shoddy toward the end. He got bored of writing," Hal noted. "And in those days you had to make books very long because they were sold on subscription, with pictures in them, with fancy bindings. And people really bought the book for its cover and for the pictures inside as much as they did for the contents. Books really had to be longer so people would think they were getting their money's worth. And Twain would have to extend a story longer than he wanted to."

Asked about his most popular Twain readings, Holbrook refuses to do requests per se anymore. "I usually have a pretty good idea of what I want to do. If I don't when I get out there I just do what comes to my mind. I think people like the Old Ram story a great deal. A lot of people have seen the Italian guide thing and like it very much. People love the ghost story and want to hear that; it's the only thing I repeat a great deal."

Carol Burnett came on deck with scenes from "As the Stomach Turns," her favorite continuing segment on her CBS–TV variety hour. "There is always somebody with a problem that I am trying to help solve," she giggled. "You know what's funny is that

some people say we get risque. But if they watch daytime television, they get away with more stuff on daytime television than nighttime television does. And it's mild compared to what those shows really talk about. There is incest and abortion and all kinds of lovely things like that!"

Even Carol Burnett reads the fan magazines. "I want to look at them and see what I am supposed to be doing," chuckled the comedienne who hails originally from San Antonio. The same inquisitiveness was expressed by a comely blonde, also an "item" in the columns. Donna Douglas, who plays Elly May Clampett on "The Beverly Hillbillies," talked fondly of her association with a series so berated by intellectuals. "People so many times speak to us about typecasting.

Our attitude is we are always glad to have a job!"

Mel Torme entertained the crowd with some original compositions, including his famous "Christmas Song." Later, he commented that other people's songs are not for him to perform. "Whether I'm a good or bad singer is really not the point. I am an original singer, a kind of unique sound because of the kind of throat I've got. I'm not trying to educate anybody or look down my nose musically. I want to do pop things, but I don't want to do them after they've been recorded by 5 other people. I'd rather go my own way and dig my own hole."

As cocktails were being served, Chris Schenkel conveyed the same philosophy on sports broadcasting. Objectivity is important to him. "We often do the Purdue-Notre Dame game, and I'm a graduate of Purdue. And I bend over so far trying not to show any interest in Purdue that a lot of people think I'm a Notre Dame fan." Chris thinks TV has created lots of instants sports experts. "Those who follow a team are just fanatic, and you can notice it by letters that you receive too."

Lee Majors of NBC's "The Men From Shiloh" recalled TV Digest's "Date With Doug McClure Contest" and chuckled about his swinger buddy, "I played tennis with Doug before and kidded him about all his marriages. He just got married again; that's the 4th time. He's a glutton for punishment and says he's got rice marks all over his back!" (With Lee was his girlfriend, Corpus Christi's own Farrah Fawcett, now a starlet in Hollywood and getting lots of film work.)

Danny Thomas sighed that he was glad to get back on television, that his story-telling techniques, which were on-stage for the anniversary party, were being solicited by scads of benefits. "People know you're doing a weekly series, and they want you to play their charity," he observed, "God, I almost lost my voice! Now I'm 'settling down' to work in a weekly series. It's not as hectic!"

Danny's TV producer, actor Richard Crenna, did some characterizations from his former television shows, including "Our Miss Brooks" and "The Real McCoys." A public relations job, I supposed he had. "That's right! Most people think a producer is somebody's uncle. 100 decisions everyday have to be made." Dick is the first to admit that breaks in show business may make up for talent. "I've done 3 series and could do another and get a lot of money," he philosophized. "You can be very bright when you have a bank account to back up your judgement. That makes you appear very bright when you say No."

Emcee Bob Hope was asked if there was anywhere he wanted to take his USO shows but hadn't been yet. "The moon, but they say Crosby and I were there years ago," he retorted. Asked where he invested his earnings, Bob replied real estate. "My first impulse was to put it into the stock market. I would have been twice as rich today. I also thought 'Thanks For the Memory' was a lousy song!"

Next Week in TV Digest:
First of a 5—week series on problems and limitations of local television stations.

Chris Schenkel interview, by Hank Moore.
First published in February, 1971.

Sports Carefully Studied, Then Reported

By HANK MOORE

Regarded as the nation's most diverse sportscaster of the day, Chris Schenkel knows many areas of participation sports. His smooth delivery and knowing calling of the shots has made him the most respected sportscaster around. The voice of ABC-TV (which is acknowledged as having the most sophisticated sports coverage on television), Chris reported NCAA football games back in the fall and is concentrating his energies this spirng on the golf tournaments and the Professional Bowlers' Tour.

The day we talked with Chris, he was home in New York City: a rarity since he logs thousands of travel miels weekly. The previous occasion was his assignment in Austin last December: the Texas-Arkansas game. In the meantime, something had happened to Texas!

"We had done the Sugar Bowl New Year's Day, and I got to the New Orleans airport in time to watch part of the Cotton Bowl," he recalled. "I couldn't believe it! I just couldn't believe it! I just figured that nobody ever could beat Texas. We televised the game where Southern California beat Notre Dame. Well, I still think that Texas is better. Nevertheless, the score didn't show that though. But, at least they were Number One in the regular season poll, so that's great."

Schenkel termed Longhorn coach Darrell Royal as "one of the fine coaches anywhere." The two have become friends through the years. "I call his wife Edith my art director because everytime I've been in Austin, I make the tour of all your art galleries there. I've picked up some Western art at The Country Store Gallery and some little pieces here and there." Chris would like to own some works by Melvin Warren, a Texas artist who is very highly priced right now.

Suffice to say, his work keeps him steadily on the go. "I should live at some midpoint like Dallas because the air traffic out of there is great," he confessed. But he gets lots of New York jobs that people don't see on the network. "They throw little things at me here like voice-overs, promos for golf, a film narration for sales presentations.

Most of the good sports films I get to do as a result of doing the events for a period of time. This is something I enjoy, because you do a telecast, and it's gone. I've done some cattle films; I grew up a farm boy and used to have some cattle in Texas, some hereford up by Fort Worth. I love it!"

Normally, Chris does the play-by-play on National Basketball Association games, but all the golf tournaments are forcing him to wait until the playoffs. (Our buddy Keith Jackson is doing the NBA games in Schenkel's place.) This weekend, he is doing the PGA, seen Saturday and Sunday over Channels 7, 10 and 12, followed by the Tournament of Champions. There will be 2 Texas tourneys in May, which I will attend: the Byron Nelson in Dallas and the Colonial in Fort Worth.

It's been only the last few years that golf coverage has come into its own as a top TV attraction. I told Chris that I believed it was before that considered an off-season stepchild, and he agreed. "The amount of

Chris with Bud Wilkinson
*...expert commentary on the
NCAA football games.*

production that goes into it is far greater than football, basketball, or anything else, because of the amount of equipment. In our big tournaments we usually have around 20 cameras, where at a football game the most we have would be 7. The costs are sorta out of the sight; but the thing that makes the difference is the rights fees aren't as high as football, baksetball, or some of the other sports."

And it's notable that golf tournaments are now sold completely out on advertising time, which isn't entirely the case with football, and which has been happening the past 3 years. "Up until that time, Hank, it was an emotional buy by a sponsor or an agency exec because he was a golfer. On paper, I don't think it made a hell of a lot of sense; but I guess it does more so now."

A golfer himself, Chris has a 12 handicap but complains, "I'm over-pro'd, Hank. I have too many professionals trying to help me; they foul you up. I occasionally play in some of the pro-ams just for the heck of it. But when you're around it that much, you lose a little interest after seeing how good they are. It takes a little edge off the desire to play." But he does still fish a lot!

I wondered if being assigned to all different kinds of sports hasn't facilitated a lot of learning about the games, some of which he might not have been an expert on at the outset. "I had the good fortune of starting

in radio," Chris explained. "I think by doing that, it made the job later a lot easier. Doing radio coverage is much more difficult because to paint a verbal picture is harder. I was fortunate to get in on all the television sports when it first started, so there was more hit-and-miss opportunity to gain the knowledge. I was with the Giant football team 13 years, when nobody really knew about pro football. When it became more prominent, I hope I'm more ready to do it."

Variety is very definitely the spice of Chris Schenkel's career. A full year of any sportsmanship attitudes. "Those who follow a team are just fanatic, and you can notice it by letters that you receive, too. They've all become experts, thanks to newspapers concentrating more on the technical side of the game, and television." Some letters are perennially charging him and colleagues with bias. "We often do the Purdue-Notre Dame game, and I'm a graduate of Purdue. And I bend over so far trying not to show any interest in Purdue that a lot of people think I'm a Notre Dame fan. We get a lot of mail saying that it's obvious I'm a Notre Dame graduate!"

A good study on objectivity through the guts, as it were, is Chris' colleague Bud Wilkinson at the Texas-Oklahoma games, which he too comments on for ABC. "Yes, it is, because here's Darrell, his star pupil, playing Oklahoma, his old team. I've never seen anybody sweat the way he does at that game. He just tries his best because he is such an honest person. He wants Darrell to do well and Chuck Fairbanks to do well; it's an emotional tug of war." Schenkel said Wilkinson had also predicted Texas would beat Notre Dame easily in the Cotton Bowl but reasoned that it was one of those times that one team did everything right, and the other team did very little right. "He wanted Darrell to come out on top, and Oklahoma's winning streak had been stopped by Notre Dame. So, he doesn't have any love for them!"

Ratings to Schenkel are a farce. Because of the costliness of the NCAA package, ABC has to cover high-rated teams to justify the investment. "As a result, I feel we should have something at the end more conclusive. And the major coaches feel the same way. But then there's the mechanics of what do you do about bowl games. Maybe they put too much emphasis on college athletics, I don't know. It's hard to evaluate it as good or bad; it would be fun to see, wouldn't it it!"

(Continued on Page 6)

More Chris Schenkel Interview . . . . .

But then opponents of collegiate athletics (and stress upon them) number among the academicians of the New Left, saying that football, for example, is not intellectual. Chris thinks there was a trend toward that kind of thinking on campuses, but that it is going back the other way. "I've noticed a big change in attitude the last 2 years; there are more students coming out to the games who don't participate. It's a bit of a revolt against the dissidents and everything else. I think that some of the faculty members, perhaps frightened that athletics have too important a role, have changed their attitude; they either think it's getting more important and want to be a part of it, or they like it less."

The 11th game rule, which is advocated by the schools that are not getting tremendous crowds in a 10-game season and need more money via attendance figures, is not favored by Schenkel, who reasserted that one sport could drive him up the wall, as it could any viewer or participant.

Football took him more studying, with talking with the coaches in the radio days and viewing game films. "I learned enough of the technical side not to make it too

difficult for everybody to understand." In more recent years, he worked hard on golf, "to really know how they do it, since I myself couldn't do it as they do it. There again, I was fortunate because I started on the Masters' Golf Tournament (1953). It was a matter of getting experience upon experience, but I think football was the hardest."

Chris confessed to getting very involved with the Super Bowl game, rooting for Dallas and for Tom Landry, whom he knew as a player with the New York Giants. I told him that I thought people really were mourning the fact that Texas and Dallas lost their 2 games in January.

"I think it's more so in college now," Schenkel commented on the extreme emotional identification with teams, players, and sportsmanship attitudes. "Those who follow a team are just fanatic, and you can notice it by letters that you receive, too. They've all become experts, thanks to newspapers concentrating more on th technical side of the

maybe there ought to be less sports on view in some seasons. "I just hope they don't overemphasize it. Personally, I just think there are too many football games on television; I'm talking from Saturday through Monday. I think it dillutes a good product but is necessary because of the size of the rights fees; otherwise, the networks couldn't break even; you've gotta have all those commercial minutes, so you've gotta have all those games. I think this will slacken off because the rights won't be quite as high in the future. The networks aren't doing too well. Those people have some sharp pencil guys too: all 3 networks are cutting back on production. So that's a pretty good indication that things will change a little bit."

***

When the camera started to move in for a closeup of Jack Benny as he was taping a guest sequence on NBC-TV's "Dinah's Place," Jack remonstrated that he didn't need extreme closeups. "But your face is your fortune," someone said. "At my age," Jack replied, "I want the camera in Pomona Every year I move the camera one town father away."

Chris with Byron Nelson
...getting an assist from the fabled golf star at ABC tourney coverage.

Don Meredith interview, by Hank Moore.
First published in November, 1970.

Don Meredith is a football fan in general. He played for the Dallas Cowboys as Dandy Don the quarterback, sometimes to cheers and sometimes to boos. And now he is commentating on the NFL Monday night games along with Howard Cosell and Keith Jackson for ABC-TV. But he keeps up with the sport and is a typical fan as a commentator.

Chatting with the former Cowboys star, I found an intense interest in the Southwest Conference NCAA teams: in SMU (where he did his collegiate gridiron thing), Baylor, and the University of Texas ("I wonder if they do those squeaker games just for television, what do you think?"). Still a Dallas resident, Don finds himself still trudging through Central Texas soil, like to an upcoming IBM meeting in Austin where he will be guest speaker. ("If you're going to hang out someplace, Austin is as good as any to hang out!")

Broadcasting to Meredith, as a Dallas Cowboy, was far from his mind. "When I retired about 2 years ago, ABC approached me about doing the sports on a local basis -up in New York," he recalled. "At that time I wasn't interested in moving to New York. I wasn't interested in being connected with football at all; I was going to give it a whirl in the old business world. Then after a year I decided heck, that I really would like to get back into it in some way, and this seemed

Meredith Returns To Cowboys This Week.....
As TV Commentator

By HANK MOORE

to be the most logical way." Pleased to be with the network, he feels the Monday night package is a good one. He was offered emceeing chores on college ball but feels better with pro.

Preliminary scouting finds him and his cohosts in the city of each game 2 days beforehand. "We visit with the different teams just as a kind of familiarization of what these teams are doing. We have a book we try to keep up with: their records and so forth. From a quarterback's standpoint, which is what I played, I've spent a lot of time studying defenses. It's been a little different because I didn't spend that much time studying the other teams' offenses. Each team I feel has a unique personality and this is more or less developed through the system that they run."

The inquisitiveness of Cosell, the factuality of Jackson, and the folksy touch of Meredith's comments, I suggested to Don, were a fresh approach in television sports coverage: definite personalities. Sort of a return to the Dizzy Dean era of calling the shots! "Possibly the viewers missed that," he asserted. "We've gotten an awful lot of comment, most of it favorable. In fact, they seem to enjoy what we're doing: Maybe we've struck on something that's pretty good!"

The Monday night telecasts are TV's most expensive football telethons. "We've got more cameras; there are more people working on this; and consequently I think the results are better. We do one game a week, and the others have regional games; so we do spend more money on it," Meredith explained.

Don feels he is still in pretty good shape and has foregone very much physical training since quitting the Cowboys early in 1969. "I play a little basketball whenever I can. Primarily I'm lazy; I like to get in that sauna bath and take the saunas, whirlpools, and rubs...play like I worked out!" And it surely shows when he is lacking in sleep time. "I've got those tell-tale eyes anyway!"

Dandy Don was said by most Cowboy

fans as either very good or very good or very bad at times. "I've never been able to explain that particular phase of athletics; why it seems sometimes you can be very well prepared. You can work hard for a game and feel good physically, and yet things just don't click well," he believes.

And Don's audience got quite loud when they thought he was not performing up to snuff with the Cowboys. "The old Christians and the lions! I think more than anything else there's been a lack of true understanding of what you're trying to accomplish out there," he chuckled. "It's a way of physically and mentally identifying with people on the field. And if their guys are not doing well, they take it personally, like I'm not doing well either, and become offended. And there's probably more individual identification with professional football than with any other sport. And that can cause some of the rowdiness or uneasiness and therefore abusive attention some of the fans give you whenever you're not doing well."

Still dabbling in the business world, Don is affiliated with a brokerage firm in Houston with the corporate finance department. "I've a piece of a couple of things that I enjoy being involved with. I don't have any great desire to build a financial castle; I'm just happy to do what I'm doing!"

What Don Meredith does yearn to do is move to Los Angeles and become an actor. "I think Namath has done it in kind of a half-hearted way," he said. "It's certainly a misconception to think here I'm a football player and now I can go become an actor. I think that's a definite insult to the acting business; there are some who have done fairly well in acting and fairly well in football. But it's more to me an expression of feelings and emotions; that's not really acting if you go out and play the part of a football player."

I noted that football itself IS a game of emotions which a lot of people don't understand; that's what prompts people to go out and bash heads. "Emotional identification,

Continued on p. 40

Don Meredith Looks To Performing

as we were talking about awhile ago," he chimed in. "You're on a testing ground each week. And if you've spent enough time and dedication and effort; and if you've done this thing fairly well, it's the self-satisfaction of doing a thing. And you don't have to read the papers to understand whether you've done this."

And scores can sometimes be deceiving as the criteria for a job well done. "A lot of the games that I received the credit for doing well, I didn't play well at all," he conceded. "They would say Meredith led the Cowboys to victory, and I knew I didn't really play well. On the other hand, they'd say Meredith had 3 interceptions, and the Cowboys lose; maybe those 3 interceptions were not necessarily my fault. Maybe the receiver ran a wrong pattern; maybe a defensive man just made a great move; and yet the interpretation of that event is too literal. Sometimes it should be more of a figurative thing."

In other words, I summed, nobody can either win or lose at a football game. Don feels football is more artistic than people give it credit. "When you think of the small percentage of individuals who rise to the level of professional athletics - less than one-half of one percent who make it to the professional ranks - that's a pretty select group in any type of profession. To me it's very artistic. You're talking about the best of the best; it's pretty rare talent which gets you there."

Monday, Nov. 16, is Don Meredith's reunion with the Dallas Cowboys since leaving the squad. He is looking forward to seeing the team and Coach Tom Landry. And we're looking forward to seeing Don again, for we'll be in the broadcast booth with them.

Broderick Crawford interview, by Hank Moore.
First published in April, 1971.

Tough Star Takes Gentle Look Back On Film & TV Successes

By HANK MOORE

HOLLYWOOD — One of the roughest, toughest guys on the silver screen is in person very definitely a straight shooter. But Broderick Crawford is sort of gentle in a heavy way. His mental notations are agile, his feelings flexible, and his ambitions depend upon both.

One of Hollywood's all-time great stars Crawford won an Academy Award Oscar in 1949 for Best Actor in the controversial "All the King's Men," exposing corrupt politics and looking at the Long dynasty in Louisiana. From 1954-59 he starred in the now-legendary TV series "Highway Patrol." Now he's visible on the tube as Dr. Peter Goldstone, father figure to CBS-TV's "The Interns."

Meeting Crawford for me was like meeting a childhood idol. Having grown up on "Highway Patrol," I was most ecstatic about discussing that series, as we had breakfast together one sunny California morning.

"Looking back, I don't know how the hell we did it," the stocky actor said of "Highway Patrol's" herculean 2-day shooting schedule, a record for any TV series ever filmed. "You had to get into a routine doing them, then had to get each one over with. But you needed a month after it. I was walking into walls!"

The series is still syndicated around the country and is still as popular as ever. "I'm ham enough to still look at it," confessed Crawford, who measures it alongside any mystery on the networks now. "The situations are still the same. The only thing that dates it are the cars."

Suffice to say, the policeman identity stuck with Crawford for years. He was asked to speak at all kinds of lawmen's functions; probably his biggest thrill was as guest speaker at a Scotland Yard banquet. "I go into the supermarket, and all the kids say, 'Are you still making Highway Patrol? Say, are you really a cop?' I'd say no; otherwise they'd hate my guts."

A trailblazer in its own right, it was "Highway Patrol" and not the real police

Broderick Crawford
...made "10–4" a household word

that originated the expression Ten-Four as a signoff. 'One of our writers just thought it up. Police use it now, and I hear it in taxis when I ride them." But the cases, according to Crawford were really from police files and were checked for accuracy. "The writers would doctor them up and put in the gunfights."

Violence on television, which has been cut down the last couple of years, is an essential ingredient, Broderick feels. "They say no violence on TV, but I look at old movies, and they're blood on all 4 walls. They don't cancel the old shows but cut violence out of the new ones, which is crazy. There's still violence on television, but in some cases they look the other way!"

Shows like "Highway Patrol" and "The Untouchables" were TV's most violent, I pointed out. " 'The Untouchables' will not be back on for quite awhile. There was too much violence for anyone," asserted Crawford, who cited the reason for his show being so strong was that it was syndicated and therefore not answerable to any of the net-

Crawford

makes a point

to intern

Stephen Brooks

in current series

works.   "We didn't have to answer to anyone's censorship, and the content wasn't sold out because of it!"

He remembered one time he ad libbed a line on "Highway Patrol" (as was often the case), and it created a furor in England. Somebody said to him "All women want money," and Crawford replied, "What women don't! I got out of it by blaming the author."

The political nature of "All the King's Men" is what made it monumental, believes its Oscar-winning star. Crawford considers his Academy Award for the picture a high point in his career and believes it was earned for the portrayal. "Nobody won so much for publicity in those days. Nobody took out full-page ads as they do today."

"King of Diamonds" was Broderick Crawford's second TV series. It was on the air for only a year because the studio was sold. He is still looking at good royalties from it and "Highway Patrol" reruns. "If they'd be honest and keep one set of books, I'd be quite rich!" (Crawford gets a percentage of the show instead of residuals, which he feels is a wise move.)

Getting back into series television after several years' absence pleases him. "You get bored. I quit for a couple of years, and they kept sending me script after script," Broderick reasoned.   " 'The Interns' is solid material, and I liked the project on first reading. I've always been an active guy physically and mentally. So here I am, knocking my brains out all over again in a television series!"

The whole film industry is "in the process of growing up, I really believe. We've got to get our growing pains in line and take off from there." Crawford believes videotape cassettes will be a great boon to actors and technicians. He further

believes that nudity is on the way out, and violence is on the way back in. "A lot of people are tired of pornography right now. I have to go along with the dames. If we didn't make such a fuss about it, it will go away; and it is. We will go back to murder and mayhem very soon. It will complete the cycle."

Oscar winner, television star: Broderick Crawford is a great student in the free form of life, much more than his 60-odd years would let on. Divorced and a bachelor, he indulges in such pasttimes as deep sea fishing, gourmet cooking, antiques, painting, and his own documentary film company.

Practical jokes and an inclination to call bluffs of those who put him on are Broderick Crawford's most striking characteristics, as witnessed by the time his son made a baseball bet with pop and lost. As retribution, Broderick made the boy polish his father's star on Hollywood Boulevard!

The Interns: Stephen Brooks, Hal Frederick, Christopher Stone (standing), Sandra Smith, Crawford

Fess Parker interview, by Hank Moore.
First published in November, 1969.

"Chit Chat"

Editor HANK MOORE

Interviews FESS PARKER

He stars on NBC-TV's "Daniel Boone" series
(Thursdays at 6:30 p.m. on Ch. 4, 6, and 42)

Fess Parker is billed in show business as an actor-writer-director-singer-composer. He is also a whiz in investments and business. But mainly, he is a nice and thoughtful guy.

I knew this 20 years ago and refreshed my memory of that fact the other day. The occasion was our second chat in 20 years. For it was in 1949-50 that Parker was the hard-working, popular-with-the-girls janitor at my father's office, the State Approval A-gency. This was when he was working his way through the University of Texas.

Although a history major with much enthusiasm for the subject, "My biggest concern was keeping off the dean's list, the bad one," he kidded.

Why study history?

"Oh, I liked it and did not have any specific objective at the time. I was just trying to graduate, kind of the path of least resistance, I guess."

Parker got into acting because he "didn't have any other job opportunities for sure. If you go where it is, you might get exposed. So that's what I did." One day, actor Adolphe Menjou was visiting the UT campus, and Parker was asked to show him around. They got along well and before he left, Menjou urged Parker to try his hand in Hollywood after finishing college.

With that in mind, he joined the Curtain Club, which was also training ground for Pat Hingle, Eli Wallach, Rip Torn, Jayne Mansfield, and John Connally. Parker, upon graduation, went to Hollywood and made his stage and motion picture debut. "Davy Crockett" made him a star.

I asked if he saw much of his Crockett co-star Buddy Ebsen these days.

"No, we're both too busy. I saw Billy Bakewell who played Major Norton in 'Davy Crocket' yesterday and said, 'Have you seen Buddy?' He said he hadn't, and I thought I might get in touch and have a visit with him one of these days."

Maybe he could do a guest shot on "Daniel Boone."

"Yeah, it would be great," exclaimed Parker. "He's so doggone busy with his other activities, it's hard to catch him."

We enjoyed you on the Dean Martin show a few weeks back.

"I understand Dean stopped drinking after that show," he mused. "He's taking up vocal lessons. I scared the hell out of him!"

Parker is ever popular at fairs and rodeos (like the '68 Heart O' Texas Fair in Waco, which he headlined). "I've been from Cheyenne to Jackson, Mississippi; from as far east as Indiana to Bomberton, Washington; to Brownsville to most of the points in between," he recalled.

Among his business holdings are an oil slick, a mobile home park, a $20 million amusements park (Frontier Worlds, being built — in Daniel Boone's old stomping grounds), and of course his TV production company.

"I'm directing a little bit now, just finished a show last week. If I like that. I'll probably hang in there with that, and may-

(Continued on Pg. 10)

More Fess Parker Interview..........

be phase out of the acting some day and try the directing field," Parker projected.

He will venture into the recording field soon. "I played in the junior high and high school bands back in my hometown (Fort Worth): the trumpet and the bass horn. I wrote some songs back in the 'Davy Crockett' era with Buddy Ebsen. I belong to ASCAP (the American Society of Composers and Publishers). Just various things here and there," Parker noted in leading up to mentioning he has just signed with RCA Victor Records to do some Country and Western Albums.

To get from one project to another, the rugged 6'6" star pilots his own twin-engine plane. "I really scare myself up there," he observed. "I'm not all that accomplished a pilot. I congratulate myself everytime I land.!

But then UT is very dear to Parker's heart. He has donated time and influence to projects furthering the school. That enthusiasm has caused him to transfer much of that educational concern to a college in his vicinity. Parker sits on the Board of Regents at Santa Clara College, where he is presently raising $1½ million for a theatre-music complex on campus.

The UT Ex-Students' Association last year named him a Distinguished Alumnus. "I was very grateful to get the award," he beamed. "There was not anything like it in my days there, and that makes me doubly pleased that they thought I was worthy of something extra unique."

Fess Parker in all probability has more warmth and humility than the real Davy Crockett and Daniel Boone put together!

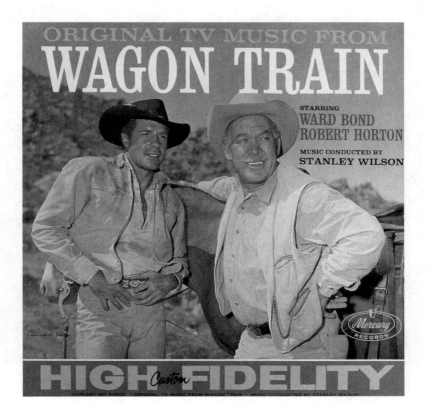

Hank More with Sonny and Cher, 1967

Hank Moore with Don Knotts, 1967

Hank Moore interviewing Herb Alpert, 1968

Hank Moore with "Beverly Hillbillies"
and "Barnaby Jones" star Buddy Ebsen, 1970

Hank Moore with Tim Conway, 1970

Hank Moore with Dick Clark, 1976

Hank Moore interviewing Ed McMahon, 1968

Hank Moore on the set of "Rowan & Martin's Laugh-In,"
with Pamela Rodgers, 1970

About the Author.

The genesis of this book started with interviews that Hank Moore conducted with television stars while he was in graduate school. They were originally written for TV Digest Magazine.

Did you ever wonder where corporations get their ideas for future growth? They are coming from Hank Moore, internationally known business advisor, speaker and author.

Hank Moore, Futurist and Corporate Strategist™, is the nation's highest level of business advisor and covers topics that one can only cover from having done them over a long career:

- Shaping business trends, challenges and opportunities.
- Corporate responsibility and ethics.
- Creating and rebuilding corporate cultures.
- New ways of doing business in the future.
- Visioning and strategic planning.
- Building coalitions, collaborations and joint-ventures.
- Crisis management and preparedness.
- International business.

Hank Moore is a Futurist and Corporate Strategist™, with his trademarked concept, The Business Tree™. Hank conducts independent performance reviews, Strategic Planning, Visioning and growth strategies for organizations of all sizes. He conducts Executive Think Tanks nationally...with the result being the companies' destinies being charted.

His client list includes more than 2,000...including 90 of the Fortune 500 companies and many public sector entities. He advises at the Executive Committee and board levels, providing Big Picture ideas.

As the nation's first Corporate Strategist™, he works with boards of directors, CEOs and executive teams of corporations...guiding them toward a profitable Vision and increased shareholder value. He facilitates decision-maker "think tanks" based purely upon his own ideas and creative concepts.

He is that rare 1 out of 100,000 senior business advisors, a Big Picture strategist, with original, cutting-edge ideas for creating, implementing and sustaining corporate growth throughout every sector of the organization. His Business Tree™ is a trademarked approach to growing, strengthening and evolving business, while mastering change.

Books by Hank Moore:

1. The Future Has Moved...and Left No Forwarding Address.

2. Power Stars to Light the Business Flame...The Business Visionaries and You

3. The Classic Television Reference,

4. The Business Tree™. 7 parts-progressions of a successful organization.

5. The High Cost of Doing Nothing.

Types of speaking engagements which Hank Moore presents internationally include:

- Conference opening Futurism keynote.

- Corporate planning retreats.

- Ethics and Corporate Responsibility speeches.

- University– College Commencement addresses.

- Business Think Tanks.

- International business conferences.

- Diversity and sexual harrassment (for top management).

- Non-profit and public sector planning retreats.

Hank Moore
Futurist, Corporate Strategist™
Website address: http://users4.ev1.net/~hankmoore/

Hank Moore's Speaking Topics and Presentation Titles

Futurism, Business Trends: The Future Has Moved...and Left No Forwarding Address.
Understanding and benefiting from trends in business, organizational transformation, capturing and building shared Vision.

Ethics and Corporate Responsibility.
Learn the lessons from the corporate scandals. How to develop a company ethics statement and program. How to show your stakeholders that your company is ethical and healthy. Understanding the scandals and what they mean to the future of business. Bullet-proofing your company from ethical fallout and controversy. Why ethics is good for business.

Business-Corporate: The High Cost of Doing Nothing™
Why good companies go bad and how to improve them.

Executive Think Tanks, Big Picture issues, The Business Tree™
Analyzing the 7 parts-components of a successful company. How to conduct Strategic Planning and Visioning processes.

Crisis Management and Preparedness: Achieving the Best by Preparing for the Worst.
Predicting and surviving any kind of crisis. Case studies, pointers and methodologies to pre-empt organizational crises.

Leadership-Mentorship: The Learning Tree™

Change: Trees in the Forest™
Distinguishing your company from the pack and move to new levels.

Investor Relations: Increasing Your Company's Book Value.
Non-profit and public sector planning retreats.

Diversity: Management Perspectives and Opportunities.
Moore was one of the authors of the Civil Rights Act of 1964. He discusses Diversity from the management perspective.

Photos of the Author Now

Hank Moore as a conference keynote speaker, with his trademarked concept,
The Business Tree ™ .

Hank Moore, discussing societal betterment programs with Lady Bird Johnson,
who served as U.S. First Lady from 1965-1969.

Hank Moore (left), with NBC News anchor Jan Carson (center) and Alberto
Gonzales at an awards banquet celebrating community leadership and steward-
ship. Gonzales is currently the Attorney General of the United States.

Hank Moore, discussing international business issues at a conference
in Kuwait, 2004

Hank Moore delivered the opening keynote address, April 28, 2005, in Sao Paulo, Brazil. The conference was sponsored by software king SAS for their business customers and collaborators.

In 1990, Hank Moore directed his favorite actress, Audrey Hepburn (right) in a series of television public service announcements for UNICEF. Later that year, both were honored by the United Nations for their humanitarian activities.

Classic TV Related Websites to Visit

Classic TV websites
http://ultimatetvshows.com
http://www.tvhistory.tv
http://www.surfnetinc.com/chuck/trio.htm
http://www.classic-tv.com
http://www.tvguide.com/games/covergallery
http://www.teevee.org
Links to show and fan websites
http://www.classictvshop.com/community/links.html
http://classictv.miningco.com
http://us.imdb.com
http://classictv.about.com/?once=true&
http://www.tv-ark.org.uk/links_new/links.html
http://www.tvparty.com
http://primetimetv.about.com/mlibrary.htm

Episode Guides for Shows
http://www.geocities.com/TelevisionCity/Stage/2950
http://epguides.com/menu
http://www.tvtome.com/tvtome/servlet/ListShowsServlet

Museum of Television and Radio
http://www.mtr.org

Academy of Television Arts & Sciences
http://www.emmys.tv

American Film Institute
http://www.afi.com

British Film Institute
http://www.bfi.org.uk

British TV website
http://www.78rpm.co.uk/tv.htm

Canadian TV website
http://www.film.queensu.ca/CBC/Index.html

Classic TV theme songs
http://www.melaman2.com/tvshows
http://www.tvsgreatesthits.com

Sources to buy Classic TV shows on DVD and VHS
http://www.shokus.com
http://www.nostalgiafamilyvideo.com
http://www.hollywoodsattic.com
http://www.kinevideo.net
http://www.tvofyourlife.com
http://www.ebay.com
http://www.half.com
http://www.mpihomevideo.com
http://www.radiospirits.com
http://www.captainbijou.com
http://members.tripod.com/~Moviecraft/index.html
http://www.moviesunlimited.com
http://grapevinevideo.com
http://www.reel.com

Appearances by favorite stars on TV this month
http://www.tv-now.com/stars/stars.html

Umbrella websites, links to other websites
http://timvp.com/tv.html
http://www.timelapse.com/tvlink
http://www.tv-now.com
http://www.classictvhits.com
http://www.geocities.com/godoftelevision

"Chit Chat"

Editor HANK MOORE
Interviews PAT PAULSEN

*stars weekly in his own series over ABC-TV,
"Pat Paulsen's Half-A-Comedy Hour"
(Thursdays, 6:30 p.m., Channel 12)*

Live From Hollywood

Week of October 25-31

Listings for Austin, Waco
San Antonio, Temple

To Hank —
a damned fine
interviewer and a very nice guy —
Ed Sullivan
april 12th
1972

"DEAR HARRIET VAN HORNE;
YOU BITCH.

SINCERELY,

ED SULLIVAN."